MW00838182

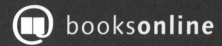 booksonline

Read this book online today:

With SAP PRESS BooksOnline we offer you online access to knowledge from the leading SAP experts. Whether you use it as a beneficial supplement or as an alternative to the printed book, with SAP PRESS BooksOnline you can:

- Access your book anywhere, at any time. All you need is an Internet connection.
- Perform full text searches on your book and on the entire SAP PRESS library.
- Build your own personalized SAP library.

The SAP PRESS customer advantage:

Register this book today at www.sap-press.com and obtain exclusive free trial access to its online version. If you like it (and we think you will), you can choose to purchase permanent, unrestricted access to the online edition at a very special price!

Here's how to get started:

1. Visit www.sap-press.com.
2. Click on the link for SAP PRESS BooksOnline and login (or create an account).
3. Enter your free trial license key, shown below in the corner of the page.
4. Try out your online book with full, unrestricted access for a limited time!

Your personal free trial **license key** for this online book is:

7tw2-vjq4-bezn-dicu

SAP® Query Reporting—Practical Guide

 PRESS

Ray Li, Evan DeLodder
Creating Dashboards with Xcelsius – Practical Guide
2010, 587 pp.
978-1-59229-335-3

Ingo Hilgefort
Inside SAP BusinessObjects Advanced Analysis
2010, 340 pp.
978-1-59229-371-1

Jim Brogden, Mac Holden, Heather Sinkwitz
SAP BusinessObjects Web Intelligence
2010, 550 pp.
978-1-59229-322-3

Mike Garrett
Using Crystal Reports with SAP
2010, 440 pp.
978-1-59229-327-8

Stephan Kaleske

SAP® Query Reporting—Practical Guide

Galileo Press

Bonn • Boston

Galileo Press is named after the Italian physicist, mathematician and philosopher Galileo Galilei (1564–1642). He is known as one of the founders of modern science and an advocate of our contemporary, heliocentric worldview. His words *Eppur si muove* (And yet it moves) have become legendary. The Galileo Press logo depicts Jupiter orbited by the four Galilean moons, which were discovered by Galileo in 1610.

Editor Eva Tripp
English Edition Editor Erik Herman
Translation Lemoine International, Inc., Salt Lake City, UT
Copyeditor Julie McNamee
Cover Design Graham Geary
Photo Credit Fotolia/Carina Hanse/Damirk/pressmaster
Layout Design Vera Brauner
Production Manager Kelly O'Callaghan
Assistant Production Editor Graham Geary
Typesetting Publishers' Design and Production Services, Inc.
Printed and bound in Canada

ISBN 978-1-59229-365-0

© 2011 by Galileo Press Inc., Boston (MA)
1st edition 2011
1st German edition published 2010 by Galileo Press, Bonn, Germany

Library of Congress Cataloging-in-Publication Data
Kaleske, Stephan.
 [Praxishandbuch SAP Query-Reporting. English]
 SAP query reporting : practical guide / Stephan Kaleske. — 1st ed.
   p. cm.
 Includes index.
 ISBN-13: 978-1-59229-365-0
 ISBN-10: 1-59229-365-4
 1. SAP R/3. 2. Business—Data processing. 3. Business—Computer programs. I. Title.
 HF5548.4.R2K35413 2011
 650.0285'53—dc22
 2010042100

Contents at a Glance

Dear Reader,

Thank you for choosing a book from SAP PRESS. As business intelligence, reporting, and analytics continue to become ingratiated into the fabric and day-to-day functions of modern business, the need for accurate, practical guidance on the available tools is critical. This book provides requisite information about one of the most commonly used SAP tools, SAP Query. SAP Query offers a great level of flexibility for retrieving and presenting data, and can be used in all areas of business and with SAP modules, including FI, CO, MM, PP, SD, etc.

Our author Stephan Kaleske has extensive, first-hand experience developing reporting programs for companies working in a vast range of industries with varying reporting needs and requirements. He brings his many years of experience to the pages of this book and provides you with practical guidance on how best to define your requirements and build reports to satisfy them. The tips and tricks provided will be of interest and relevance to both beginner and experienced SAP professionals.

Once you've finished reading the book, I'd love to hear your feedback, so feel free to drop me a line at the email address below.

Thanks again for purchasing a book from SAP PRESS!

Erik Herman
Editor, SAP PRESS

Galileo Press
100 Grossman Drive, Suite 205
Braintree, MA 02184

erik.herman@galileo-press.com
www.sap-press.com

Contents

PART II SAP Query Functions

PART V   Real-Life Examples

Preface

Often, the enthusiasm in the room is palpable at the end of one of my customer appointments. Most of my customers are small- or medium-sized enterprises that usually want to extract specific data for a specific topic from the system to do the following:

- Optimize processes
- Support corporate management
- Improve master data quality

Frequently, the topics that arise extend beyond the limitations of the SAP components, and, for this reason, a suitable standard analysis is not always possible. Generally, my contacts (key users, heads of departments, managing directors, and executive boards) do not have the requisite knowledge of ABAP to use an individual report to query the information they require. So why are they so enthusiastic? The answer is SAP Query. SAP Query makes it possible to generate reports across components and according to specific requirements. After reading this book, you will become a confident user of SAP Query, and I have no doubt that you will be as enthusiastic as my many customers about the options available to you!

The undisputed strengths of SAP systems include their wide range of functions, their many integration options, and the "merciless" plausibility check they perform on data entered. The data stored in the system is extremely valuable to any enterprise. However, it is even more important to make this highly valuable data basis available to the relevant groups, as required.

In my projects, the average customer actively uses approximately 100 queries. This high number of queries demonstrates the importance of SAP Query functions for both the user and developer.

During a project, I actively impart my knowledge to the customer so that, at the end of the day, he or she has real added value. This is also my goal for this book. In other words, by reading this book, you will quickly obtain tangible added value. Remaining true to my motto of "Growth through knowledge," I will provide you with a tool that you can use to quickly obtain the results you require. I do not view my consulting mandate as one of explaining a detailed function and then immediately providing an answer to every topic, but rather one of designing or presenting an entire process. It is completely acceptable and even sensible to develop a solution jointly because you, as an SAP user, may be more knowledgeable than I in certain areas because you have specialized in one or more of these areas.

In my work, it is important to me that I am not solely regarded as being a component consultant. Component limitations do not exist for me. Rather, I examine how a solution could look and, more often than not, SAP Query proves to be the fastest and best solution. SAP Query is not aware of any (component) limitations. Furthermore, you can easily link tables from different areas with each other and analyze them.

I have written this book from an SAP application viewpoint rather than a developer viewpoint. My goal is to show you real-life solutions that will make your daily work easier. In this book, you will find many good suggestions that will make it a rich source of information for you.

I also wish to invite you to actively participate in dialog — let's exchange ideas! Twice a year, I host an informal workshop where my customers and I exchange our most recent practical experiences. You are more than welcome to attend such active information exchanges. You will always find the latest information on my website *www.ZLex.de*.

I would like to take this opportunity to thank you for your interest in SAP Query. I would also like to thank everyone who contributed questions and ideas to this book. It is always a pleasure to work with you on developing solutions.

While writing this book, I had to postpone or cancel numerous appointments with customers. I would therefore like to take this opportunity to thank all my customers for the faith and understanding they have shown me. In particular, I wish to thank:

Mr. Georg Alef

Ms. Eva Ackermann

Mr. Marcus Bethge

Dr. Achim Degner

Mr. Dirk Engel

Mr. Giuseppe Evangelista

Mr. Franz Feinäugle

Mr. Bernd Feyerabend

Mr. Christoph Flicker

Mr. Sven Gerum

Ms. Antje Gössel

Mr. Andreas Grigoleit

Mr. Andreas Gruber

Mr. Willy Hartung

Mr. Michael Hinge

Mr. Stefan Holtkamp

Mr. Dietmar Jung

Mr. Erwin Kaiser

Mr. Jürgen Kegel

Mr. Hans-Jörg Kern

Mr. Andreas Köstler

Ms. Karin Krewerth

Mr. Stephan Kury

Ms. Elisabeth Lämmle

Mr. Lars Landwehrkamp

Mr. Klaus Lehmann

Mr. Rudi Leisinger

Mr. Ralf Linha

Ms. Karin Meierhoff

Mr. Oliver Meyer

Ms. Doris Mies

Mr. Christoph Militzer

Mr. Michael Müller

Ms. Dorothea Nußbaumer

Mr. Herbert Nusser

Mr. Stephan Püschl

Mr. Michael Reinken

Mr. Dieter Reiser

Mr. Wolfgang Riexinger

Mr. Jürgen Roller

Mr. Klaus Rucziczka

Ms. Sylvia Schäfer

Ms. Annett Scheibner

Mr. Sven Scherer

Mr. Hendrik Schmidt

Ms. Antje Schneider

Ms. Ute Schusser

Mr. Alfred Simon

Mr. Frank Sommerhalter

Dr. Peter Spieker

Mr. Dirk Ullwer

Ms. Aleksandra Voigt

Mr. Harald Wagner

I would also like to thank those unnamed persons with whom I discussed ideas and collaborated on developing the best solutions. All that remains is for me to wish you a very pleasant read and many "enlightening moments" during the course of this book!

Stephan Kaleske

This introductory chapter describes the objectives and target audience of this book. It also provides an overview of the content of each chapter. Here, you will learn how to deepen your knowledge and get the best from this book.

Introduction

Do you want to query specific information directly in the SAP system — without any programming whatsoever and within a short space of time? When you use SAP Query, you do not need any other programs or servers. Consequently, you can retrieve up-to-date data directly from the SAP system.

In this book, we will use real-life customer examples and sample solutions to demonstrate how you can use SAP Query to retrieve data that will optimally support the daily work you do within your enterprise. Within a very short time, you will be able to prepare information that is not available in standard SAP reports.

Target Audience of this Book

This book provides specific information about SAP Query for all user departments. In other words, we will map requirements from the following areas: Logistics (SD, MM, PP, and so on), Financial Accounting (FI, CO, etc.), the HR department (SAP ERP HCM), and Basis. Furthermore, the information in this book can be applied to any industry in any country.

Component-independent and industry-independent

SAP users at all knowledge levels can use this book with a view to covering their reporting requirements more fully. Even readers who do not have extensive prior knowledge will benefit from reading this book. However, you should have some user knowledge of an SAP component. This book is particularly suitable for the following:

- Key users
- Administrators
- Project managers
- Members of a project team
- End users
- Developers
- Analysts

Structure of the Book

This book is divided into five parts.

Part I, **Introduction to SAP Query,** provides you with a basic introduction to query reporting.

Query reporting in context

In **Chapter 1**, Introduction to SAP ERP Reporting, you will be introduced to query reporting tools in context. You'll see the distinction between SAP Query and other SAP report generators. You will also learn when to use the report tools Report Painter and Drilldown Reporting. Finally, you will become familiar with standard SAP reports.

Localizing tables

In **Chapter 2**, Overview of SAP Tables and Table Links, you will learn about the options available to you for determining the most important SAP tables. You will also learn how to use the Data Browser, the F1 help, logical databases, archiving tables, and the where-used list.

QuickViewer

In **Chapter 3**, QuickViewer, you will learn how to use the simplest query tool, QuickViewer, to create reports. We will also show you how to insert the data basis into a query report. We will pay particular attention to the selection and layout options, especially the graphical layout mode.

Relationships between query objects

In **Chapter 4**, Overview of SAP Query, we will provide an example that explains the most important query terms to you. Here, you will learn about the relationships among the query area, user groups, the InfoSet, and SAP Query itself.

Query utilities

In **Chapter 5**, Query Utilities, you will learn how to obtain an overview of existing query objects in the system. You will get to know the most important query object directories. You will also learn how to call an object description. Finally, we will introduce you to the trash folder and the query copy program.

In **Part II, SAP Query Functions,** we will take a closer look at the most important functions of SAP Query.

In **Chapter 6**, InfoSet in Detail, we will describe the InfoSet. In particular, we will show you the data basis for creating a report. First, you will learn how to use a table join to link several tables together and then how to structure individual data fields into field groups.

InfoSet in detail

In **Chapter 7**, SAP Query in Detail, you will get to know all aspects of SAP Query. We will show you how to use SAP Query to create your own report, how to use the output formats available to you, how to select selection and layout fields, and how to use other options available to you when designing a basic list.

SAP Query in detail

In **Chapter 8**, Selection and Layout Variants, we will show you how to design the selection screen. Here, you will learn how to use a specific data selection to analyze the information you require. You will also learn how to create your own layout and selection variants for recurring reporting requirements. Finally, we will show you various other options associated with layout and selection variants (e.g., multiple selection, in particular).

Selection and layout variants

In **Chapter 9**, Traffic Light Icons, Drilldown, Graphics, and ABC Analyses, we will introduce you to the report drilldown and icons. You will also learn how to integrate report jumps to transactions, ABAP reports, or other reports into your analysis. Finally, you will learn how to use your own symbols or icons (e.g., traffic lights) to highlight key data.

Report drilldown and traffic light icons

In **Part III, Designing User-Friendly Reports,** we will show you how to design reports that users will find easy to use

In **Chapter 10**, Summarized Data Output with Statistics and Ranked Lists, you will learn about ranked lists and statistics. You can use ranked lists to display the top entries in a selection, while statistics enable you to group and aggregate the data in your report according to different characteristics.

Ranked lists and statistics

ABAP
fundamentals/
ABAP Dictionary

In **Chapter 11**, ABAP Fundamentals in the InfoSet, we will introduce you to the ABAP Dictionary. You will learn how data fields are defined in the SAP system and how you can define your own data fields in an InfoSet. In the additional data fields, you will use basic ABAP commands to select data content and process it further. You can insert both additional fields and additional tables into your InfoSet.

Integration
with Excel

In **Chapter 12**, Integration with Microsoft Excel, you will learn how to use the tool Excel Inplace to display data in an Excel interface within the SAP system.

In **Part IV, Query Management,** we will describe the most important functions used in query management:

Transport system/
transaction
creation

In **Chapter 13**, Transport System, you will learn how to transport query objects. Here, we will discuss the various transport options available to you in the context of the local or standard query area. If your query objects are stored locally (i.e., they were created for a specific client), you will learn how to export data from one client and import it into another client. We will also show you how to create your own query transactions within the transaction for user role management.

Table index,
table view, and
function modules

Chapter 14, Data Retrieval and Function Modules, will build on the knowledge that you acquired in Chapter 11 (ABAP Dictionary). You will learn how to use an additional table index to improve query performance. For recurring table relationships, table views will be created in the ABAP Dictionary. Finally, you will learn other ways to insert additional ABAP code into an InfoSet. Here, we will pay particular attention to data retrieval through the use of function modules.

Authorizations

To conclude this topic, **Chapter 15**, Authorizations and Transaction Creation, will show you how to assign authorizations. Here, we will list the most important authorization objects for you. You will also learn which authorization objects are relevant when creating query objects. In particular, we will discuss the SAP_QUERY authorization object.

Examples from
Sales and
Distribution,
Financial
Accounting,
and Production
Planning

In **Part V, Real-Life Examples, Chapter 16**, of the same name, we will introduce you to three analyses that are frequently used in real life. In the first example, you will see how different customers create a sales evaluation. Here, we will also explain which crucial points must be considered to ensure that data is displayed correctly. The second real-life example will relate to the analysis of open items from Financial Accounting (FI), while the third example will concern an analysis from Production Planning (PP). Confirmations for operations will also be analyzed here. Traffic light icons will also be used to highlight variances between actual times and target times.

In the **appendix**, you will find a list of the most important SAP tables.

Working with This Book

To make it easier for you to work with this book, we have used the following symbols to highlight certain sections.

Tips highlighted using this symbol are real-life recommendations that will make your work easier. **[+]**

Notes highlighted with this symbol will give you information about important requirements or implications that you must always consider. **[«]**

This symbol represents examples that will explain the topic under discussion in greater detail and show you how to use the individual functions in your enterprise. **[Ex]**

Additional Material on the Publisher's Website

On the publisher's website, *www.sap-press.com*, you can register yourself as the owner of this book to gain access to exclusive bonus material. Simply log on using your personal access code, which is printed at the beginning of this book. **www.sap-press.com**

In particular, the publisher's website describes and provides more than 100 immediately usable queries from all enterprise areas. Based on real-life examples (toolkit), you can query specific information directly from the following SAP modules: SD (incoming orders, sales volume, credit limit, and customers), MM (stock, creditors), PP (orders, work centers), FI (open items, payment data, and dunning data), and many other application areas.

Contacting
the author

For more information about query reporting, please visit the following website: *www.zlex.de/query/*. If you wish to make suggestions or provide feedback to the author, please send an email to *Info@Zlex.de*.

PART I
Introduction to SAP Query

SAP Query is used to create analyses in real time without any great effort. Such analyses are used to optimize processes and master data, and to support corporate management. In your SAP ERP system, you can use the SAP Query functions without the need for any additional installations or license fees.

1 Introduction to SAP ERP Reporting

For enterprises, quickly and accurately accessing business information is vital. To this end, SAP provides an extensive portfolio of tools for report creation. The most important tools are as follows:

▶ Query reporting tools

▶ Report Painter/Report Writer

▶ Drilldown Reporting

▶ SAP NetWeaver Business Warehouse (SAP NetWeaver BW)/SAP BusinessObjects

The term *query reporting tools* comprises the following tools:

▶ SAP Query

▶ QuickViewer

▶ InfoSet Query

This chapter introduces you to SAP Query, Report Painter, and Drilldown Reporting, and distinguishes among these three tools and SAP NetWeaver BW. In addition, you will learn about frequently used standard SAP reports. After obtaining an overview of the basic requirements for report creation in Section 1.1, ABAP Report Generators, we will compare the three aforementioned query tools in Section 1.2, Query Reporting Tools. Here, you will learn when it is advisable to use the query reporting tools to query information directly in the SAP ERP system. In Section 1.3,

Comparing Analysis Tools: SAP Query and SAP NetWeaver BW, we will highlight the advantages of SAP Query over SAP NetWeaver BW.

If you need reports with summarized figures (totals), which is often the case in Financial Accounting (FI), we recommend that you use the following tools: Report Painter/Report Writer and Drilldown Reporting. In Section 1.4, Cumulated Analyses with Multilevel Hierarchies, you will see how SAP ERP is used in different enterprises with different business requirements. For the most important reporting requirements, which are often the same for many customers, a standard report is frequently available in SAP ERP. Before you create a new report, you should always check whether an existing report already covers your requirements (see Section 1.5, Using Standard Reports).

1.1 ABAP Report Generators

Analyzing requirements

At the start of every report, there is a specific requirements specification. After the data basis has been clarified, the user decides how to format the data and answers the following questions:

► What does the selection screen look like?

► Which field contents do you want to output?

► Which report jumps (drilldown) are useful?

► How do you want the data to be formatted?

  ► Output length, decimal places, unit

  ► Color display

► How do you want to summarize or display the data?

  ► Summation levels

  ► Excel display

Business and technical expertise

For example, a developer can use an ABAP report to format the data. However, a good ABAP developer requires time to output structured data. He needs not only technical expertise but also business knowledge, in particular.

Because the business requirements of an enterprise are often challenging, both detailed technical knowledge and industry knowledge are essential. In addition to technical knowledge, a good consultant, key user, user, or developer must have some business knowledge to create the best analyses.

If you have a good level of technical knowledge, you must acquire the relevant business expertise. Because the analysis requirement is based on many years of real-life experiences, the question of simplified technical analysis options arises. Is it always necessary to create an analysis program from scratch? Are there easy ways to create ABAP code? The goal is to generate a good report and to accces a simple report generator, either to accelerate the implementation speed or simply due to a lack of programming knowledge. Table 1.1 provides an overview of the most important report generators for you.

Simplified report creation via the report generator

Report Generator	Transaction	Focus in Real Life
SAP Query	SQ01	All SAP components
SAP NetWeaver BW		All SAP components
Report Painter	FGRP	▶ FI: General ledger, special ledger ▶ CO: Overhead costs, product costs, Profit Center Accounting
Drilldown Reporting		▶ FI: General ledger, customers, vendors, special ledger ▶ CO: Product costs, Profitability Analysis, Profit Center Accounting ▶ TR: Cash Management, Treasury ▶ IM: Investment Management ▶ PS: Project System
LIS		▶ SD: Sales and Distribution, shipping, billing ▶ MM: Purchasing, inventory management, invoice verification ▶ QM: Quality Management ▶ PM: Plant Maintenance ▶ PP: Production Planning and Control

Table 1.1 Overview of the Most Important Report Generators for You

The term "query
reporting tools"

SAP provides different utilities for creating ABAP code for an analysis. We already mentioned the most important reporting tools in the introduction, namely Report Painter/Report Writer, Drilldown Reporting, and SAP NetWeaver BW. The Logistics Information System (LIS) is another tool. The term *query reporting tools* is often used in different contexts, both in literature and in real life. Frequently, the term SAP query reporting is also used to describe the SAP NetWeaver BW reporting tools. However, this book concerns only those query reporting tools within the SAP ERP system.

In the next section, we will explain which query reporting tools are available to you.

1.2   Query Reporting Tools

This section provides a first impression of the functional scope of query reporting tools. We will compare the various options and application areas of SAP Query, InfoSet Query, and QuickViewer against each other and explain them in detail.

When we speak of query reporting tools, we mean the following three tools:

- ▶ SAP Query
- ▶ InfoSet Query
- ▶ QuickViewer

Functions of query
reporting tools

The order in which these tools are listed reflects their decreasing functional scope. QuickViewer is the easiest tool to use, but it provides the lowest functionality of all three query tools. An overview of the most important functions is provided in Table 1.2.

Development
of query
reporting tools

In Release 4.6, SAP renamed one of its query reporting tools to SAP Query. Prior to Release 4.6C, it was known as the *ABAP Query Tool*. In the SAP solution portfolio, this tool is still listed under the ABAP development tools because it was originally intended for developers who wanted an easier way to generate ABAP code.

Criterion	SAP Query	InfoSet Query	QuickViewer
Transactions	SQ01, SQ02, SQ03	SQ10	SQVI
Functionality	Calculated additional fields, drilldown	Calculated additional fields, drilldown	–
Output	Basic list, ranked list, statistics	Basic list, ranked list, statistics	Basic list
Table logging	No	Can be activated	No

Table 1.2 Differences Among the Query Reporting Tools

To enable end users to create their own individual reports, InfoSet Query (initially intended for the Human Resources area) and QuickViewer (a particularly easy-to-use tool for occasional users) were developed in Release 4.6C. At the same time, the query tools were completely revised in terms of their performance and the way in which they create ABAP code. The user interface was also simplified.

SAP release changes

In the course of this further development, SAP changed many terms. Table 1.3 provides an overview of these terminology changes.

Terminology changes

Area	Term Before Release 4.6	Term as of Release 4.6
Tool name	ABAP Query	SAP Query
Data pool	Functional areas	InfoSet
Structuring of data	Functional groups	Field groups
Output format	ABAP List Viewer (ALV)	SAP List Viewer (ALV)

Table 1.3 ABAP/SAP Query Terms According to Release

However, all three query reporting tools have the same purpose, namely to create ABAP code easily and thus generate individual analyses.

You can use the following data sources as a data basis for these analyses (see Figure 1.1):

Data sources

▶ Individual database table

▶ Table join

▸ Logical database

▸ InfoSet

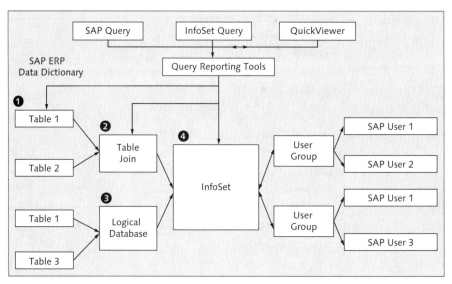

Figure 1.1 Relationships Between SAP Query Functions

Data source: database table

In some cases, it is sufficient to query an individual database table (**❶**). If you have the necessary authorization, you can also use the Data Browser to query the database directly. However, if you want to easily limit access and have a user-friendly query, it may make sense to create a query. It may also be productive to query only one database table (if this table already contains most of the information you require) and to read additional information in separate additional fields.

Data source: table join

Due to its simplicity and high implementation speed, QuickViewer has proven successful for one-time ad hoc analyses. In comparison to querying the table directly in the database, you can use QuickViewer to query several tables that are linked via fields. If two or more tables are linked with each other, this is known as a table join (**❷**).

Logical database

Logical databases (**❸**) contain information that has already been compiled for the creator of the report. Logical databases are the basis for linking SAP tables with each other. Even though a query is easily possible, the predefined data basis carries the risk of unnecessary data content being queried. Consequently, the simplified query is synonymous with lower performance.

An InfoSet (❹) is, for the most part, comparable with a table join. In QuickViewer, a transaction is the basis for defining the table join (data basis) and selecting the selection and layout fields. For SAP Query and InfoSet Query, a separate transaction is used to create the data basis as an InfoSet. An InfoSet can have a table, table join, or logical database as its data basis.

InfoSet

QuickViewer is frequently used in real life. A report can be created in just a few minutes, simply by using one transaction (SQVI) and knowing the database table(s). The newly created QuickViewer report is available locally but only to the creator of the report. If another user requires this report, it cannot be simply forwarded to the user. With SAP Query, however, it is possible to convert the new QuickViewer report into an SAP query. For detailed information about QuickViewer, see Chapter 3, QuickViewer.

Using QuickViewer

Creating an SAP query is not much more difficult than generating a QuickViewer report. Even though three transactions are used to create a report, report creation is also easy here if you are familiar with the logic. The use of SAP Query is usually preferred over the use of QuickViewer or InfoSet Query because it not only provides more options but also demands a more structured working method.

Using SAP Query

SAP Query enables you to specifically format data for individual information objects. In real life, master data is frequently queried using SAP Query. Consequently, numerous analyses exist for the following master data objects, in particular:

Master data reports

▶ Customers

▶ Vendors

▶ Materials

▶ Conditions

▶ Credit limit

▶ Work centers

- General ledger accounts
- Fixed assets

Displaying data
in an ALV layout
or in Excel

These analyses enable the user to analyze his data individually. In real life, data displayed in an ALV layout or in Microsoft Excel is often received very positively. Because reports are individual, you can easily recognize duplicates or incorrect field content. You can then double-click the report to correct or adjust the data content directly.

Transaction
data reports

With SAP Query, you can also select transaction data according to specific criteria. The status or document flow for orders is queried in this way, and you can specifically optimize the business process on this basis. For example, you can analyze the associated delivery or billing status for a sales order. If the actual status differs from the target status, the relevant departments, customers, or vendors can be informed in good time and specific measures can be taken. In particular, icons (e.g., a red traffic light) are used to highlight critical statuses. The following data objects, in particular, are analyzed in real life:

- Sales orders
- Deliveries
- Billing documents
- Purchase orders
- Production orders
- Open items

Corporate
management

Many enterprises also use SAP Query for corporate management. Many customers require analyses for incoming orders or sales, for example. In addition, many enterprises create stock analyses or target production quantity analyses to display fact-based enterprise results.

Distinguishing
between SAP
Query and SAP
NetWeaver BW

If you have large datasets and complex cross-module analyses, you soon reach the limitations of SAP Query. However, the use of SAP NetWeaver BW is undisputed in such cases. Be that as it may, not all (small and medium-sized) enterprises use a SAP NetWeaver BW system, or they only use some aspects of SAP NetWeaver BW. In the next section, we will discuss the criteria for and against SAP Query (when compared with SAP NetWeaver BW).

1.3 Comparing Analysis Tools: SAP Query and SAP NetWeaver BW

If your enterprise has sufficient resources (time, money, and technical expertise), we recommend using SAP NetWeaver BW or SAP Business-Objects alongside SAP Query. Examples of SAP BusinessObjects products include Crystal Reports (formatted reporting), Xcelsius Enterprise (dashboarding), and Web Intelligence (ad hoc analysis).

Required resources

Table 1.4 compares and contrasts the most important distinguishing characteristics between SAP Query and SAP NetWeaver BW, especially in terms of the resources used.

Criterion	SAP Query	SAP NetWeaver BW
License fees, interfaces, maintenance, and hardware	Part of the SAP ERP license	Additional license fees frequently necessary (especially if you also want to use SAP BusinessObjects)
Installation	Can be used immediately	Additional installation and hardware frequently necessary
System configuration	Query transactions immediately available	Must be configured independently
Individual real-time analysis	Access to live data with drilldown in real time	Data usually updated in an overnight job

Table 1.4 Comparing Analysis Tools: SAP Query and SAP NetWeaver BW

In terms of resource usage, there are many advantages to using the SAP Query reporting tools:

Advantages of query reporting tools

▶ In contrast to SAP NetWeaver BW/SAP BusinessObjects, you can use SAP Query without needing to procure additional licenses.

▶ Because report creation via SAP Query occurs directly in the SAP ERP system, no additional maintenance is necessary.

▶ The need for a separate system installation or configuration is eliminated as a result of using the query tools directly in the SAP ERP system.

▶ You do not have to configure any interfaces or restore them after you perform a system copy.

▶ You can already create reports even if you have very little system knowledge. In particular, you require little or no knowledge of ABAP. Even after just a short time, you can create your own queries or analyze existing analyses.

▶ The time needed to create reports is comparably low because reports can be created from a single source (business knowledge can be applied directly).

▶ Individual information can be queried promptly, and the data already stored in the database is available immediately (in real time). In transactions, you can use a drilldown to navigate directly to the display screen or change screen for data.

Query reporting tools enable SAP users to analyze specific master data objects and process information without the need for a lengthy training phase. As the report recipient/key user, you can create a new report from scratch (on the basis of the data analysis) and only include absolutely necessary information in your reporting environment. You decide which fields you want to output in a list, which selection criteria you will provide, or how you want the data to be formatted.

We recommend using SAP NetWeaver BW to query mass data. If you want to query extensive datasets at a highly aggregated level, it is more productive to use SAP NetWeaver BW because of its runtime. For financial analyses, you can use Report Painter to create aggregated analyses.

1.4   Cumulated Analyses with Multilevel Hierarchies

Analyzing hierarchy nodes

The purpose of corporate management reports is to analyze data at a summarized level. If you want to obtain an overview of your enterprise's key performance indicators (KPIs), a top-down analysis will accomplish this goal for you. For example, a top hierarchy node is displayed in Cost Center Accounting. This hierarchy node is then gradually expanded in accordance with the hierarchy levels. If variances arise, the values are initially called for each account and then for each line item. This means that the report user initially obtains the data information at a highly summarized level and can display this data in greater detail, if necessary. In the system, you can maintain hierarchies for many objects. In Financial Accounting (FI), in particular, a good hierarchy structure (summarization of characteristics) can cover many reporting requirements.

1.4.1 Summarization Hierarchies

In the SAP system, separate transactions are used to maintain summarization levels. Depending on the purpose of the report, the information characteristics (e.g., cost centers) must be summarized in accordance with different criteria. For example, an enterprise summarizes its cost center information in accordance with its responsibilities on one hand and in accordance with functional viewpoints on the other. Different time-based groupings are also required. For the current fiscal year, actual values must be queried in accordance with the first grouping while, for the subsequent year, planned values must be queried in accordance with the second grouping.

Summarization criteria

To fulfill your analysis requirements, the SAP software enables you to group master data objects at multiple levels and in accordance with different criteria. In the SAP system, a hierarchy (also technically known as a set) is used to group master data. Table 1.5 lists the most important transactions for summarizing master data.

Master data hierarchies

Master Record	Create	Change	Display
Financial statement version	OB58	FSE2	FSE3
Cost elements	KA01	KA02	KA03
Standard cost centers	–	OKEON	OKENN
Alternative cost centers	KS02	KS02	KS03
Statistical key figures	KK01	KK02	KK03
Activity types	KL01	KL02	KL03
Internal orders	KO01	KO02	KO03

Table 1.5 Transactions for Master Data Hierarchies

Master Record	Create	Change	Display
Standard profit center	KCH1	KCH5N	KCH6N
Alternative profit center	KCH1	KCH2	KCH5
CO-PA characteristics	KES1	KES2	KES3
Sets, general	GS01	GS02	GS03

Table 1.5 Transactions for Master Data Hierarchies (Cont.)

Querying hierarchy nodes in the query

In the context of queries, you can also query the information in master data hierarchies. For example, when analyzing work centers, you can display the assigned cost center. In the query, you can then determine the associated cost center node on the basis of the cost center. You can query a summarization level in SAP Query. If you want to display the information characteristics at multiple levels, Report Painter and Drilldown Reporting report tools will usually accomplish this goal for you.

1.4.2 Report Painter

Database tables

Report Painter accesses database tables in the same way SAP Query does. Because Report Painter is usually used in real life, we will not discuss Report Writer. Report Writer — considered by most users to be too technical — can be regarded as a precursor to Report Painter. Almost all of the Report Writer functions have been incorporated into Report Painter. Because there are still some minor functional differences between the two tools, and some of the Report Writer reports delivered by SAP still exist, both tools continue to coexist in the system.

Reporting tables

The most important related database tables are grouped together to form reporting tables. Reporting tables are predefined and comprise a certain number of characteristics and key figures. The relationships between the database tables, the reporting tables, and the characteristics and key figures are shown in Figure 1.2.

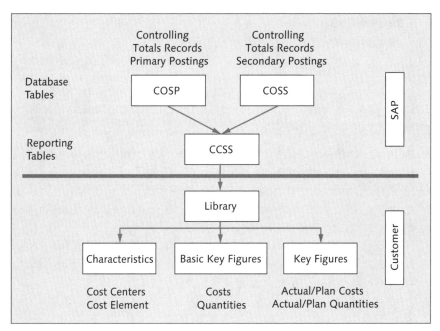

Figure 1.2 Relationships Among Database Tables, Reporting Tables, and Report Painter Libraries

SAP has defined database tables and reporting tables. Approximately 60 reporting tables are delivered in the standard SAP ERP system. You can structure the contents of the reporting tables in libraries. A library represents a selection of characteristics and key figures associated with a particular reporting table. Therefore, please check whether the reporting tables delivered by SAP contain the analysis characteristics and key figures you require.

Libraries

Report Painter is particularly suitable for the following areas:

Areas in which Report Painter can be used

▶ Cost Center Accounting

▶ Internal orders

▶ Analyses in accordance with cost of sales accounting

▶ Profit Center Accounting

▶ Reconciliation ledgers (if the new general ledger is not used)

▶ Special ledgers

▸ General ledger

▸ Project System (PS)

▸ Product Cost Planning

You should examine the use of Report Painter in these areas. The following two examples demonstrate the advantages associated with using Report Painter in this context.

Example 1: Controlling report

Figure 1.3 shows the first example, namely a controlling report. The controlling report analyzes account groups in individual rows. In a master data hierarchy, individual accounts are grouped together. Planned, actual, and variance costs are displayed in the columns. In addition, key figures are calculated in the lower section of the report. As in Excel, specific column and row positions are used as a basis. Report Painter is an excellent reporting instrument in Overhead Cost Controlling and Profit Center Accounting, in particular.

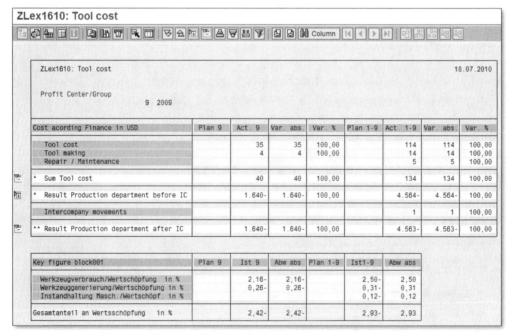

Figure 1.3 Example of a Controlling Report in Report Painter

You can also create very good analyses in FI. In real life, Report Painter is very often used to create a provisions report. Figure 1.4 shows you the creation screen for a Report Painter report.

Example 2: Provisions report

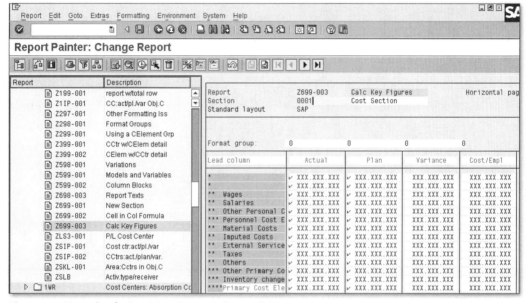

Figure 1.4 Example of a Provisions Report in Report Painter

The different applications are displayed on the left-hand side of the screen as libraries. You now obtain a report generator as an Excel display. By double-clicking the rows and columns, you can use the contents you require. The two axes are displayed in the original report display accordingly. This display is also known as WYSIWYG (What You See Is What You Get).

The Report Painter interface is comparable with an Excel spreadsheet. Consequently, planned or actual values for each period or fiscal year are usually displayed in the columns. In the rows, the data is displayed in accordance with an expandable summarization group (e.g., a cost element); in other words, the report structure is fixed in terms of the columns and rows displayed. If you now want to analyze other char-

Characteristics and key figures

acteristics or key figures in the rows or columns, you must adjust the report accordingly.

Distinguishing between Report Painter and Drilldown Reporting

The Drilldown Reporting tool affords you the flexibility to change the characteristics in the report display. This tool has many interactive functions, which we will describe in the next section.

1.4.3 Drilldown Reporting

Drilldown Reporting provides you with an interactive analysis of your cumulated data. The Drilldown Reporting function is used in FI, in particular. Table 1.6 shows the most important transactions for report creation.

Master Record	Report Overview	Create Form	Change Form	Display Form	Create Report	Change Report	Display Report
GL accounts New GL	FGI0	FGI4	FGI5	FGI6	FGI1	FGI2	FGI3
GL accounts Classic GL	FSI0	FSI4	FSI5	FSI6	FSI1	FSI2	FSI3
Customers	FDI0	FDI4	FDI5	FDI6	FDI1	FDI2	FDI3
Vendors	FKI0	FKI4	FKI5	FKI6	FKI1	FKI2	FKI3
Profit centers	KE80	KE81	KE82	KE83	KE84	KE85	KE86
Projects	CJE0	CJE1	CJE2	CJE3	CJE4	CJE5	CJE6
CO-PA totals records	KE30	KE34	KE35	KE36	KE31	KE32	KE33
CO-PA line items	KE30	KE94	KE95	KE96	KE91	KE32	KE33

Table 1.6 Transactions for Creating Reports in Drilldown Reporting

Example: Key figure reports

You can use the Drilldown Reporting tool to create key figure reports, in particular. For example, you can create valuable key figure reports in Profitability Analysis (CO-PA) and Financial Accounting (FI). An example of a key figure report is shown in Figure 1.5.

```
Formular          ZLEX99SAVE   ZLex Group ReportBlatt 1  / 1
```

	IST &3FY 1 - &1PT	in %	IST &3FY 1 - 12	in %	IST &1FY 1 - &1PT	in %	IST LJ in % &3FY 1 - 12	PLAN &1FY 1 - &1PT
KEY FIGURES								
Liquidity								
Cash Ratio ❶ (Cash/Sh-t liab. > 20-30)	0	←xxx,xx	0	←xxx,xx	0	⊞xxx,xx	0	0
Quick Ratio (Cash+Rec./Sh-t liab. > 100)	0	←xxx,xx	0	←xxx,xx	0	⊞xxx,xx	0	0
Current Ratio (Cu.Ass./Sh-t liab. > 200)	0	⊞xxx,xx	0	⊞xxx,xx	0	⊞xxx,xx	0	0
Intensity of Cash (Cash/Assets)	0	⊞xxx,xx	0	⊞xxx,xx	0	⊞xxx,xx	0	0
Assets & Liabilities								
Intensity of Stock (Stock/Assets)	0	⊞xxx,xx	0	⊞xxx,xx	0	⊞xxx,xx	0	0
Stock turnover (months)	0	0	0	0	0	⊞xxx,xx	0	0
Receiv. turnover Third Party (months)	0	0	0	0	0	0	0	0
Receiv. turnover Intercompany (months)	0	0	0	0	0	0	0	0
Reveiv. turnover Total (months)	0	0	0	0	0	0	0	0
Payables turnover Total (months)	0	0	0	0	0	0	0	0
Gross turnover / current assets	⊞ xxx.xxx.xxx	0	⊞ xxx.xxx.xxx	0	⊞ xxx.xxx.xxx	0	0	0
Gross turnover / current assets in days	⊞ xxx.xxx.xxx	0	⊞ xxx.xxx.xxx	0	⊞ xxx.xxx.xxx	0	0	0
IC Loans to Equity (Thin capital. Rule)	0	⊞xxx,xx	0	⊞xxx,xx	0	⊞xxx,xx	0	0
Profitability								
Salary Costs to Gross Margin on Sales	0	⊞xxx,xx	0	⊞xxx,xx	0	⊞xxx,xx	0	0
Gross Margin on Net Sales	0	⊞xxx,xx	0	⊞xxx,xx	0	⊞xxx,xx	0	0
EBITAD Margin (EBITAD/Net Sales)	0	⊞xxx,xx	0	⊞xxx,xx	0	⊞xxx,xx	0	0
EBIT Margin (EBIT/Net Sales)	0	⊞xxx,xx	0	⊞xxx,xx	0	⊞xxx,xx	0	0
Income Margin (Result b. tax/Net Sal.)	0	⊞xxx,xx	0	⊞xxx,xx	0	⊞xxx,xx	0	0
Earnings Margin (Result a. tax/Net Sal.)	0	⊞xxx,xx	0	⊞xxx,xx	0	⊞xxx,xx	0	0
Covenants								
Equity Ratio (Equity/Liabilities)	0	⊞xxx,xx	0	⊞xxx,xx	0	⊞xxx,xx	0	0
Interest Coverage Ratio (EBIT/Int.Res.)	0	⊞xxx,xx	0	⊞xxx,xx	0	⊞xxx,xx	0	0
Borrowing Ratio (EBITAD/Bank Debts)	0	⊞xxx,xx	0	⊞xxx,xx	0	⊞xxx,xx	0	0

Figure 1.5 Drilldown Reporting — Key Figure Report

When creating a Drilldown Reporting report, you must first define a form that will contain field contents at field level. As in Excel, a field can represent row 3, column 4, for example. In real life, key figures such as EBIT (Earnings Before Interest and Tax) are determined (❶).

Form in Drilldown Reporting report

The most important part of a Drilldown Reporting report is the creation of the report form. You can also use Report Painter technology to create the form. You therefore require very little additional knowledge to create your own Drilldown Reporting report.

SAP delivers numerous reports in the standard system. For each application area, there is one central transaction with which you can execute Drilldown Reporting reports:

Drilldown Reporting reports in the standard system

▸ FGI0 — New General Ledger (New GL)

▸ FSI0 — Classic General Ledger

▸ FDI0 — Accounts Receivable Accounting

- FKIO — Accounts Payable Accounting
- KE80 — Profit Center
- KE30 — CO-PA (Totals Item and Line Item Reports)
- CJEO — Project Reports

[+] **Using Report Templates**

Before you create a new report, take a look at the previously mentioned transactions to see if the report you require already exists. Frequently, it is useful to use an existing report as a template for a new report.

Figure 1.6 shows various balance sheet reports with different time periods for the classic general ledger.

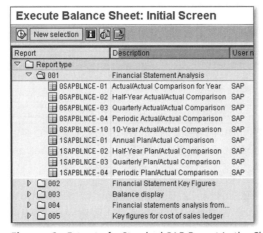

Figure 1.6 Extract of a Standard SAP Report in the Classic General Ledger

Cash flow reports   Predefined key figure reports are delivered in addition to the various reports for financial statement analysis. Four sample reports for displaying the cash flow are available, for example. One advantage of the Drilldown Reporting tool is the flexible selection of analysis characteristics. Open customer items were analyzed in Figure 1.7.

Here, you will see the four areas of the Drilldown Reporting tool:

The navigation bar (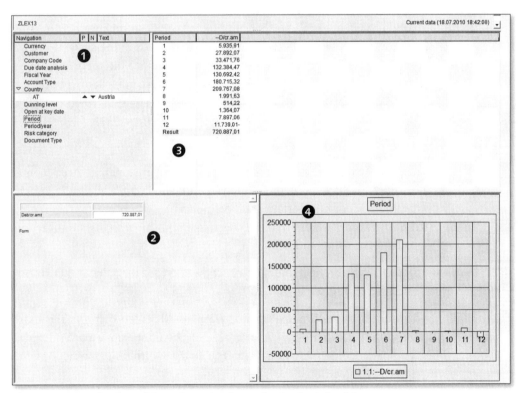❶) contains various characteristics for a specific data selection. In our example, open items were selected for Austria. The PERIOD/YEAR characteristic was then selected.

Navigation bar

In the lower-left screen area (❷), you can define predefined key figures. In our example, the debit/credit amount is shown.

Key figures

The selected data is also displayed in the breakdown (❸). In our example, you see when the open items for Austria fall due. You could now use drag and drop to further analyze these values (e.g., in accordance with the CUSTOMER criterion).

Breakdown

Area (❹) is a graphical representation of the data that you have selected.

Graphic

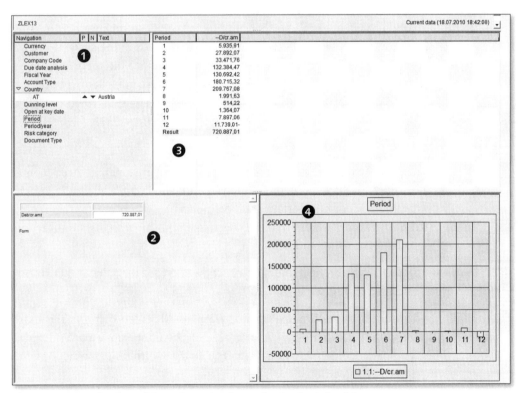

Figure 1.7 Example of a Drilldown Reporting Report for the Analysis of Open Customer Items

In summary, Report Painter and Drilldown Reporting are excellent tools for creating reports in FI. These tools are also considerably faster than using SAP Query or standard SAP transactions for a summarized display of single records, especially when you want to display cumulated data and use multilevel hierarchies.

In addition to the summary reports shown in this section, SAP ERP has numerous excellent standard reports. In the next section, we will introduce you to a selection of these reports.

1.5   Using Standard Reports

Not every analysis is customer-specific, and it is not always necessary to create a new (query) report. In the standard system, there are many good predefined analyses that provide the information you require. This section shows how you can find standard analyses in the system. Before you create a new report, you should check whether the report you need already exists in the standard system. The most important reports for real-life scenarios are also listed.

1.5.1   SAP Area Menus

One way to identify standard reports is to use area menus. Area menus are menu trees that are predefined by SAP and contain the most important transactions for certain areas of application. There are approximately 1,500 area menus. You can call the area menus by entering a transaction code in the command field.

Sales and Distribution area menu (Transaction SD01)

In the command field, enter Transaction SD01 for the Sales and Distribution area menu (see Figure 1.8).

Instead of the entire SAP menu, your initial screen displays the most important transactions in the Sales and Distribution menu. Under the SALES • QUOTATIONS menu path, you find six different transactions for analyzing quotations.

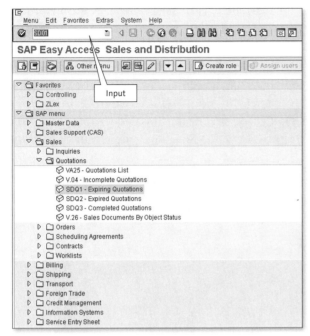

Figure 1.8 Calling the Sales and Distribution Area Menu

You can use Transaction SE43 (Area Menu) to find the SAP area menu. Enter Transaction SE43 in the command field to display the AREA MENU MAINTENANCE screen (Figure 1.9).

Area menu maintenance (Transaction SE43)

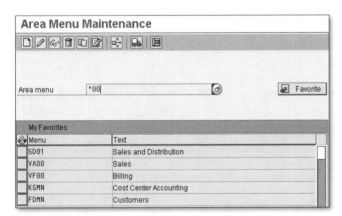

Figure 1.9 Displaying Area Menus in Transaction SE43

Matchcode
(Transaction SE41)

Here, you can use the matchcode F4 to select the relevant menu for you. You either search through all 1,500 area menus (approximately), or you use the explanatory text to restrict the number of menus. For example, you could use the text "Sales" to find an area menu. Because many important area menus have the ending MN or 00, you could perform a *MN or *00 search in the area menu. By entering an asterisk before the two zeros, you get all area menus that end with MN or 00. Call the matchcode F4 in Transaction SE41, and enter your restriction (see Figure 1.10).

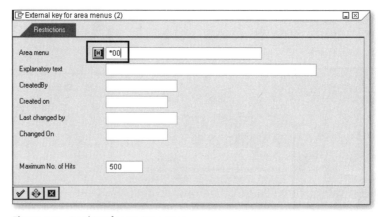

Figure 1.10 Looking for an Area Menu

You obtain approximately 125 different area menus in your search result. The actual transactions are listed on the left-hand side of the result. For example, your search result contains Transaction VA00 for the SALES area menu (see Figure 1.11).

Sales area menu
(Transaction VA00)

If you now enter Transaction VA00 in the command field, a menu branch containing the relevant transactions from the Sales area is displayed. Expand the INFORMATION SYSTEM • QUOTATIONS path in the menu branch, and the system displays six transactions for analyzing quotations.

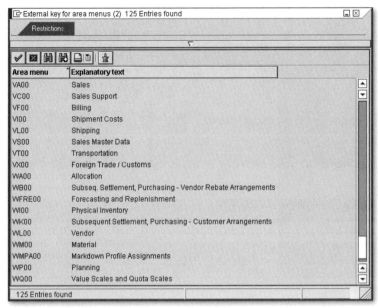

Figure 1.11 Displaying Area Menus Ending with 00

1.5.2 Finding a Report in the SAP Menu

You can also find standard reports by searching the entire SAP menu for a term. To do this, enter Transaction SEARCH_SAP_MENU in the command field (as shown in Figure 1.12).

Transaction SEARCH_SAP_MENU

Figure 1.12 Entering "search_sap_menu" in the Command Field

After you have entered the command "search_sap_menu" or pressed the key combination $\boxed{\text{Ctrl}}$ + $\boxed{\text{F}}$, the system displays the SEARCH IN MENU

Finding transactions

TREE dialog box. You can enter any term here. You can also use an * as a wildcard. For example, if you search for "Customer master*", the transaction for calling the customer master record is displayed. Alternatively, enter the term "Quotations" in the FIND field (see Figure 1.13).

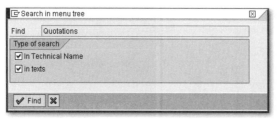

Figure 1.13 Entering the Search Term "Quotations" in Transaction "search_sap_menu"

After you have chosen the button with the green checkmark to confirm the search term "Quotations", the system displays the relevant menu paths on the next screen. You now have an accurate overview of the menu item that contains the transactions for analyzing quotations (see Figure 1.14).

Search for a Transaction Code or Menu Title

Node	Transaction code	Text
Nodes	V.04	Display Incomplete Quotations
Preceding node		Inquiry and Quotation
Preceding node		Service Agreements
Preceding node		Report Selection
Preceding node		Information System
Preceding node		Equipment and Tools Management
Preceding node		Logistics
Nodes	SDQ1	Expiring Quotations
Preceding node		Inquiry and Quotation
Preceding node		Service Agreements
Preceding node		Report Selection
Preceding node		Information System
Preceding node		Equipment and Tools Management
Preceding node		Logistics
Nodes	SDQ2	Expired Quotations
Preceding node		Inquiry and Quotation
Preceding node		Service Agreements
Preceding node		Report Selection
Preceding node		Information System
Preceding node		Equipment and Tools Management
Preceding node		Logistics

Figure 1.14 Search Result for the Term "Quotations" in the SAP Menu

In this way, you find the same transactions as the ones you found when searching the area menu. However, because menu branches are displayed when you search the SAP menu, we generally recommend that you search the SAP menu directly.

1.5.3 Searching the Menu for Standard Reports

You can perform a search directly in the actual application for which you require an analysis. In the standard SAP menu, select the following menu branch, for example: LOGISTICS • SALES AND DISTRIBUTION • SALES • INFORMATION SYSTEM • QUOTATIONS. After you have expanded the QUOTATIONS menu item, you find six transactions for analyzing quotations (see Figure 1.15).

Searching an SAP component

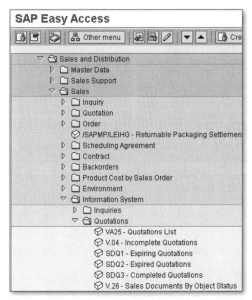

Figure 1.15 Searching the SAP Menu for Transactions for Analyzing Quotations

In addition to searching the information system for the relevant application, you can also search the INFORMATION SYSTEMS menu item. As well as the application components from the LOGISTICS, ACCOUNTING, and HUMAN RESOURCES areas, a cross-application menu branch with analyses is also available (see Figure 1.16).

"Information Systems" menu item

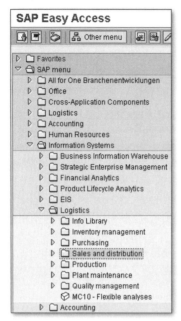

Figure 1.16 Standard SAP Menu: Information Systems

In addition to the reports available under INFORMATION SYSTEMS, SAP has created additional transactions that are not yet available in the standard menu. We will introduce you to these transactions in the next section.

1.5.4 Important Standard Transactions

On feedback from its customers, SAP has revised many transactions and equipped them with improved functions. However, existing transactions have not been changed. Instead, they coexist with the newly revised transactions, which have the suffix N.

List of Quotations (Transaction VA25 and VA25N)

For example, Transaction VA25N is now available in addition to the former Transaction VA25 for querying quotations (List of Quotations).

Transaction VA25 has six selection fields (see Figure 1.17). However, the new transaction (VA25N) is considerably more flexible because its new selection screen contains the new and improved functions for analyzing quotations (see Figure 1.18). Additional display functions are available for the report, which now has a modernized layout. Furthermore, you can display and change quotations directly.

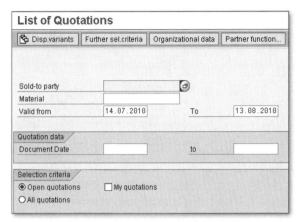

Figure 1.17 Transaction VA25 — List of Quotations

List of Quotations

Docum.Data			
Document Number		to	
Sales Document Type		to	
Sold-To Party		to	
Document Date		to	
Material		to	
Valid From		to	
Purchase Order Number			

Persons Responsible			
Partner Functions Responsible			
Personnel Number Responsible		to	
Created By		to	

Organizat. data			
Sales Organization		to	
Distribution Channel		to	
Division		to	
Sales Office		to	
Sales Group		to	

Selection Crit.
○ Open Quotations
◉ All Quotations

Figure 1.18 Transaction VA25N — List of Quotations

Table 1.7 contains a selection of transactions that are not available in the SAP menu.

Application	Transaction	Description
Sales and Distribution	VA05N	List of Sales Orders
Sales and Distribution	VA15N	List of Inquiries
Sales and Distribution	VA25N	List of Quotations
Sales and Distribution	VA35N	List of Scheduling Agreements
Sales and Distribution	VA45N	List of Contracts
Sales and Distribution	VF05N	List of Billing Documents
Purchasing	ME80AN	General Analyses (Inquiry)
Purchasing	ME80FN	General Analyses (Purchase Order)
Purchasing	ME80RN	General Analyses (Contract, Scheduling Agreement)
Purchasing	ME81N	Analysis of Purchase Order Values

Table 1.7 Transactions with Extensive Options

The new transactions provide highly flexible options. In the Purchasing transactions, for example, you can navigate directly to the purchasing documents (e.g., purchase order) or the material master. In the purchasing analyses, you can also display the purchase schedule lines and purchase order history.

1.6 Summary

In SAP ERP, SAP provides the following three query reporting tools for data queries: SAP Query, InfoSet Query, and QuickViewer. You can use these tools immediately in the SAP ERP system without any extensive training or additional costs for online data queries.

When analyzing mass data and highly summarized financial key figures, we recommend that you use SAP NetWeaver BW or Report Painter. The Report Painter technology is also used in the Drilldown Reporting tool. In addition, the standard system already contains numerous analyses.

In real life, there are numerous application scenarios in which SAP Query has advantages over SAP NetWeaver BW and Report Painter. In query reporting, it is important to find the correct table with the relevant data content. We will therefore explain how to find the relevant tables in the next chapter, Overview of SAP Tables and Table Links.

In this chapter, you will learn how to use the Data Browser to display table contents. We will then show you how to find the relevant tables yourself. We will also introduce you to the most important SAP database tables. Finally, we will explain possible links between SAP tables.

2   Overview of SAP Tables and Table Links

If you want to create a report, you must know its data basis. Therefore, you must look at the transactions used to create the data records for the report, create several sample data records for the report or create sample data, and then view your new data records in the database. You can only localize the data content in the database if you know the actual application transactions.

Any information entered in the system is stored in a database table. In this chapter, we will show you how to display this data. You will then learn how to find the relevant database tables yourself.

Because many analyses are based on just a few tables, we will introduce you to the relationships that exist between the most important SAP tables in Section 2.3, Table Links. First let's look at the Data Browser in the system. You can use the Data Browser to view SAP ERP database tables and get an overview of their content and structure.

2.1   Data Browser

This section shows you how to use the Data Browser to display data in the SAP system directly in the database.

If the data you require is contained in one table only, the current display may already fulfill your reporting requirements. At the very least, the data display will help clarify the data content, so that you can find the correct data for your report or check this data. For a one-time analysis, it may suffice to export multiple tables to Excel.

In the SAP system, a distinction is made among the following table categories:

▶ TRANSP — transparent table

▶ INTTAB — structure

▶ CLUSTER — cluster table

▶ POOL — pool table

▶ VIEW — table view (generated view structure)

The transparent tables and the table view are important for you. Only for these two table categories, which are defined in the Data Dictionary, can you use the Data Browser to query the contents directly.

Transparent table

The transparent table has a one-to-one relationship with a table in the database. In a transparent table, you can call the application's master data or transaction data directly. You can therefore query data in a transparent table directly.

Structure

A structure represents a combination of fields. No data is stored in the structure itself. Instead, the purpose of a structure is to store data temporarily so that it can be processed further or be used in calculations. Lastly, any data temporarily imported into a structure is output in the system. A structure therefore contains data when a program is running.

Cluster tables and pool tables

Cluster tables and pool tables comprise several tables. Consequently, a simple data display is not possible here. HR frequently uses such table categories to store summarized data objects.

Table view

Finally, the SAP system knows the table view. No data is stored in the view itself. Rather, the view represents a view of transparent tables. You can use a view to display selected data from one or more tables. The system contains numerous valuable views, which can display data from several tables. For your query report, you can use an existing view or create your own. If you use an existing view, it will be easier for you to create a query.

To use the Data Browser to view database tables, follow these steps:

1. Log on to your SAP system. The SAP EASY ACCESS initial screen is displayed.

2. Left-click in the SAP command field and use Transaction SE16 or SE16N to call the Data Browser. Alternatively, enter the letter "N" in the command field (see Figure 2.1). Then press the Enter key.

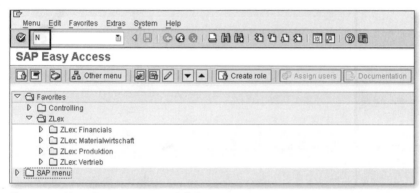

Figure 2.1 Using Transaction N to Call the Data Browser

3. The system then displays the GENERAL TABLE DISPLAY screen. You are now in the Data Browser and can display table contents and existing tables.

4. Enter the table name "DD02L" in the TABLE field (see Figure 2.2).

5. For the table DD02L (SAP Tables), you can now determine the number of hits for different SELECTION CRITERIA.

When you use the Data Browser, you can determine the number of materials, customers, vendors, and so on, for a plant, company code, sales/purchasing organization, or document type.

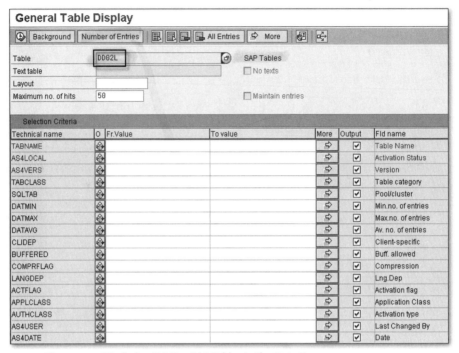

Figure 2.2 Displaying Existing SAP Tables in the Data Browser

Number of entries in the Data Browser

6. The SAP ERP system contains approximately 310,000 database tables. You can choose the NUMBER OF ENTRIES button to display the number of tables in your system. This button is directly above the input field in which you entered the table name DD02L. By limiting the selection, you can find not only the scope of data but also the data that is actually relevant for you.

The system then displays a dialog box with the number of entries found (see Figure 2.3). The system used for the purposes of this book (SAP ERP 6.0) contains 311,260 tables. In transparent tables, you can analyze the data directly.

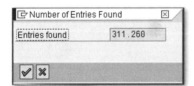

Figure 2.3 Number of SAP Tables (Release SAP ERP 6.0)

To find the transparent tables, proceed as follows:

1. In the TABLE CATEGORY field, enter the value "TRANSP" (see Figure 2.4) or use the matchcode F4 to select the characteristic value TRANSP.

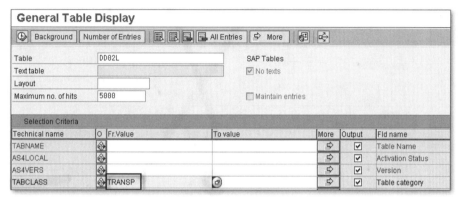

Figure 2.4 Selecting Transparent Tables in the Data Browser

2. You have now queried the table DD02L (SAP Tables) without restricting the selection. Enter "TRANSP" in the Table category field, and choose the Number of Entries button again.

   You now get a considerably lower hit list of approximately 71,000 entries (see Figure 2.5).

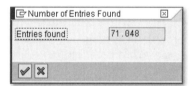

Figure 2.5 Querying Table DD02L with the Characteristic TRANSP

You do not have to know everything about the approximately 71,000 transparent tables. In real life, it frequently suffices to have an overview of only the most important tables for the analysis object you require. In the next section, we will show you how to find the tables that you require for your analysis.

2.2   Table Determination Options

Although often it is very easy to find a table, in some cases, it can also be extremely challenging. There are many ways to determine an actual table. The most important ones are shown in Table 2.1.

Transaction	Application	Explanation
F1 help	Field help	Click in the data field. The F1 help displays technical information about the field.
SE36	Logical databases	These are hierarchically related tables for an object, which are fully preconfigured by SAP.
ST05	Table trace	This transaction is performed in one SAP mode, while the table accesses are recorded in a second mode.
SARA	Archiving	All dependent tables are displayed for an archiving object.
SE80	Where-used list	In the ABAP Dictionary, the related tables are found on the basis of the technical attributes of a field.

Table 2.1   Options for Finding a Table

[+]   **Using the F1 Help to Find a Table**

Using the F1 help to find a table is easy. You do not require any special authorizations for the table trace or for displaying archiving objects.

In the next section, we will describe in greater detail the most frequently used method for finding a table, namely the F1 help. In our example, we want to find a table that will help us analyze the sales documents entered in the system.

2.2.1   F1 Help

You can use the F1 help to find a database table by following these steps:

1. Call Transaction VA03 (Display Sales Order). Click in the ORDER field (see Figure 2.6).

Figure 2.6 Displaying a Sales Order

2. Press the ⌷F1⌷ help key. The system displays a window in which an explanation of the ORDER field is provided (see Figure 2.7).

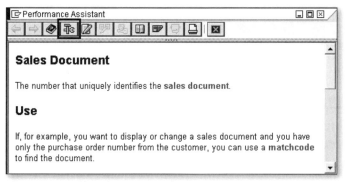

Figure 2.7 Field Explanation — Sales Document

3. Choose the TECHNICAL INFORMATION button ⌷⌷ in the toolbar. A large amount of technical information about the current program appears. Here, you will also see the table in which the sales document information is stored, namely a transparent table (see Figure 2.8).

Technical information

The sales document number is in the table VBAK and field VBELN. As described in the previous section, you can now use the Data Browser to display all sales documents in your system.

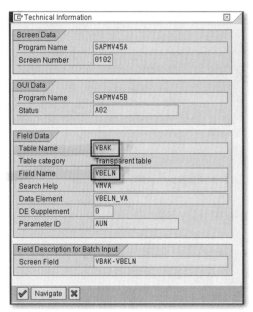

Figure 2.8 Technical Information about the Sales Document Field

The table information is not always as unique as it is in this example. If you use the F1 help, structures are displayed for other fields such as address data. Consequently, the other methods described next are also applied in real life.

Header data and item data

Essentially, most objects have header data and item data. For example, the sales document contains header data information (the document number or sales organization) that applies to the entire document. Other information (e.g., the material number or ship-to party) is stored in the item data. If you now add more data to an item, you do not need to change all of the header data. The same is true for changes. If, for example, you change the material number in a sales document, only the relevant header data changes.

If the information about an analysis object is contained in several tables, it makes sense to display them as related tables in the SAP system. SAP has adopted this train of thought by defining *logical databases* for the most important data objects.

> **Logical Databases** [«]
>
> Logical databases already contain a hierarchical table structure for the most important data objects. On one hand, the logical databases perform the table search for you. On the other hand, the links between the tables are already predefined. SAP ERP contains approximately 250 predefined logical databases.

Logical databases can also be the basis for a query report. If your queries are manageable in terms of data volume and complexity, you should use a logical database to perform a query.

With a logical database, you can work in the SAP system as follows:

1. Enter Transaction SE36 in the command field, or choose the following menu path: TOOLS • ABAP WORKBENCH • DEVELOPMENT • PROGRAMMING ENVIRONMENT • LOGICAL DATABASES. The system then displays the menu window shown in Figure 2.9.

Displaying a logical database

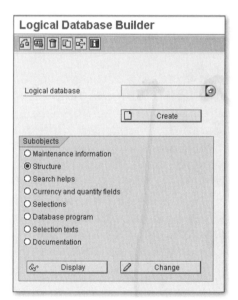

Figure 2.9 Calling the Logical Database Builder

2. Click in the LOGICAL DATABASE field, and select the matchcode [F4]. The system now displays the search window shown in Figure 2.10, which you can use to select logical databases.

Searching the logical database

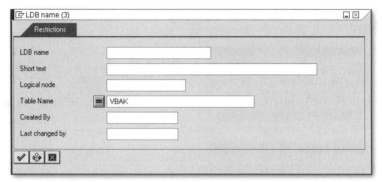

Figure 2.10   Logical Database with the Table VBAK

Using a table
to determine a
logical database
3. If you already know a relevant table, it is relatively easy to find related tables. In this case, we know that the sales documents are stored in the table VBAK. Therefore, to analyze sales documents, search all logical databases for the table VBAK (see Figure 2.11).

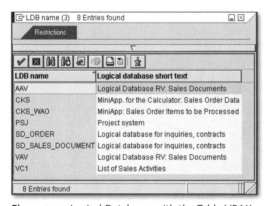

Figure 2.11   Logical Databases with the Table VBAK

Displaying a
logical database
4. Eight logical databases have been found. Now take a look at the first logical database AAV — Logical Database RV: Sales Documents. To do this, select the entry AAV. You then return to the initial screen for logical databases (see Figure 2.12).

5. At this point, we are not interested in the technical possibilities associated with the logical database because that is beyond the scope of this book. Select the Structure option, and then choose

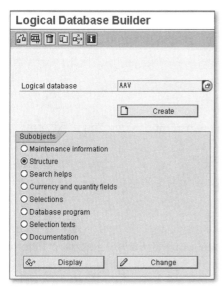 | . The system then displays the hierarchical structure of the logical database AAV (see Figure 2.13).

Figure 2.12 Displaying the Structure of the Logical Database AAV

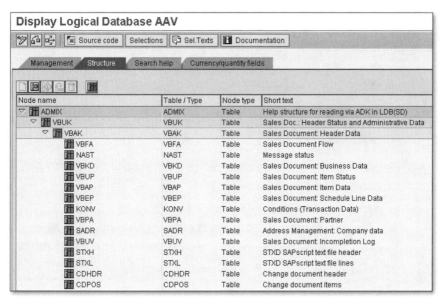

Figure 2.13 Table Structure of the Logical Database AAV

In addition to the table VBAK (Sales Document: Header Data), 15 other tables are displayed.

In this way, you have obtained the most important database tables for analyzing sales documents. Now take a look at other logical databases. For example, you can search all logical databases that are associated with the already known material master table MARA.

2.2.2   Table Trace

The table trace is another option for determining tables. You need administrator authorizations for the table trace. Here, you work in two screens. In one screen, you call the transaction for which you want to analyze the data; in a second mode, you log all table accesses while you execute the transaction.

1. Call Transaction VA03 (Display Sales Order). In your system, enter an existing sales document number in the ORDER field (see Figure 2.14).

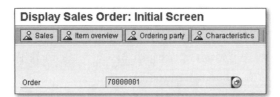

Figure 2.14   Displaying a Sales Order

2. Call a second screen mode in which you call Transaction ST05. Select the SQL TRACE selection as shown in Figure 2.15.

3. Choose the ACTIVATE TRACE button on the right-hand side of Transaction ST05 (Performance Analysis).

4. In your first mode, switch to Transaction VA03, and press the [Enter] key. The system logs all database accesses at this moment in time.

5. After you have executed Transaction VA03 (Display Sales Order), return to Transaction ST05 (Performance Analysis).

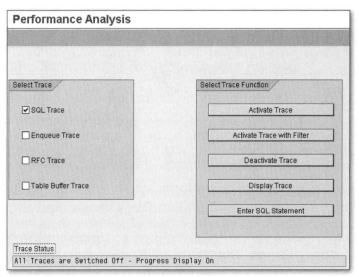

Figure 2.15 Activating Performance Analysis

6. Click the DEACTIVATE TRACE button on the right-hand side of the screen. The system displays the window shown in Figure 2.16.

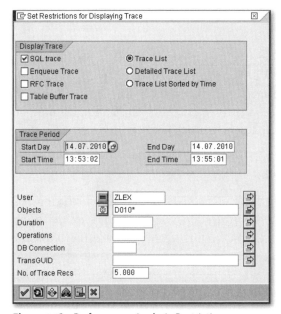

Figure 2.16 Performance Analysis Restrictions

Performing a
table trace

7. In the DISPLAY TRACE screen area, select only the SQL TRACE option. Leave the remaining data on this screen unchanged. If necessary, restrict the trace period and user further. After you have confirmed your entries on this screen (either with a green checkmark ✔ or by pressing the ⌨Enter key), the system displays the screen shown in Figure 2.17.

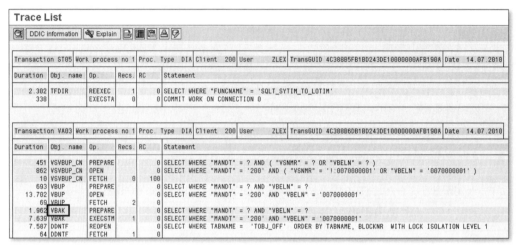

Figure 2.17 Displaying a Trace List

Displaying the
trace result

The relevant database tables are now listed in the OBJ. NAME column in the trace list. The table VBAK (Sales Document: Header Data) and all other database tables associated with displaying a sales order are shown. The relevant fields are also displayed on the right-hand side, and our own sample data is displayed next to these fields.

2.2.3 Archiving Object

The next option for finding tables, that is, the use of an archiving object, also requires administrator authorizations. SAP provides you with the option of archiving object data. Archiving objects are the basis for archiving. For example, in the case of the SALES DOCUMENT archiving object, the tables VBAK (Sales Document: Header Data), VBAP (Sales Document: Item Data), and so on are bundled together. The SALES DOCU-

MENT archiving object contains all tables associated with processing sales documents.

To archive an object, follow these steps:

1. Call Transaction SARA (Archive Administration: Initial Screen) to access the screen shown in Figure 2.18.

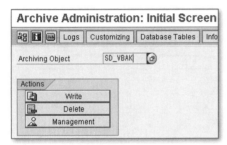

Figure 2.18 Archive Administration — Initial Screen

2. You can now use the matchcode F4 to search for the relevant archiving object. Select the archiving object SD_VBAK from the 525 archiving objects available.

3. Choose DATABASE TABLES. You now get an overview of all tables associated with the selected archiving object (see Figure 2.19).

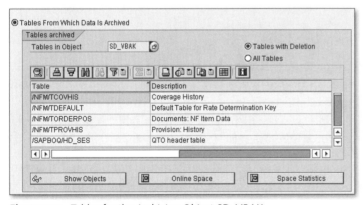

Figure 2.19 Tables for the Archiving Object SD_VBAK

4. On the same screen, you get additional help to identify the relevant archiving object. As you can see in Figure 2.20, you can also use the table VBAK (Sales Document: Header Data) to determine the archiving object.

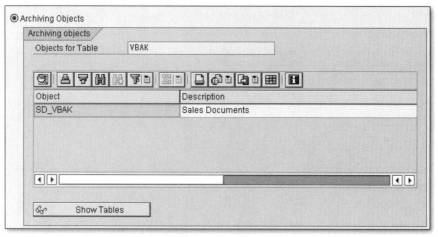

Figure 2.20 Finding Archiving Objects for Table VBAK

5. Enter the now familiar table VBAK in the OBJECTS FOR TABLE field.

6. You now get the archiving object SD_VBAK, and you can display the database tables associated with this archiving object.

2.2.4 Where-Used List

If the preceding options prove to be unsuccessful in finding your table, the where-used list may help you further. The where-used list helps you find tables on the basis of the table fields or technical attributes of the fields. For example, you can display the tables in which a particular field occurs. To use the where-used list, follow these steps:

1. Call Transaction VD03 to display a customer master. Then display an existing customer in your system. Your system now displays the DIS-PLAY CUSTOMER: GENERAL DATA screen (see Figure 2.21).

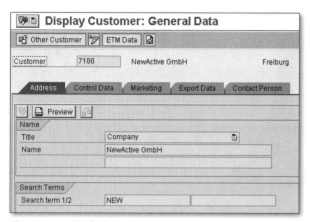

Figure 2.21 Displaying a Customer

2. Position your cursor on the NAME field. Press the $\boxed{\text{F1}}$ key and display technical information about the NAME field (as shown in Figure 2.22).

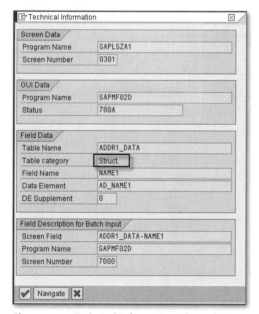

Figure 2.22 Technical Information About the Name Field

Structure
as technical
information

▶ The system displays the TABLE NAME ADDR1_DATA, which is a structure for data storage. Consequently, you cannot use this information directly in a query report. NAME1 is displayed as the FIELD NAME. The structure temporarily saves the data from a transparent table. To transfer the data from the transparent table to the structure, the fields of the transparent table and structure must be identical. Because the structure field must have the same structure (data type) as the underlying table, we can search for the relevant table on this basis.

3. Call Transaction SE85 (Object Navigator). You now see an overview of all relevant development objects (see Figure 2.23). In the Object Navigator, open the third menu path, ABAP DICTIONARY.

4. Open the FIELDS folder, and double-click the TABLE FIELDS entry.

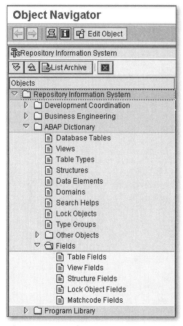

Figure 2.23 Object Navigator — Display

5. After you have double-clicked the TABLE FIELDS menu item, a selection screen in which you can search table names is displayed on the right-hand side. Now enter "Name1" in the FIELD NAME field (as shown in Figure 2.24).

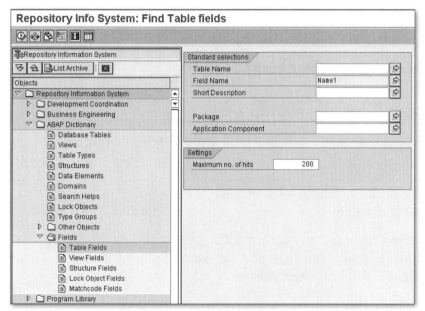

Figure 2.24 Repository Information System — Table Search

6. You can now list all tables that contain the NAME1 field. To get an overview of all relevant tables, choose ⊕ (Execute) or press the F8 key. The system will now search all tables that contain the NAME1 field (Figure 2.25).

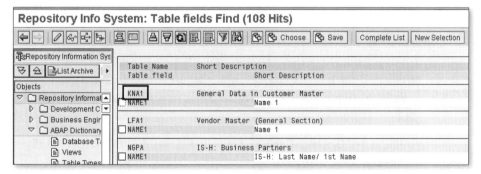

Figure 2.25 Transparent Tables with the Name1 Field

7. Among the 108 tables found, you also find a table called KNA1 — GENERAL DATA IN CUSTOMER MASTER. The data from the customer display screen is stored in this table.

2.3   Table Links

This section uses two analysis objects — customer master and sales document — to explain the relationships between tables.

2.3.1   Customer Master

The customer master comprises three data areas:

▶ General data

▶ Company code data

▶ Sales area data

If you call a customer master, you need to restrict the data display further. As you can see in Figure 2.26, you can select data for a particular company code or actual sales area.

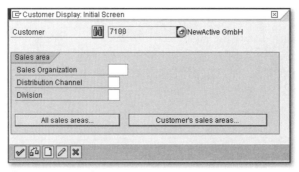

Figure 2.26   Display — Customer

If you find the three data areas in the database, you will find the following descriptive table names (Please note: the table names are based on a German system):

▶ KNA1 — General Data in Customer Master/**Ku**ndenstamm (**a**llgemeiner Teil) in German

▶ KNB1 — Customer Master (Company Code)/**Ku**ndenstamm (**B**uchungskreis) in German

▶ KNVV — Customer Master Sales Data/**Ku**ndenstamm **V**ertriebsdaten in German

Customer master tables usually start with the prefix KN (**Kun**denstamm in German). Most database table names contain four characters. You identify the application area (component) by the third character in the database table. The letter A for General (**A**llgemein in German) is used for the customer master. In other words, this data is not associated with Accounting or Sales and Distribution. The letter B represents Accounting data (**B**uchhaltungsdaten in German), while V, when used as the third character, represents customer master information from Sales and Distribution (**V**ertrieb in German).

Logic applied when naming customer master tables

If you use the Data Browser to search for all tables beginning with KNV (KNV*), you will find a total of 10 database tables with customer sales data (**Kun**den**v**ertriebsdaten in German) (see Figure 2.27).

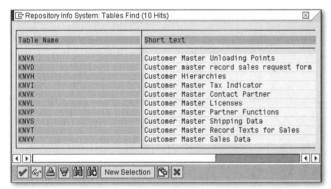

Figure 2.27 Database Tables for Customers from Sales and Distribution

In the SAP system, tables have very descriptive names. For example, all customer tables (**Kun**dentabelle in German) start with the prefix KN. This logic is also applied to many other SAP objects (sales documents, for example).

2.3.2 Sales Document

In the previous section, Customer Master, we established that both general customer data and special customer data exists for the Accounting area and Sales and Distribution area. The relationship between general data and special data also exists for transaction data. When we speak of

Header data and item data

transaction data, we mean header data and item data. A sales document therefore has header data and item data.

If, in sales documents, you consider the tables associated with orders, you will identify the logical naming structure:

▶ VBAK — Sales Document: (Order) Header Data/**V**erkaufs**b**eleg: (**A**uftrags-)**K**opfdaten in German

▶ VBAP — Sales Document: (Order) Item Data/**V**erkaufs**b**eleg: (**A**uftrags-)**P**ositionsdaten in German

Logic applied when naming sales tables
You see that the sales document tables start with the prefix VB (**V**erkaufs**b**eleg in German). You identify the type of sales document by the third character. Here, the tables for sales orders have an A (for Auftrag in German) as their third character. Because you know that the sales invoice documents have an R (for Rechnung in German) as their third character, you can, once again, use the Data Browser to search for the relevant tables (see Figure 2.28).

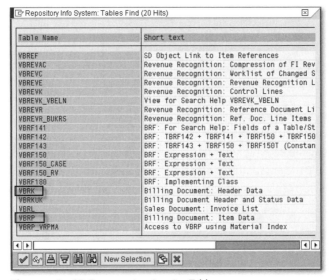

Figure 2.28 SD Documents—Invoice Tables

The INVOICE sales documents follow the same logic as the ORDER sales documents. The Data Browser finds 20 tables, including the following:

- VBRK — Sales Document Invoice Header Data (Billing Document: Header Data)/**V**erkaufs**b**eleg **R**echnung **K**opfdaten (Faktura: Kopfdaten) in German

- VBRP — Sales Document Invoice Item Data (Billing Document: Item Data)/**V**erkaufs**b**eleg **R**echnung **P**ositionsdaten (Faktura: Positionsdaten) in German

This logic may be helpful when searching for tables. The following tables are frequently relevant in conjunction with analyzing sales document header data:

Sales document header data tables

- VBAK — Sales Document: Header Data/**V**erkaufs**b**eleg **K**opfdaten in German

- VBFA — SD Document Flow/**V**ertriebs**b**eleg**f**luss in German

- VBKD — Sales Document: Business Data/**V**erkaufs**b**eleg: **K**aufmännische **D**aten in German

- VBPA — SD Document: Partner/**V**ertriebs**b**eleg: **P**artner in German

- VBUK — SD Document: Header Status and Administrative Data/**V**ertriebs**b**eleg: **K**opfstatus und Verwaltungsdaten in German

- VBUV — Sales Document: Incompleteness Log/**V**erkaufs**b**eleg: **U**nvollständigkeitsprotokoll in German

Frequently, the sales document item data is similar to the sales document header data (in terms of its table names). Instead of K for header data (**K**opfdaten in German), the last letter is P for item data (**P**ositionsdaten in German). The following are the most important database tables for analyzing sales document order items:

Sales document item data tables

- VBAP — Sales Document: Item Data/**V**erkaufs**b**eleg: **P**ositionsdaten in German

- VBEP — Sales Document: Schedule Line Data/**V**erkaufs**b**eleg: **E**inteilungsdaten in German

- VBFA — SD Document Flow/**V**ertriebs**b**eleg**f**luss in German

- VBKD — Sales Document: Business Data/**V**erkaufs**b**eleg: **K**aufmännische **D**aten in German

- VBPA—SD Document: Partner/**V**ertriebs**b**eleg: **P**artner in German

- VBUP — SD Document: Item Status/**V**ertriebs**b**eleg: **P**ositionsstatus in German

- VBUV — Sales Document: Incompleteness Log/**V**erkaufs**b**eleg: **Unv**ollständigkeitsprotokoll in German

Now that you know these tables, it is very easy to further analyze data and format it. Some tables obtain information about the order header and order items. If the data applies to a certain item, the item is listed in the relevant table. Otherwise, the item remains empty (see Figure 2.29).

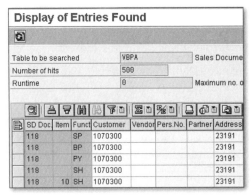

Figure 2.29 Sales Document Partner Table

If we take a look at the most important tables for the sales document order (sales order), we see that most tables start with VB (**V**erkaufs**b**eleg in German). Therefore, a generic table search is also conceivable here. The most important tables and their relationships are listed in the appendix to this book.

2.4 Summary

You are now better equipped to deal with future analyses because you know how to analyze tables in the Data Browser and find the tables relevant for you. In the next chapter, you will learn about QuickViewer in greater detail. You will soon be able to create a report that analyzes transaction texts.

In this chapter, you will learn how to create a simple report yourself. With QuickViewer, you can quickly create an analysis. Finally, you will learn how to create your own selection screen and define display fields for your report.

3   QuickViewer

Of the three query reporting tools (QuickViewer, InfoSet Query, and SAP Query), QuickViewer provides the easiest way to create a report. In this book, we will start by discussing the query reporting functions of QuickViewer for instructional purposes.

QuickViewer is especially suitable for ad hoc queries. In particular, QuickViewer is suitable for users who occasionally create analyses or will do so only once. Any reports generated using QuickViewer are available only to the creator. However, you can convert such reports into SAP Query reports. In Section 7.2.2, Converting QuickView into a Query, in Chapter 7, we will discuss how to convert a QuickViewer report into an SAP Query report.

In this chapter, we provide an overview of the three steps associated with creating a QuickViewer report. The table TSTCT is the data basis for your report. The SAP transactions texts are stored in this table. You will become familiar with the QuickViewer initial screen and learn how to create a QuickViewer report, step by step. Finally, we will explain how to use the basis mode and layout mode, which are available to you as an alternative to creating your report.

3.1   QuickViewer Overview

Because the other two query reporting tools, InfoSet Query and SAP Query, have more extensive functions, it is a good idea to use Quick-

Selection fields

Viewer to show the basic procedure for query reporting. All three query reporting tools access uniform data sources. The process for selecting the selection fields and designing the selection screen is identical for all three reporting tools. For our sample report, you will define three selection fields.

List fields The methodology applied when selecting the fields to be displayed is the same for all three query reporting tools. In the sample report, you will determine three display fields. To get to know the various options within QuickViewer, you will create your first analysis step by step. Specifically, you need to complete only three steps to create a QuickViewer report:

1. **Create and name a report.**
   Enter a report name, and choose CREATE. Then enter a name for your QuickViewer. The name you choose will appear as a report header. You can also enter a comment in relation to the report.

2. **Choose a data source.**
   Select a table, logical database, InfoSet, or table join as a possible data source.

3. **Define selection fields and layout fields.**
   Define the actual selection fields for your selection screen. You can restrict the selected data in accordance with these fields. In addition, define the layout fields for your report output. These fields can be displayed when you output the report.

Table TSTCT To display the QuickViewer functions, you will analyze the SAP transaction texts. To get to know the data basis and learn how to display table fields, you will first use the Data Browser to take a look at the database table for the transaction texts TSTCT.

3.2   Sample Data for Table TSTCT

Language-
dependent
table entries
In our example, we will query the database table TSTCT. This table contains all SAP transactions and associated transaction descriptions. Because the transaction description is language-dependent, it is listed in all languages installed in the system. Consequently, multiple transaction

texts exist for a transaction. You will therefore restrict the selection to English texts. Our analysis will display English texts for all transactions that start with VA0.

You will view the desired result in the Data Browser. Within the Data Browser, you must make the entries numbered in Figure 3.1.

Data Browser

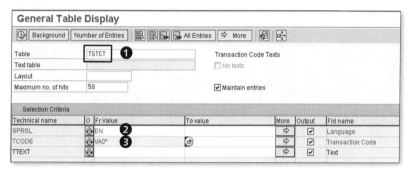

Figure 3.1 Querying the Table TSTC in the Data Browser

After you have used Transaction SE16N or N to call the Data Browser, enter the following information:

▶ Enter "TSTCT" in the TABLE field (❶). This database table contains the SAP transaction texts.

▶ Enter "EN" as the SAP abbreviation for English in the LANGUAGE field (❷).

▶ Enter "VA0*" in the TRANSACTION CODE field (❸). The symbol * (asterisk) represents a placeholder for any number of characters. By entering the asterisk, the system selects all entries that start with VA0.

You should then obtain a result list with eight hits as shown in Figure 3.2.

After you have displayed the table TSTCT in the Data Browser, the next step is to query the table in QuickViewer.

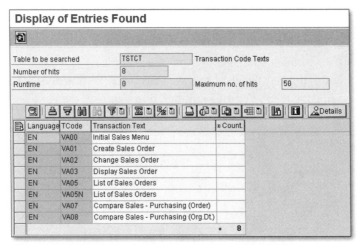

Figure 3.2 Selection Result when Querying the Table TSTCT

3.3 QuickViewer Initial Screen

You can use Transaction SQVI (QuickViewer) to create very simple analyses without any programming knowledge by following these steps:

1. Log on to your SAP system, and enter Transaction "SQVI" as shown in Figure 3.3.

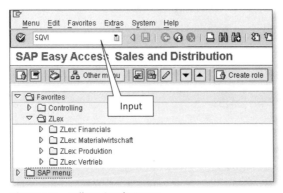

Figure 3.3 Calling QuickViewer

2. After you have pressed the ⌈Enter⌉ key, you access the QuickViewer initial screen (see Figure 3.4).

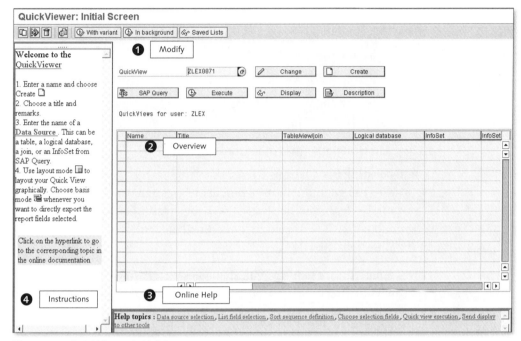

Figure 3.4 QuickViewer Initial Screen

The initial screen for the QuickViewer transaction provides you with a lot of functions and information. To simplify matters, the following is a brief overview of the different screen elements in Transaction SQVI:

▶ **Editing functions (❶)**
In this screen area, you can perform the central functions for Quick-Viewer editing. Here, you can create, change, display, or execute a new QuickView. You can also navigate to SAP Query Transaction SQ01 (see Chapter 7, SAP Query in Detail).

▶ **Report overview (❷)**
In this screen area, the system displays all of the QuickViewer reports currently created in the system with your user.

▶ **Online help (❸)**

In this screen area, you can call the ONLINE HELP for the most important functions. You can obtain additional information about the following:

- ▶ Selecting the data source
- ▶ Selecting the list fields
- ▶ Defining the sort sequence
- ▶ Selecting the selection fields
- ▶ Executing the QuickView
- ▶ Directing output to other tools

▶ **Operating instructions (❹)**

Here, you get more information about creating QuickViewer reports. You also learn the necessary steps for creating a QuickView. If you double-click the keywords underlined in blue, you will access the online help directly.

Now that you are familiar with the QuickViewer initial screen, you can create your QuickViewer report in three steps.

3.4   Steps for Creating a QuickViewer Report

To create a QuickViewer report, you must perform three steps:

1. Define a QuickView name and description.

2. Select a data source.

3. Define selection fields and layout fields.

These steps are described in the following subsections.

3.4.1   Defining a QuickView Name and Description

QuickViewer reports are created in the editing options area within the QuickViewer initial screen (❶). To create a new QuickViewer report, proceed as follows:

1. Enter a name for your report. After you have assigned a name to the report, choose CREATE (see Figure 3.5).   **Report name**

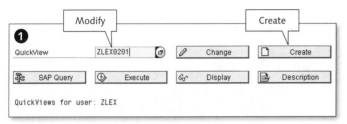

Figure 3.5   Creating a QuickViewer Report

The system displays a window entitled CREATE QUICKVIEW ZLEX0201: CHOOSE DATA SOURCE (see Figure 3.6).   **Data source**

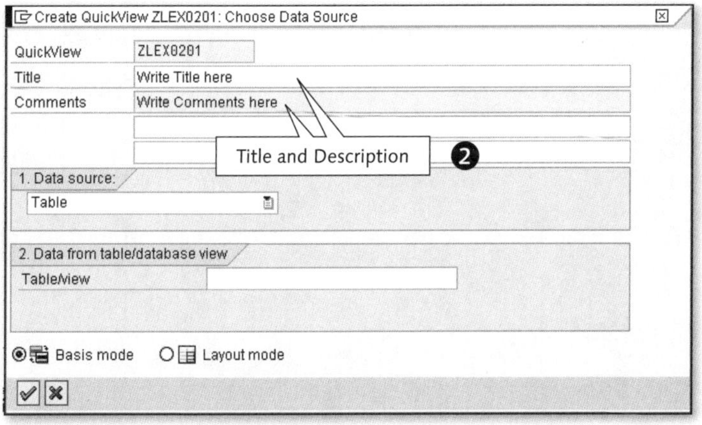

Figure 3.6   Entering a QuickView Title

2. In this window, enter a title for your analysis. Enter, for example, transactions and their descriptions in the TITLE field. You can enter some explanatory text in the COMMENTS field (❷).   **Title and comment**

In the next report creation step, described in the next section, we need a data basis.

3.4.2 Selecting a Data Source

In the second step, you select a data source for creating your report. To do this, use the dropdown menu in the DATA SOURCE area (see Figure 3.7). You can choose from the following four options:

▶ Table

▶ Table join

▶ InfoSet Query

▶ Logical database

The easiest way to create a report is to use a single table as a data source (❸). In our example, this is the table TSTCT.

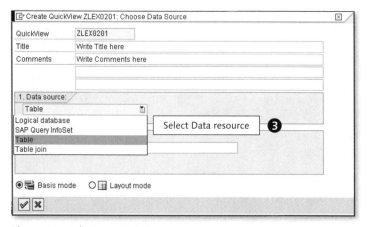

Figure 3.7 Selecting a Data Source

Table join
A second option is to use a table join to create a report. When you use a table join, you can define two or more tables as a data source for your report. In our example, you can use the table TSTC, for example, as a data basis instead of the table TSTCT. The tables TSTC and TSTCT are then linked with each other for the purposes of your analysis. You then have the option of displaying the transaction, associated transaction text, and associated ABAP program in a report.

InfoSet
A third option is to use an InfoSet as a data source. The InfoSet is a view of a data source. We will discuss how to use and create InfoSets in Chapter 6, InfoSet in Detail.

Finally, you can select a logical database as a data source for your report. **Logical database** Logical databases are special SAP programs that comprise finished table links. The logical database automatically selects the data in the background. The logical databases available in the standard SAP system are listed with their associated tables in the appendix to this book.

Use the database table TSTCT as a data source. Enter the table "TSTCT" as shown in Figure 3.8 (❹).

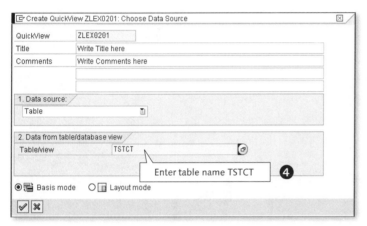

Figure 3.8 Selecting the Table TSTCT as a Data Source

After you have entered the table TSTCT, choose ✓ to confirm your entry. You then access basis mode so that you can design your report (see Figure 3.9).

All of the fields in the table TSTCT are available to you when designing your report. You can choose which fields you want to include in the selection screen and which fields you want to display in the list display. You must now select the selection fields and layout fields.

3.4.3 Selecting Selection Fields and Layout Fields

Your report is almost complete. In a third and final step, you can select your selection fields and layout fields. The system displays a split screen (see Figure 3.9).

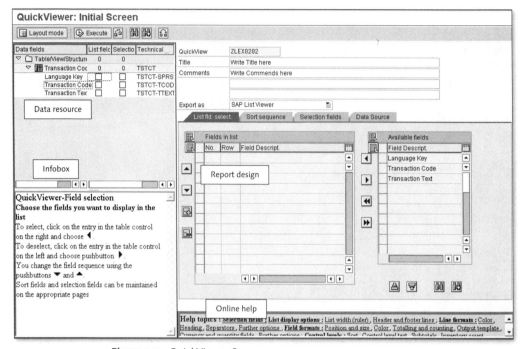

Figure 3.9 QuickViewer Screen

Selecting selection fields and layout fields

The system displays the tables used in your QuickView (data source) on the left-hand side, and it displays the data source again on the right-hand side (the report design area). In both areas, you can select the selection fields and layout fields for your report from the data source. The functionality is redundant here to meet the requirements of different users.

Online help and operating instructions

As already described in Section 3.3, QuickViewer initial Screen, you also have the option of navigating to the SAP online help here. In addition, operating instructions are provided in the information box. The operating instructions explain how you can select selection fields and layout fields for your report. Simply select the list fields and selection fields you require by selecting the relevant boxes ☑ in the data source area. Figure 3.10 shows you how to select the list fields.

Select all possible list fields. In addition to the list fields, select all possible selection fields (see Figure 3.11).

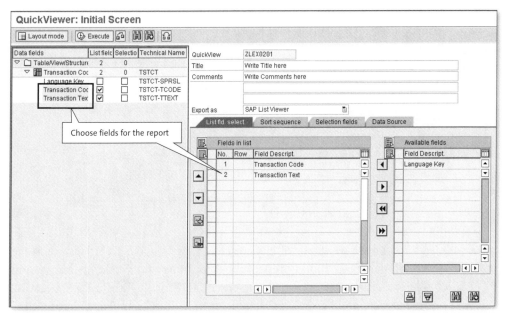

Figure 3.10 Selecting List Fields

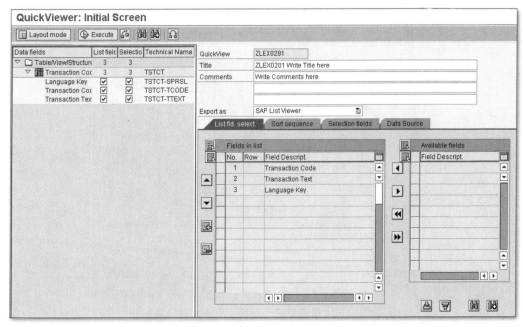

Figure 3.11 Selecting List Fields and Selection Fields

Your report is now complete. To call the report, choose 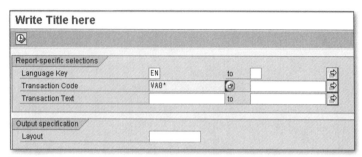 Execute . The system then displays a selection screen (see Figure 3.12).

Figure 3.12 Selection Screen

Searching for report data

You now have the flexibility to select report data in accordance with the following selection criteria: language, transaction code, or transaction text. As the selection criteria, enter "EN" for English in the LANGUAGE KEY field and "VA0*" in the TRANSACTION CODE field. Then choose 🔽 to display all English transactions that begin with VA0. You then obtain a list as your selection result (see Figure 3.13).

ZLEX0201 Write Title here

ZLEX0201 Write Title here

Language	TCode	Transaction Text
EN	VA00	Initial Sales Menu
EN	VA01	Create Sales Order
EN	VA02	Change Sales Order
EN	VA03	Display Sales Order
EN	VA05	List of Sales Orders
EN	VA05N	List of Sales Orders
EN	VA07	Compare Sales - Purchasing (Order)
EN	VA08	Compare Sales - Purchasing (Org.Dt.)

Figure 3.13 Report Output

Formatting the list output

Your list output contains three columns. In QuickView, you can now use all known ALV layout (ALV = SAP List Viewer) functions. You can also format a QuickViewer report yourself. In addition to basis mode, you can also edit the QuickViewer report in layout mode. To exit the report, double-click ⟳ to return to QuickViewer basis mode. Here, you can switch from basis mode to layout mode. In the next section, we will discuss layout mode.

3.5 Layout Mode

The layout mode in QuickViewer enables you to optimize your report's design. For example, you can assign different colors to your columns, or you can change the output format of your fields. To switch from basis mode to layout mode, choose the LAYOUT MODE button on the upper-left side of the screen (see Figure 3.14).

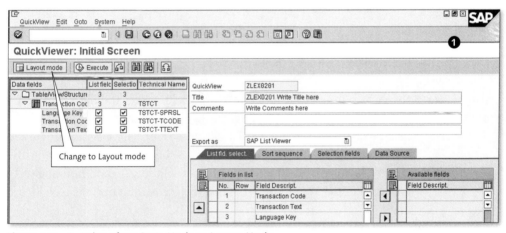

Figure 3.14 Switching from Basis Mode to Layout Mode

The right-hand side of the screen area of the QuickViewer design screen now changes. The system displays the different options available to you for editing your report. For example, you can delete fields, identify fields as totaling fields or sort fields, insert headers and footers, or use colors to change the format of the report (see Figure 3.15).

Totaling or sort fields, headers, and footers

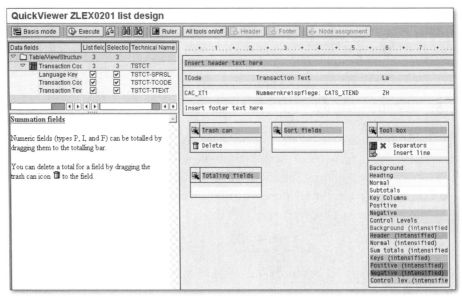

Figure 3.15 Layout Mode Display

Formatting options for a field

To activate the design functions for a field, select the data field CAC_XT1 below the TCODE heading on the right-hand side of your screen. This field is then surrounded by a blue border. The view on the lower left-hand side of your screen changes to show detailed data about the TRANSACTION CODE field in the LIST FIELD window. In addition to a technical name, the system offers you some formatting options (see Figure 3.16).

Now experiment with the new formatting options by making the following changes:

1. Change the length (OUTPUT LENGTH) of the TRANSACTION CODE field from 20 characters to 10 characters.

2. Change the OUTPUT POSITION of the TRANSACTION CODE field from 1 to 50.

3. Select the KEY (INTENSIVE) option in the LIST FIELD COLOR box.

4. Do not output null values. Even though you can select this field, this change will not be applied to your report because this editing option is only relevant for numeric data fields.

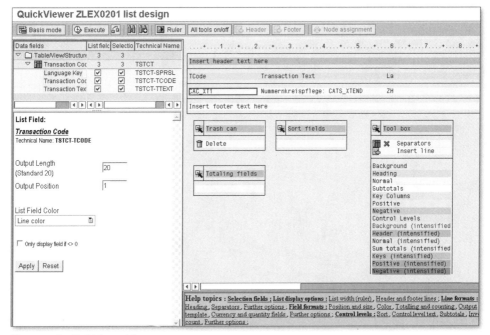

Figure 3.16 Field Formatting

After you have made your changes, choose APPLY on the lower-left side of the screen so that your settings are applied. The TRANSACTION CODE field in your list changes position and color. View the effects of your format changes by choosing ⊕ Execute to execute your report.

Apply field formatting

3.6 Summary

QuickViewer is a very simple query reporting tool that enables you to quickly create a report. QuickViewer is particularly suitable for occasional users because of its ease of use. In other words, QuickViewer is suitable for simple one-off reporting requirements. However, if you want users other than the report creator to execute the report, you must convert the QuickView into an SAP query. The query not only allows you to make the report generally available, but it also provides you with flexible options in terms of creating reports. We will discuss the procedure for creating a query in Chapter 4, Overview of SAP Query.

In this chapter, you will learn how to use SAP Query as a query reporting tool. In particular, we will explain the relationships between the transactions relevant for report creation. Finally, you will learn how to create an SAP query.

4 Overview of SAP Query

Of all the three query reporting tools, SAP Query provides you with the most options. Thanks to its flexibility, SAP Query is divided into several transactions. These transactions are linked with each other in a logical manner. They help you assign the necessary authorizations and structure your reporting requirements in a logical manner.

All query objects are created with reference to a query area. A distinction is made between storage in a global query area (cross-client) and storage in a standard query area (client-specific). For the query area, it is necessary to manage user groups in the system. On one hand, a user group comprises individual users. On the other hand, InfoSets are assigned to the user group.

The InfoSet represents the data basis for the query. The specific table fields available in the query are defined in the InfoSet. In the query itself, you can then decide which fields in the InfoSet you want to make available to the user as selection fields and layout fields.

In this chapter, you will get to know the functions associated with the following three transactions:

▶ SQ03 — User Group
▶ SQ02 — InfoSet
▶ SQ01 — SAP Query

4.1 Fundamentals

To use SAP Query as intended, you should know the relationships among the following four query objects:

- ▶ Query areas
- ▶ User groups
- ▶ InfoSets
- ▶ SAP queries

[Handwritten margin notes: step1 : check → / step2 : create → / step 3 : create → / step 4 : create → / → system → user profile → own Data → parameter tab. / Ck : SQ01 → Environment → Par ID : AQW / → ⊙ Std Area (client - specific)]

To highlight these relationships, we have provided a graphical illustration of the query objects with in Figure 4.1.

Query area Each time your query objects are accessed, this data access is ruled in the context of the *query area* (❶). For example, your user groups, InfoSets, queries, and all other query objects are stored differently in the database. The differences between the two query areas in the SAP system (standard area/global area) are described in the next section.

User group In the SAP Query application, *user groups* (❷) are used to further structure your query objects (see Section 4.3, User Group). For example, your user master is assigned to a user group so that you can also further control the authorization. You can also assign the InfoSet to one or more user groups. Similarly, you call SAP Query on the basis of the user group.

InfoSet The *InfoSet* (❸) helps you to further structure the data content. For example, you can restrict the data that you require for your SAP query. The InfoSet can use different data sources as a data basis. As in the case of QuickViewer, you can use a table join, table, or logical database as a data basis. In addition, the InfoSet enables you to use a data retrieval program as a data source.

[Handwritten margin notes: QuickViewer → only for yourself / Infoset → All users]

Query Finally, you can define your *SAP query* (❹) on the basis of the InfoSet. An SAP query intentionally contains only those data fields that you previously selected in the InfoSet. You create a query on the basis of a user group. When you create a query, you are forced to select a user group. If you want to use a certain InfoSet as a data basis for the query, you must assign it to a query area.

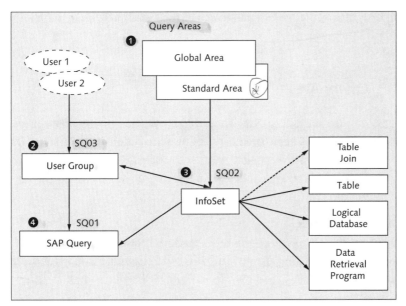

Figure 4.1 SAP Query — Relationships

The following sections provide an example that examines the following four query objects: query area, user group, InfoSet, and SAP query. For three of the query objects (user group, InfoSet, and SAP query), it is important to select the correct query area (global or standard query area).

You must define the user groups once only. They govern the access options of your users and support you in structuring your SAP queries according to target groups. During productive operation, you will use the SAP InfoSet and SAP query most frequently.

In the following sections, we will use a specific example to guide you through the individual steps associated with creating an SAP query. You will create a new user group, new InfoSet, and a new query.

In Chapter 3, QuickViewer, you learned how to access the database table TSTCT (Transaction Texts). You will now use a table join as a data source. The table join links the following two tables:

▶ DO10TAB — Database Tables
▶ TSTC — Transactions

In an SAP query, the first step is to select the right query area (global or standard query area).

4.2 Query Areas

When you create a query, you should always select the correct query area on the initial screen of the relevant transaction (SQ03, SQ02 or SQ01). Depending on the query area, the system will display different user groups, InfoSets, and queries. SAP distinguishes between the following two query areas:

- **Global query area** → request a transport
  New query settings are generally made in the Customizing client. New or changed user groups, InfoSets, and so on require a transport request.
- **Standard query area** → No transport request
  The settings are made without any recording, mainly in the production client, and they can be exported from one client/system and imported into another client/system.

These two query areas therefore control data storage on the basis of the client:

- Client-specific storage: standard area
- Cross-client storage: global query area

In particular, this setting determines whether or not your SAP query is integrated into the SAP transport system. You have the option of creating the SAP query directly in the production client or treating your SAP query as an additional development object and creating the report in the Customizing client.

Advantages and disadvantages associated with the standard query area

There are advantages and disadvantages to both procedures. If you create an SAP query in the standard area, your analysis is available directly in the client in which you create the query. If the analysis is missing in another client (for test purposes), you must export the query objects and import them into another client. For simple and manageable analyses, however, creating a standard area gives you great flexibility. Not only can you make your changes directly, you can also test and release them.

If, on the other hand, you create your SAP query in a global area, you must take note of the transport system you use. In other words, you create your query objects in the Customizing client. From a technical development perspective, it makes considerably more sense to create the query in the global area than in the standard area. However, you cannot immediately check your report results in the global area because suitable test data may be missing.

In Chapter 13, Transport System, we will show you how to transport the query objects to other clients/systems, irrespective of the query area.

Use of the query area is generally a company policy decision. Many medium-sized customers create queries in the standard area so that suitable reports are quickly available to the user and management.

In the SAP system, you select the query area as described next. When creating a query, you work with the following three transactions:

▶ SQ03 — User Group

▶ SQ02 — InfoSet

▶ SQ01 — SAP Query

For all three transactions (SQ03, SQ02, and SQ01), you can choose between the standard area and global area under the menu path ENVIRONMENT • QUERY AREAS (see Figure 4.2).

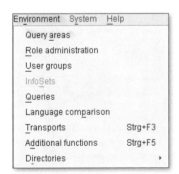

Figure 4.2 Selecting the Query Area

For all three transactions, the system displays the screen shown in Figure 4.3.

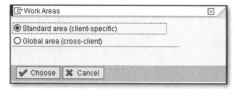

Figure 4.3 Selecting the Query Area

For this example, you select STANDARD AREA (CLIENT-SPECIFIC) so that you can create your analysis directly in a test client.

If you, together with your SAP administration team or project management team, have decided in favor of a particular query area, you can specify this query area for your additional activities. For query functions, you also have the option of defining default values on the PARAMETERS tab in your user master.

Specifying user parameters for the query area
When you enter the value "AQW" as a PARAMETER ID, the system then displays the text ABAP QUERY: QUERY AREA in the SHORT DESCRIPTION column. The parameter ID AQW is therefore the abbreviation of ABAP Query Work Area.

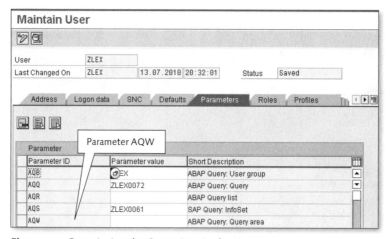

Figure 4.4 Preassigning the Query Area in the User Master

If the parameter value is not filled (see Figure 4.4), the standard area for your user is found. If, on the other hand, you work in the global area, you enter "G" in the PARAMETER VALUE field.

> **Checking your Query Area Selection**
>
> In real life, selecting the query area is one of the most common sources of error. Frequently, a search is performed for query objects that exist in the system. Check whether you are in the correct query area.

[+]

SQ01/SQ02/SQ03
↳ Environment
↳ Query Area
① standard area
(Client-specific)

In the next section, you will learn how to create a user group.

First step :

4.3   User Group   — *SQ03*

User groups can be freely selected and created in the system with 12 characters. The users in the system are then assigned to the user groups. Therefore, users can be assigned to a user group. For example, users 1 and 2 can be assigned to user group 1. User 1 can also be assigned to user group 2. You can also assign any number of InfoSets to each user group. Here, InfoSet 1 can also be assigned to user groups 1 and 2.

Naming a user group

1. To create user groups, call Transaction SQ03. The system then displays the initial screen shown in Figure 4.5.

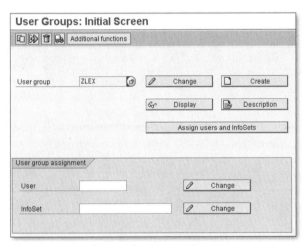

Figure 4.5   Initial Screen for the User Group

2. On this screen, you can copy, rename, or delete an existing user group. In this example, create the user group ZLEX by entering "ZLEX" in the USER GROUP field, and choose CREATE. The system then displays a dia-

log box in which you can assign a descriptive long text to your user group (see Figure 4.6).

Figure 4.6 Naming a User Group

3. In this dialog box, give your user group a descriptive name.

Naming a
user group

4. Because approximately 130 user groups are provided in the SAP system, we recommend that you remain in the customer namespace (e.g., Z as the initial letter) when naming the user group.

5. If you choose SAVE, the system will issue the following success message: "User group ZLEX has been saved."

[»]   **Selecting the Standard Query Area**

If the system displays a dialog box entitled ERROR IN OBJECT PROCESSING, or you obtain a transport request, choose the red X to cancel the transaction. You are now in the global query area. Therefore, select the standard area (see Section 4.2, Query Areas).

6. Assign the new user group ZLEX to multiple users by choosing ASSIGN USERS AND INFOSETS (see Figure 4.7).

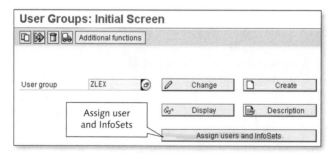

Figure 4.7 Assigning Users to a User Group

The system then displays the user assignment screen shown in Figure 4.8.

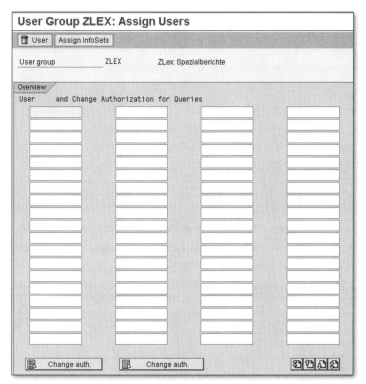

Figure 4.8 Assigning Users and InfoSets to a User Group

7. You can now display the users assigned to a user group, or you can enter new users yourself. The screen template provides you with the options listed in Table 4.1.

Icon	Shortcut	Function
🗑 User	Shift + F2	Delete user group
Assign InfoSets	F5	Assign InfoSets
🗒 Change auth.	–	Select the ALL USERS change authorization

Table 4.1 Icons in the User Groups Area

101

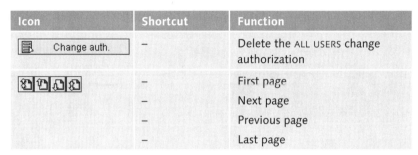

Icon	Shortcut	Function
📋 Change auth.	–	Delete the ALL USERS change authorization
🔲🔲🔲🔲	–	First page
	–	Next page
	–	Previous page
	–	Last page

Table 4.1 Icons in the User Groups Area (Cont.)

Assigning users to a user group
To take a closer look at the screen functions, enter existing system users in the user group that you have just created. In our example, the users DE241, SKALESKE, and ZLEX were assigned to the user group ZLEX.

Query change authorization
You have the option of selecting or deselecting a field behind the respective user names. If extensive authorizations (SAP_ALL) have not been assigned yet, the user can only change the queries associated with the user group if the field is assigned a checkmark. In our example, only the user ZLEX can change the queries in the user group ZLEX (see Figure 4.9).

Figure 4.9 Assigning Three Users to a User Group

Deleting users from the user group
If you have assigned too many users to a user group or if a user leaves your enterprise, you can simply delete this user. To do this, select the relevant user and then choose 🗑 User (DELETE USER). You can now display the InfoSets assigned to the user group. To do this, choose ASSIGN INFOSETS (see Section 4.4, InfoSet).

You can assign the change authorization to all users in a specific user group, or you can delete this authorization. If you want to assign the authorization to all users, choose ⊞ Change auth. (SELECT CHANGE AUTHORIZATION). However, if you want to remove the authorization for changing the SAP query from all users, choose ⊞ Change auth. DESELECT CHANGE AUTHORIZATION). If more than 85 users are assigned to the user group, you can use the buttons ⊞⊞⊞⊞ to scroll between the individual users.

Now you can assign the relevant users to your user group, save this assignment, and exit the transaction for managing user groups. Because you have now returned to the SAP Easy Access initial screen, let's move on to InfoSets.

4.4   InfoSet — *second step : SQ2*

In this section, you will learn how to define the actual data basis for your SAP query.

1. To access the initial screen for the InfoSet, call Transaction SQ02. The system displays the initial screen shown in Figure 4.10.

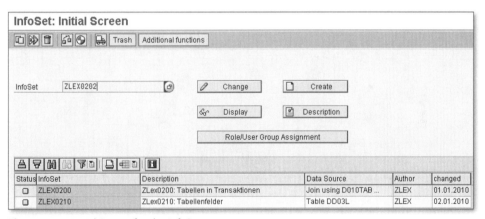

Figure 4.10   Initial Screen for the InfoSet

2. Numerous functions are available in the InfoSet, which are described in Chapter 6, InfoSet in Detail. Enter the InfoSet name "ZLEX0203" in the INFOSET field.

3. Choose ☐ Create as shown in Figure 4.11.

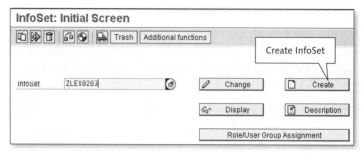

Figure 4.11 Creating an InfoSet

4. The system displays the screen shown in Figure 4.12. Here, enter a name for your InfoSet, and specify the associated data source.

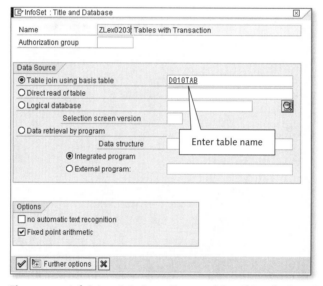

Figure 4.12 InfoSet — Entering a Name and Specifying the Data Source

Naming an InfoSet

5. Enter a descriptive name for your InfoSet in the NAME field. Select TABLE JOIN USING BASIS TABLE as the data source, and then enter the table "D010TAB". For a table join, you must specify two or more tables as a data basis. Press the [Enter] key or choose ☑. You can now access the graphical overview of the table relationships (see Figure 4.13).

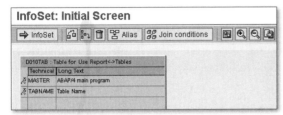

Figure 4.13 InfoSet — Table Links

6. In this window, you will link the relevant database tables with each other. You will now link the table TSTC (TRANSACTION CODE) with the existing table D010TAB (TABLE FOR USE). To do this, choose [icon] (INSERT TABLE). The system displays the window shown in Figure 4.14.

Creating a table join

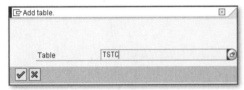

Figure 4.14 InfoSet — Inserting an Additional Table

7. In this window, you can now enter additional tables for your table join. In the TABLE field, enter the table name "TSTC". The table TSTC is then linked with the previous table D010TAB (see Figure 4.15).

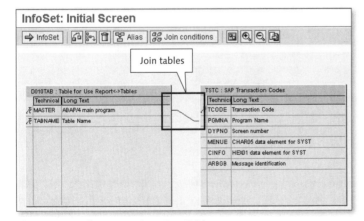

Figure 4.15 InfoSet — Linking Two Tables

Link suggestion in the table join

The system now suggests a link to you. The system searches for fields that have the same field length and attribute in both tables. The term attribute means, for example, that it concerns a numeric or alphanumeric field. Generally, the standard suggestion produces the correct result.

8. Choose 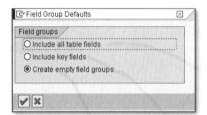 (BACK) to exit the transaction and display the window shown in Figure 4.16.

Figure 4.16 Field Group Defaults

9. You can now choose from the following three options:

▸ You can transfer all table fields to the InfoSet.

▸ You can transfer only key fields to the InfoSet. (Key fields are all key fields in a database table.)

▸ You can create an empty field group.

10. Choose the third option, CREATE EMPTY FIELD GROUPS. The system now automatically creates a field group for each table. Initially, the newly created field groups do not contain any data fields (see Figure 4.17).

[+]   **InfoSet as a Data Basis for the Query**

The InfoSet is the data basis for the SAP query to be created. The fewer fields you add to your InfoSet, the easier it is to create a query because only the fields that you transfer to the field groups are available in the query as selection fields.

Transferring table fields to the field group

11. Transfer the two data fields ABAP/4 MAIN PROGRAM (MASTER) and TABLE NAME (TABNAME) from the table D010TAB to field group 01 TABLE FOR USE REPORT ↔ TABLES. To do this, click the data fields, and use drag and drop to move them to field group 01 TABLE FOR USE REPORT ↔ TABLES.

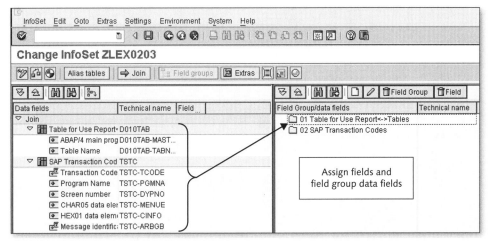

Figure 4.17 InfoSet — Data Fields and Field Groups

12. In addition, select the first two fields in the table TSTC (Transaction Code/Program Name), and use drag and drop to move them to field group 02 SAP Transactions Codes. After you have assigned the fields to the field groups, the data fields are colored blue. The assigned field group is displayed behind each data field (see Figure 4.18).

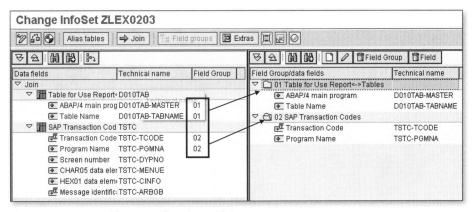

Figure 4.18 Data Fields Assigned to the Field Groups

The following four fields are now available in the query as a data basis: ABAP/4 main program (MASTER), Table Name (TABNAME), Transaction Code (TCODE), and Program Name (PGMNA).

L↳ save.

Message : Generate Infoset ?

yes

See = prior page

[»]

> **Assigning an InfoSet to a User Group**
>
> To use the InfoSet for a query, you must assign it to a user group. The user group controls the authorization and helps you structure your query objects. A query is always created in reference to a user group.

13. Choose 🔙 (BACK) to exit editing mode for the InfoSet. The system now displays the initial screen for the InfoSet (see Figure 4.19).

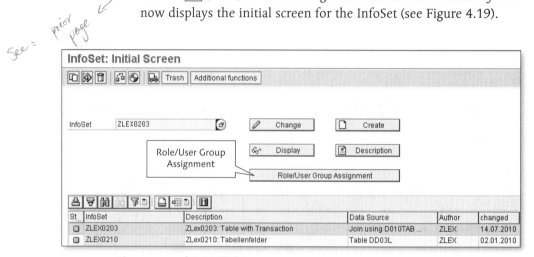

Figure 4.19   nfoSet Initial Screen

14. Assign the InfoSet directly to a user group by choosing ROLE/USER GROUP ASSIGNMENT. You now access the transaction for managing user groups. All of the user groups defined in the system are displayed on this screen (see Figure 4.20).

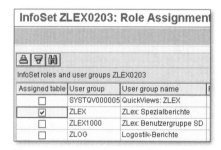

Figure 4.20   Assigning an InfoSet to a User Group

108

15. Assign the InfoSet to the user group ZLEX.

16. If you are using another user group in your system, assign the Info-Set to a user group of your choice. The InfoSet is now available as a data basis for your query report.

In the next section, we will show you how to create your first query report.

4.5 SAP Query — step 3 = SQ01

To create your SAP query report, follow these steps:

1. Call Transaction SQ01 to display the initial screen for query editing. An SAP query is always assigned to a user group. The user group currently selected is displayed as a header on the query initial screen. Check whether the system displays the user group that you selected or the user group ZLEX (see Figure 4.21).

Selecting a user group

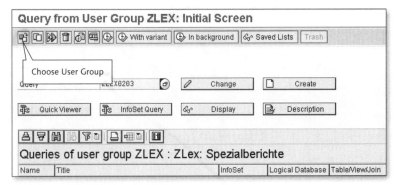

Figure 4.21 SAP Query — Initial Screen

2. If you want a user group other than the one displayed in the header, you can change the user group by choosing 🔲 to change the user group (as shown in Figure 4.21). You then obtain an overview of the user groups available in the system (see Figure 4.22).

Changing user group

Figure 4.22 User Group Overview

3. Select your user group. The system then displays your user group in the header of the query initial screen.

4. Assign the name ZLEX0203 to your query report, and choose ▢ Create (see Figure 4.23). The system then displays a window that lists all of the InfoSets in your selected user group.

Figure 4.23 Creating an SAP Query

5. Select the InfoSet ZLEX0203 (see Figure 4.24).

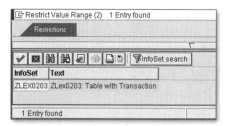

Figure 4.24 Selecting an InfoSet for SAP Query Creation

In real life, it has proven beneficial to assign the same name to the Info-Set and query. This ensures consistency and, if changes are required, you immediately know the name of the InfoSet assigned to the query. If you require different queries for an InfoSet, the basic query name is usually retained, and a suffix is added to each query name. For example, a second query for the InfoSet ZLEX0203 would be named ZLEX0203-01.

In the next step, you will access a window in which you can assign a name to your query (see Figure 4.25).

Figure 4.25 Query Screen for Specifying the Title and Format

In Chapter 7, SAP Query in Detail, we will describe all of the options available to you when creating or changing queries. For now, follow these steps to create a query:

Naming a query

1. Enter a query name in the TITLE field.

2. Entering the InfoSet name in the title is often beneficial. Therefore, enter "ZLEX0203: Table with Transaction" as the title. This title will be displayed as the header on your selection screen.

3. Choose BASIC LIST below the screen header. The system then displays a screen with the header QUERY ZLEX0203 LAYOUT DESIGN (see Figure 4.26).

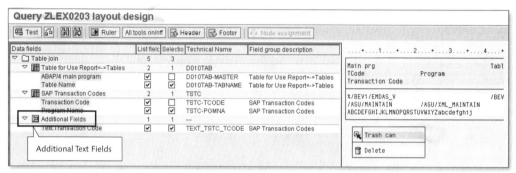

Figure 4.26 SAP Query: Layout Design

4. Select the fields (list fields) that will be displayed in your report.

5. You can also determine the fields for your selection screen. The system displays exactly those field groups and fields that you selected in the InfoSet. Select all of the fields as list fields.

6. Select the TABLE NAME and TRANSACTION CODE fields as selection text. To ensure that your field is selected, check the boxes next to the fields in the columns with the headers LIST FIELDS and SELECTION FIELDS.

7. An additional group of fields is displayed in the ⬚ Additional Fields area on your query editing screen. For the most important table fields, the system automatically offers the associated text fields for your query design. For the TEXT:TRANSACTION CODE field, select the boxes in the columns with the headers LIST FIELDS and SELECTION FIELDS.

8. Your query is now complete. Choose ⬚ Test to view the result of your new report immediately. The system then displays a TEST QUERY window (see Figure 4.27).

9. You can restrict the number of data records to be selected. In the MAXIMUM field, enter the value 99999 and choose ✓ to confirm your entry. You now have access to the selection screen for your analysis (see Figure 4.28).

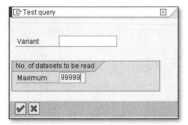

Figure 4.27 Executing an SAP Query

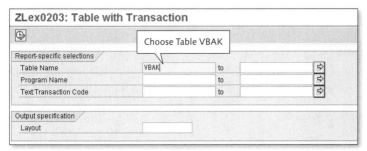

Figure 4.28 SAP Query: Selection Screen

10. In the TABLE NAME field, enter the table "VBAK". (We will describe the other options on the selection screen in Chapter 8, Selection and Layout Variants.)

11. Choose ⊕ (EXECUTE) to execute your report. The system now displays the result list for your report (see Figure 4.29).

ZLex0203: Table with Transaction

ZLex0203: Table with Transaction

Table Na..	TCode	Transaction Code	Program
VBAK	VA01	Create Sales Order	SAPMV45A
VBAK	VA02	Change Sales Order	SAPMV45A
VBAK	VA03	Display Sales Order	SAPMV45A
VBAK	VA05	List of Sales Orders	SAPMV75A
VBAK	VA07	Compare Sales - Purchasing (Order)	SDBANF02
VBAK	VA08	Compare Sales - Purchasing (Org.Dt.)	SDBANF01
VBAK	VA11	Create Inquiry	SAPMV45A
VBAK	VA12	Change Inquiry	SAPMV45A
VBAK	VA13	Display Inquiry	SAPMV45A
VBAK	VA14L	Sales Documents Blocked for Delivery	SDLIEFSPE
VBAK	VA15	Inquiries List	SAPMV75A
VBAK	VA21	Create Quotation	SAPMV45A

Figure 4.29 SAP Query: Result List

For the table VBAK (SALES DOCUMENT: HEADER DATA), the system displays additional columns with information about the transaction code (TCODE), transaction code name, and ABAP program names. Your report shows you all SAP system transactions that use the table VBAK as a data basis. As a result of your selection, you can see whether the standard SAP system already contains a specific transaction that meets your requirements.

4.6   Summary

You have now created your first complete report. Consequently, you now know the most important transactions and how they relate to each other. To create the next analysis, you will use the following transactions:

▶ SQ03 — User Group

▶ SQ02 — InfoSet

▶ SQ01 — SAP Query

In Chapter 5, Query Utilities, you will learn how to quickly obtain an overview of the existing user groups, InfoSets, and SAP queries.

In this chapter, you will learn how to get an overview of the query objects that exist in the system. You will also learn useful descriptions for existing query objects. Finally, we will introduce you to some copy functions as well as trash management.

5   Query Utilities

In this chapter, we will show you transactions and reports that you can use to get an overview of the query objects currently available in the system (user groups, InfoSets, queries, etc.). In addition, we will introduce you to some utilities for transporting and copying queries. After reading this chapter, you will be able to answer the following questions:

- Which query objects are in the standard area or global area?
- How are individual query objects currently named? How have, for example, the following query objects been named?
    - User groups
    - InfoSets
    - SAP queries
- Which user groups have been used, and which InfoSets and queries have been assigned to the user groups?
- Who created which InfoSets when, and who has which authorizations?
- To what extent have SAP queries been used, and who created or changed these queries?
- In which form do the descriptions for the query objects exist in the system?
- How can you copy, delete, or transport query objects?

5.1 Overview of Query Utilities

People involved

When doing the groundwork for creating a report, you need to address not only the technical aspects but also the organizational aspects. To achieve the best project result, you should involve project management, system administration, and the relevant user department in the creation of the report. In real-life scenarios, employees with specific module or process knowledge are best able to create the majority of reports. SAP Query is so easy to use that its implementation is usually only a content-related challenge rather than a technical challenge. Because query reports essentially read data rather than change data, an employee from the user department can create the required report.

Naming convention

Each enterprise and organization also has a different structure. Therefore, each enterprise has its own focal points in terms of reporting. In real-life situations, it is often too idealistic to have a generally valid naming convention for query objects.

Customer namespace

Always use the customer namespace for your SAP query objects. In other words, always use the letter Z or Y as the first character in a query object name. In real-life scenarios, the first letter is frequently followed by an abbreviation that represents the user department. Here, you can distinguish between a customer analysis and an SAP analysis. A user transaction can also be named in the same way as the query objects.

Renaming query objects

You can rename your query objects at any time. Suitable SAP tools are also available for copying query objects. SAP provides numerous useful programs for getting an overview of the query objects in the system (user groups, InfoSets, queries, etc.). Table 5.1 provides an overview of helpful ABAP programs.

Purpose	Content	ABAP Report		Program Name
Complete directory	▶ InfoSets ▶ User groups ▶ Queries ▶ Transport datasets	RSAQ	SUMM SA38 → RSAQSumm	Content directory of all query objects

Table 5.1 Useful Query Utilities

↗ SA38

Purpose	Content	ABAP Report		Program Name
Directory	Users/user groups	RSAQ	USGR	Directory of users and user groups
Directory	Query	RSAQ	DEL0	Query directory
Directory	Lists	RSAQ	QLRE	Directory of saved lists
Description	User groups	RSAQ	SHBG	User group description
Description	InfoSet	RSAQ	SHSG	InfoSet description
Description	Query	RSAQ	SHQU	Query description
Editing	Copy function	RSAQ	COPY	Special copy function
Editing	Trash	RSAQ	PBAS	Trash management
Editing	Transport	RSAQ	R3TR	SAP Query transport tool

Table 5.1 Useful Query Utilities (Cont.)

SA38

You can call these useful utilities directly as an ABAP program or in the individual query transactions. The technical names of the ABAP programs have eight characters and always start with RSAQ. The last four characters of the ABAP program are somewhat descriptive, for example, COPY for copy functions and PBAS for trash management.

Report name for ABAP auxiliary programs

To help you quickly familiarize yourself with the SAP system, Figure 5.1 provides a graphical overview of the most important auxiliary programs in the standard system. We have divided these programs into four categories. Under (❶), you will find a program that you can use to obtain a complete overview of the query objects in the system. You can use different auxiliary programs (❷) to list the individual query objects.

Query overviews

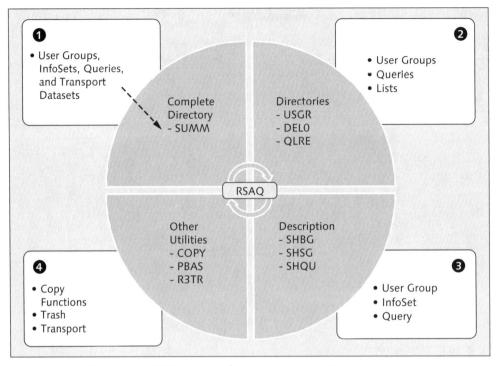

Figure 5.1 ABAP/4 Programs for Query Management

Query descriptions The third group of auxiliary programs (❸) contains useful descriptions for the query objects. For example, there is a very good report for describing an InfoSet. Before Release 4.6, an InfoSet was known as a functional area. Consequently, the ABAP report is still called RSAQSHSG. The last two characters of the ABAP program show that this program has existed in the system for a long time.

Query editing functions The fourth category of ABAP programs helps you to copy query objects. The trash folder and transport transaction are also introduced here (❹).

In the following sections, we will describe the various utilities in greater detail.

5.2   Overview of Query Objects

You can use special directories to get an overview of the query objects that exist in the system. For example, the ABAP program RSAQSUMM provides a complete overview of the query objects. Alternatively, you can call Transaction SQ02 (InfoSet), which calls a complete overview (*see* Figure 5.2).

Report
RSAQSUMM

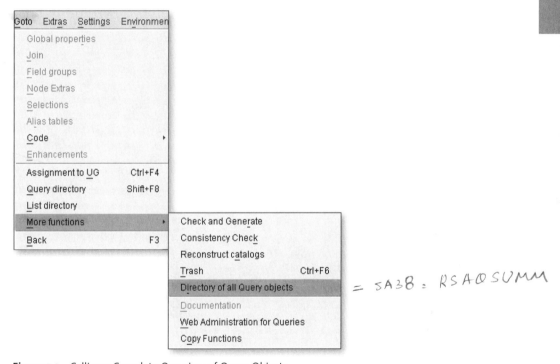

= SA38 : RSAQSUMM

Figure 5.2   Calling a Complete Overview of Query Objects

Follow these steps to...

1. Access the report window RSAQSUMM in which you can call the query objects for the global area or standard area. Select INFOSETS and QUERIES (see Figure 5.3) and then enter your user group.

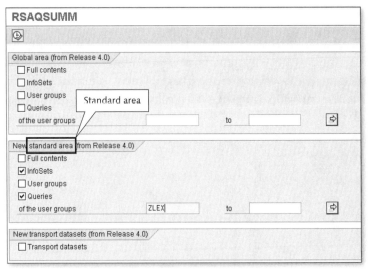

Figure 5.3 Selecting InfoSets and Queries According to User Groups

2. After you have chosen ⊕ to execute a report, you get a list of query objects in a user group (see Figure 5.4).

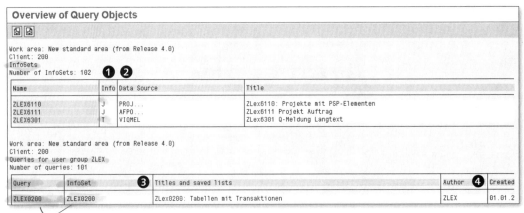

Figure 5.4 Overview of Query Objects in a User Group

Query Name
SiB = InfoSet Name

InfoSets and queries according to user group

This report already provides basic information about the user group ZLEX. For example:

▶ **Which data source (Info) is used by the InfoSets in the user group ZLEX? (❶)**
Here, INFO indicates the different data sources. T indicates an individual table, while J indicates a table join. If the column is not filled (blank), a logical database represents the data basis. The fourth alternative is to enter a D in the column (D for data retrieval program).

▶ **Which database table is used as a data basis for the InfoSet? (❷)**
In this part of the report, the table name is displayed for an InfoSet that contains a table. If, in the case of a table join, at least two tables are used, the leading table is displayed. If there are three dots after the table name, this means that additional tables are used. In our example, there are three dots after the table name AFPO.

▶ **Which queries exist for the individual InfoSets? (❸)**
In this example, a query Zlex0200 exists for the InfoSet Zlex0200 (ZLEX0200: TABLES WITH TRANSACTIONS). You should name the query in the same way as the InfoSet.

▶ **Who created or changed the InfoSet or query and when? (❹)**
In the case of InfoSets and queries, the name of the person who created the query is listed with the date. The last person to change the InfoSet or query is also specified with the date.

This report provides you with an initial insight into the system. You obtain important information and can identify which analyses already exist. You also learn how the various query objects are named.

5.3 Query Objects

The system provides you with other overviews as well. For example, some directories list user groups and their associated users. An overview of available queries and an overview of saved lists are also available.

5.3.1 Overview of User Groups

You can use Transaction SQ03 (User Groups) to display all user groups and the users assigned to each group. In Transaction SQ03, you can also use the menu branch to select the overview (see Figure 5.5).

J – join table
T – individual table

SQ3 :

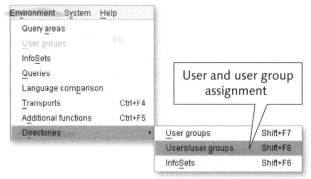

Figure 5.5 Directory of User Groups and Assigned Users

Follow these steps:

1. You obtain a selection screen for this report. Here, you can make a selection according to USER NAME or USER GROUP (see Figure 5.6).

Figure 5.6 Selecting Users and User Groups

Overview of users for the user group

2. For your selection result, you get an overview of the users and user groups. A traffic light icon displays the change authorization for the user and assigned user group. A red traffic light means that the user does not have any authorization to change an SAP query. On the other hand, the green traffic light enables the user to change SAP queries (see Figure 5.7).

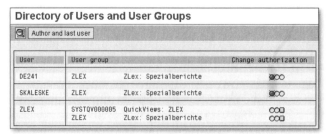

Figure 5.7 Displaying Users for the User Group

5.3.2 Query Overview

A query directory, which you can call from the selection screen, provides additional information about a particular query. For example, you can display a particular InfoSet or user group. You can also list the specific tables and fields used for a particular query. To use a query directory, call the query directory for your user, and select the following two flags: LIST TABLES USED and DISPLAY FIELDS USED (see Figure 5.8).

SA3B = RSAQ DELO

(P117)

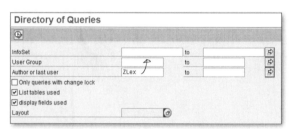

Figure 5.8 Selection Screen for the Query Directory

For your report result, the system displays a list in the ALV layout. This report lists all selected queries and their associated InfoSets. The system also displays the actual database tables and table fields (see Figure 5.9).

Directory of Queries

InfoSet	User group	Query	Query Properties	Table	Short Description	Field Name
ZLEX0061	ZLEX	ZLEX0072	ZLex0072: Query Table with Transaktion	D010TAB	Table for Use Report<->Tables	D010TAB-MASTER
					Table for Use Report<->Tables	D010TAB-TABNAME
				TSTC	SAP Transaction Codes	TSTC-PGMNA
					SAP Transaction Codes	TSTC-TCODE
ZLEX0200		ZLEX0200	ZLex0200: Tabellen mit Transaktionen	D010TAB	Table for Use Report<->Tables	D010TAB-TABNAME
				TSTC	SAP Transaction Codes	TSTC-TCODE

Figure 5.9 Query Directory with Information

5.3.3 Directory Lists

The final report of interest is a directory of saved lists. You can save selected lists here. You can use the report RSAQQLRE to get an overview of the lists saved in the system.

Report RSAQQLRE

5.4   Calling Query Object Descriptions

The various query object directories provide a good overview of the structures available. In addition to directories, the system provides additional descriptions for query objects.

5.4.1   User Group Description

Report RSAQSHBG   As a first step, you can view the user group descriptions by using the ABAP Editor or another development tool to call the ABAP report RSAQSHBG directly. Alternatively, call Transaction SQ03. In Transaction SQ03, you can call the report from the menu path USER GROUP • DESCRIPTION (see Figure 5.10).

Figure 5.10   Calling a User Group Description

You now get an overview of the users assigned to the user group you have selected. The system also shows you which users have change authorization for the queries assigned to the user group, who created the user group, and when it was created (see Figure 5.11).

The user group description is kept very simple. The InfoSet description, on the other hand, is more extensive. We will discuss this in the next section.

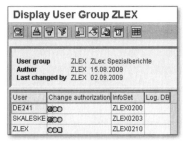

Figure 5.11 Description of the User Group ZLEX

5.4.2 InfoSet Description

You can display the InfoSet description directly in the associated transaction. Call Transaction SQ02, and select the INFOSET • DESCRIPTION entry in the menu path (see Figure 5.12).

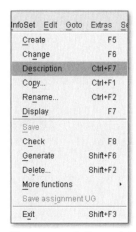

Figure 5.12 Calling an InfoSet Description

After you have called your report, you get a very useful and extensive description of the relevant InfoSet. The following information is displayed:

Information about the InfoSet description

▶ A: General information

▶ DP: Data retrieval program

▶ JO: Join

▶ AL: Alias tables

- ► SG: InfoSets and fields
- ► ZT: Additional tables
- ► ZF: Additional fields
- ► ZS: Additional structures
- ► AB: Selections
- ► CO: Code

Table links
We will explain the exact components of an InfoSet in greater detail in Chapter 6, InfoSet in Detail. The InfoSet description is a good and clear summary. At a glance, you get all of the InfoSet information you need: the name of the person who created the InfoSet, the name of the last person to change the InfoSet, and the table links. In this example, an inner join is used to link the tables D010TAB and TSTC with each other. Here, the table fields D010TAB-MASTER and TSTC-PGMNA were used to link the tables (see Figure 5.13).

Figure 5.13 Author, Additional Structures, and Alias Tables in an InfoSet

In the InfoSet, all of the tables and table fields used in a table join are listed in a clear and transparent manner. Here, two fields in the table D010TAB TABLE FOR USE REPORT ↔ TABLES and two fields in the table TSTC SAP TRANSACTION CODES are listed and sorted according to field group. The ADDITIONAL TABLES and ADDITIONAL FIELDS used in the InfoSet are also listed (see Figure 5.14).

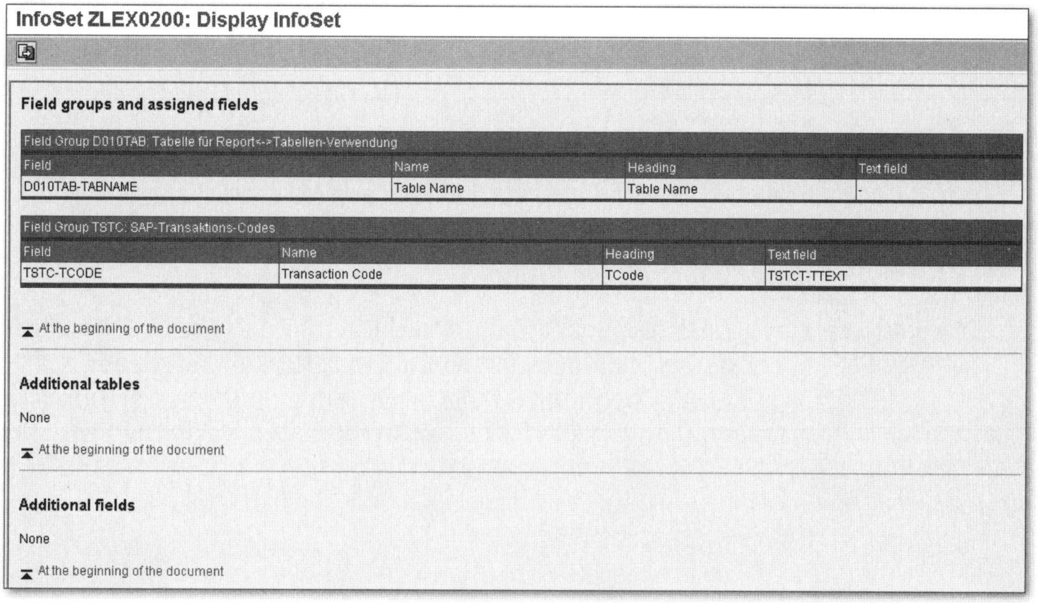

Figure 5.14 Field Groups, Additional Tables, and Additional Fields in an InfoSet

The InfoSet provides further options. For example, the ADDITIONAL STRUCTURES, SELECTIONS, and individual code (CODE) are displayed in the InfoSet description (see Figure 5.15). You can use SELECTIONS to influence the data selection and design the selection screen for your report yourself. An InfoSet is highly flexible. In other words, you can insert your own ABAP code. In real life, however, the code from a function module is frequently inserted.

Field groups, additional fields, and additional tables in an InfoSet

The InfoSet description is very detailed yet clear. You also can export the InfoSet description to an HTML file. For the HTML export, choose 🔲 (EXPORT) in the upper-left screen area.

Downloading the InfoSet description

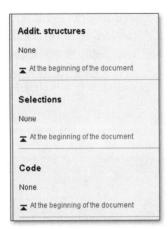

Figure 5.15 Additional Structures, Selections, and Code for an InfoSet

5.4.3 Query Description

Very good descriptions are also available for the query reports contained in the system. Call the ABAP report RSAQSHQU or Transaction SQ01. In Transaction SQ01, choose the menu path Query • Description (see Figure 5.16).

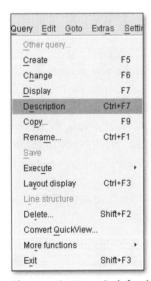

Figure 5.16 Menu Path for the Query Description

The query description lists relevant information about your report. In the general description part, for example, you get information about the author, creation date, InfoSet used, and so on (see Figure 5.17).

Query creator and creation date

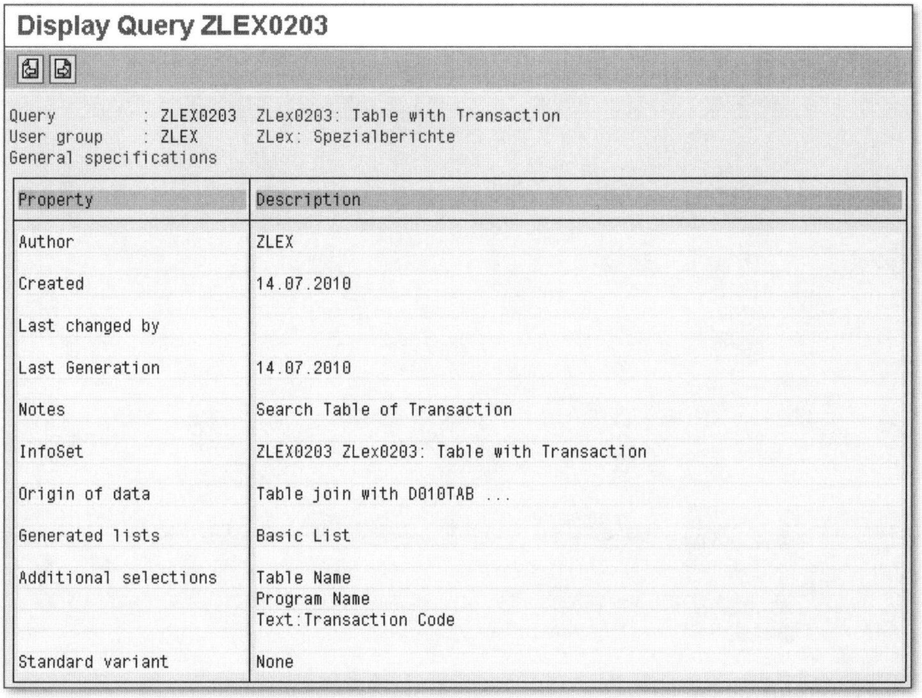
Display Query ZLEX0203

Query : ZLEX0203 ZLex0203: Table with Transaction
User group : ZLEX ZLex: Spezialberichte
General specifications

Property	Description
Author	ZLEX
Created	14.07.2010
Last changed by	
Last Generation	14.07.2010
Notes	Search Table of Transaction
InfoSet	ZLEX0203 ZLex0203: Table with Transaction
Origin of data	Table join with D010TAB ...
Generated lists	Basic List
Additional selections	Table Name Program Name Text:Transaction Code
Standard variant	None

Figure 5.17 Query Description Part 1

In the second part of the description, you get information about the individual table fields. Information about the sort sequence, summation, and so on is also listed here (see Figure 5.18).

Table fields, sort sequence, and summation in the query

In addition to the overviews and descriptions of query objects, the standard SAP system also provides a very useful utility for editing query objects.

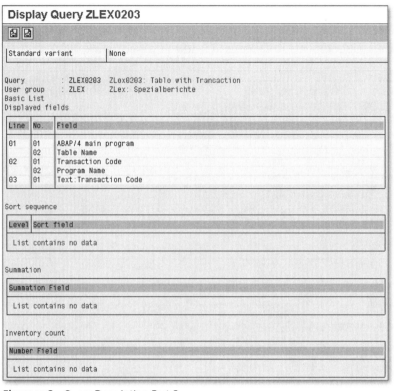

Figure 5.18 Query Description Part 2

5.5 Editing Functions for Query Objects

A special utility is available for copying query objects. You can use this special program to copy queries and InfoSets from one user group to another user group. Furthermore, you can manage the trash folder in which all deleted query objects are stored temporarily. SAP also provides a highly flexible instrument for the query transport. You can use the utility for transporting query objects not only to perform the transport but also to export query objects from one client and import them into another client. In other words, you can create query objects directly in the production client. You then export the query objects to a local file and, in a second step, import your query objects. For more detailed information about the transport system, see Chapter 13, Transport System.

5.5.1 Copy Function

You can execute the copy program in the ABAP report RSAQCOPY or you can call Transaction SQ02 and select the menu path GOTO • MORE FUNCTIONS • COPY FUNCTIONS (see Figure 5.19).

Program: RSAQCOPY

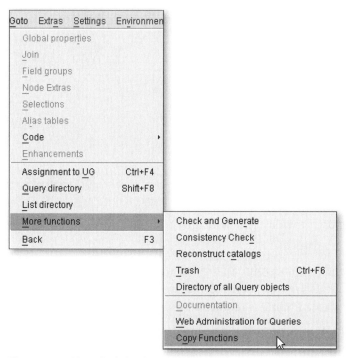

Figure 5.19 Menu Path for Copy Functions

You now access a selection screen in which you have the choice of several options. For the copy function, you, once again, have to specify a global query area or standard query area. Deselect the GLOBAL QUERY AREA flag because we were previously active in the standard area. To see the effects of your copy process, you can perform a TEST RUN (see Figure 5.20).

Copy function in the context of the query area

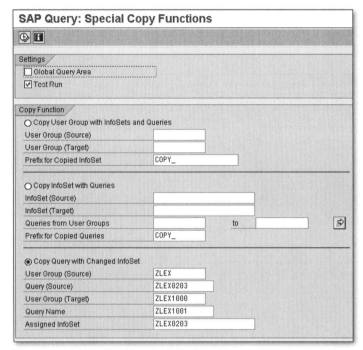

Figure 5.20 Input Template for Copy Functions

The copy report provides you with three options for copying query objects:

1. The first option is to group all of your queries from one user group into another user group. Because the previous InfoSets are retained, the newly created InfoSets require a prefix.

2. The second option is to copy the InfoSets and queries. Once again, the newly created queries require a prefix.

3. The third and final option is to copy queries and change the InfoSet.

Basically, the result of your copy process is the creation of new query objects. You can also copy existing query objects again (see Figure 5.21).

Deleting query objects If you copy too many objects at once or no longer require the query objects, you can delete these objects. Deleted objects move to the trash folder temporarily.

SAP Query: Special Copy Functions

Copy query ZLEX0203 of user group ZLEX in standard area

Test mode only (not written to database)

Query ZLEX1001 has been added

Figure 5.21 Result of the Copy Process

5.5.2 Trash Folder

If you execute the delete operation in the query transactions, the query element disappears from the active display. However, the query element is not permanently deleted. As in the case of Windows programs, the query object is initially moved to the trash folder.

Temporary delete operation

As the user, you can also display the contents of the trash folder. Call the ABAP program RSAQPBAS or Transaction SQ02. Here, you access the trash folder via the menu path GOTO • MORE FUNCTIONS • TRASH (see Figure 5.22).

Contents of the trash folder

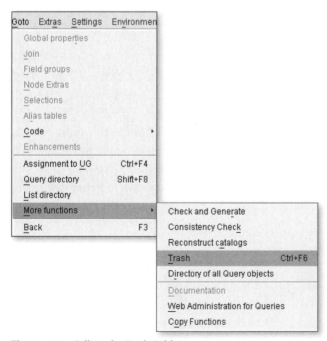

Figure 5.22 Calling the Trash Folder

Retrieving
deleted objects In trash management, you now have the option of retrieving query objects that have been deleted from the application (see Figure 5.23). To start the retrieval process, select the object you require, and choose ⊞ (RETRIEVE) or press F5 . If you want to permanently delete the query element, select the object you require, and choose 🗑 (DELETE) or press Shift + F2 .

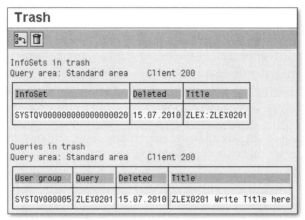

Figure 5.23 Trash Management

5.5.3 Query Transport

Program
RSAQR3TR For the sake of completeness, we will now list the ABAP program for the query transport or for exporting and importing query objects. We will discuss the ABAP program RSAQR3TR in greater detail in Chapter 13, Transport System. In the global query area within the transport system, you can use this program to export query objects from one client and import them into another client. If you work in the standard area, you can transfer query objects across the system by downloading the query objects from one client and uploading them into another client (see Figure 5.24).

SAP Query: Transport tool

Transport Action Selection

- ◉ Export
- ○ Download
- ○ Display
- ○ Import
- ○ Upload
- ○ Delete
- ○ Copy Standard Area -> Global Area
- ○ Copy Global Area -> Standard Area

- ☑ Test run
- ☐ Overwriting allowed (only with import/upload/copy)
- ☐ Transport query variants (only with export/import/copy)
- ☐ Transport of Query Layout Variants
  (Only with Export/Import/Copy)
- ☐ Transport of Report-Report Interface of Queries
  (Only with Export/Import)

Transport Option Selection

- ◉ Transport user groups
- Import option   REPLACE
- User groups   [   ] to [   ]

- ○ Transport InfoSets
- Import option   REPLACE
- InfoSets   [   ] to [   ]

- ○ Transport InfoSets and queries
- Import option   REPLACE
- InfoSets   [   ] to [   ]
- Queries   [   ] to [   ]

Figure 5.24 Editing Screen for the Transport Tool

5.6 Summary

You can use a complete directory to quickly get an overview of the query objects available in the system. Directories of user groups, queries, and saved lists are also available. Additional information is provided in the form of user group, InfoSets, or query descriptions.

You can also use a highly flexible copy function. You can copy and change your query objects in the context of user groups. You can delete superfluous query objects, which means that they are temporarily moved to the trash folder. If you accidentally delete query objects, you can undo this action. Finally, you can use the query transport tool to transfer query objects across the system (i.e., to other clients).

PART II
SAP Query Functions

In this chapter, you will learn about the data basis for your report. You will use a table join to link several tables together, you will structure your data into field groups and create individual additional fields for your report.

6   InfoSet in Detail

In Chapter 4, Overview of SAP Query, you learned about the InfoSet in the context of creating query reports. Because the InfoSet is a central component of an SAP Query reports, this chapter introduces the additional InfoSet functions. So far, you know the following about InfoSets:

▶ An InfoSet is a prerequisite for an SAP query.

▶ You must create the InfoSet before you create the query.

▶ The data source for the query is defined in the InfoSet.

▶ Only the fields available in the InfoSet can be used in the query.

▶ The fields available in the InfoSet can be further restricted for a query.

The InfoSet provides you with numerous additional options. Therefore, to refresh your memory and to cement this process in your mind, you will recreate the already familiar InfoSet for querying tables and their associated transactions in this chapter. When creating the InfoSet, you will get to know or deepen your knowledge of the following points:

▶ Using data sources (table join, table, logical database, and data retrieval program)

▶ Using automatic text recognition

▶ Designing the table join (left inner and outer join/alias tables)

▶ Creating field groups and assigning fields

▶ Enhancing the additional fields, additional tables, additional structures, or code in the InfoSet

▶ Inserting selections (parameters, selection criteria)

In addition to the already familiar data sources (table join, tables, and logical databases), you can also design more flexible data retrieval in the InfoSet. As you will see in Section 6.1, Data Sources, the InfoSet enables you to use a data retrieval program to define the data basis.

Unlike QuickViewer, an InfoSet has the advantage of automatic text recognition. In other words, in the case of a table field, the system automatically provides another text field in the background for selection in the query. Section 6.2, Automatic Text Recognition includes an example to demonstrate this function.

Additional options are also available to you when designing the table join. For example, you can design the table relationship as a left inner join or left outer join. The differences between both joins are explored in Section 6.3, Table Join.

After you have designed the table join, you will learn how to create and change field groups in Section 6.4, Field Groups. You can create and name the fields groups according to your own criteria. You can also define the content of the field groups.

InfoSets are also extended to include fields that will be used as a data source. In an InfoSet, for example, you can use the aforementioned data sources as a basis and also make the data basis more flexible. Here, you have the option of assigning additional fields, tables, or structures that you have named to your InfoSet. As you will learn in Section 6.5, Individual Additional Fields, you can even add your own code to the InfoSet.

Finally, in Section 6.6, Selection, we will show you how you can influence the data to be selected in the InfoSet by defining your own selections there (parameters and selection criteria). Consequently, you can define field contents on the selection screen or fixed characteristic values in the background.

You will now create a new InfoSet for the already known table D010TAB (TABLE FOR USE REPORT ↔ TABLES) in conjunction with the table TSTC

(SAP Transaction Code). This new InfoSet will reinforce the knowledge you have already acquired as well as introduce you to many other new functions.

6.1   Data Sources

To create an InfoSet, follow these steps:

1. Select a data source (e.g., table join, table, or logical database).

2. Call Transaction SQ02 (InfoSet: Initial Screen). In the INFOSET field, enter the name "ZLEX0061". Then choose ⬜ Create (see Figure 6.1).

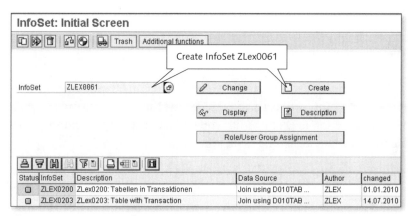

Figure 6.1   Creating an InfoSet

3. The system displays the DATA SOURCE window (see Figure 6.2). In the DESCRIPTION field, enter the text "ZLEX0061: Tables with Transaction Code". Select TABLE JOIN USING BASIS TABLE as the data source, and enter "D010TAB".

Selecting a data source

The following are available as possible data sources for your InfoSet:

▸ Table join

▸ Table

▸ Logical database

▸ Data retrieval program

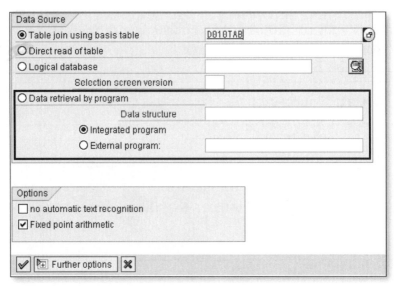

Figure 6.2 Data Sources for an InfoSet

Table join as a
data source

The first option, the *table join*, is the most frequently used option in real-life scenarios. You can use two or more data tables as a basis for your InfoSet. In Section 6.3, Table Join, you will learn about the options available to you when designing table joins.

Table as a
data source

If you require only one *table* as a data basis for your InfoSet, you can use the DIRECT READ OF TABLE option. If you use direct reading of the table as the data basis for your InfoSet, you can also use a cluster table as a data basis. For example, the cluster table BSEG (Document Segment: Accounting) contains a large amount of important information.

Logical database
as a data source

The third option is to use a *logical database* as a data source. Logical databases are predefined hierarchical table structures used by SAP for frequent analyses. SAP has already established the table links and additional arithmetic operations for you. The logical databases are extremely powerful and can affect performance as a result of their extensive table links and programming logic. You should therefore consider whether you want to access a predefined table structure with a lot of individual information or whether a separate table join or table as a data basis is sufficient for your requirements.

If these three potential data sources are insufficient as the basis for your InfoSet, the fourth option is to use an individual *data retrieval program*. In Chapter 14, Data Retrieval and Function Modules, we will explain how to use a data retrieval program and provide an example.

Data retrieval program

When you create the InfoSet, the system also automatically provides additional fields in the background. Consequently, your InfoSet automatically makes text fields from other tables available to the query as additional fields. Thanks to automatic text recognition, the InfoSet finds the associated text table for each characteristic. If, for example, you insert the table TSTC (SAP Transaction Codes) into the InfoSet, the associated text from the table TSTCT (Transaction Code Texts) is automatically added to the field TSTC-TCODE in the InfoSet.

Automatically generated text fields

6.2   Automatic Text Recognition

The InfoSet has automatic text recognition, which is active in the dialog box for creating the InfoSet. The Options area contains the no automatic text recognition flag, and the Class for text identification field contains the text CL_TEXT_IDENTIFIER (see Figure 6.3). Do not change this default setting. As a result of this setting, the standard SAP system automatically adds other data fields to the InfoSet in the background.

Example of Automatic Text Recognition   **[Ex]**

Let's assume that you insert the table TSTC (SAP Transaction Codes) into your InfoSet. The table TSTC contains the field TSTC-TCODE (Transaction Code). In addition to the characteristic TSTC-TCODE (Transaction Code), the associated transaction code text is made available to the InfoSet as additional information. In other words, for your query, the associated name field from the table TSTCT-TTEXT (Transaction Code Text) is automatically added to the field TSTC-TCODE as an additional field.

You do not have to add the tables and their characteristic names (e.g., TSTCT) to your InfoSet. The table fields in your InfoSet, for which a text field is already provided, are displayed with another icon. For example, the icon preceding the table field ▦ (Text Icon) also contains a small uppercase T (see Figure 6.4).

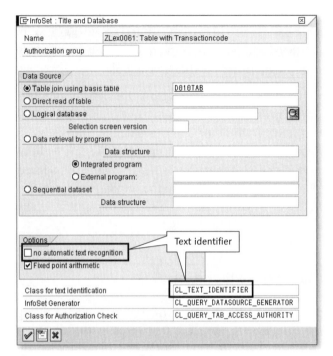

Figure 6.3 Creating an InfoSet

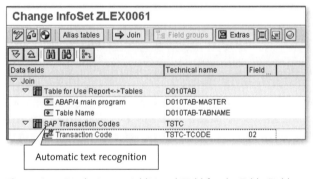

Figure 6.4 Displaying an Additional Field for the Table Field

You have now named your InfoSet ZLEX0061 and entered a table join with the table D010TAB as a data source. Choose ✓ to confirm your entry. You now access the screen in which you can edit your table join. After you have named your InfoSet and selected the table D010TAB as a data source, you access the graphical interface for designing your table join.

6.3   Table Join

The table join in the InfoSet shows the leading table D010TAB with the table fields on the left-hand side of the screen (see Figure 6.5). The table D010TAB contains two key fields. If you call your analysis, the system performs a data search on the basis of the key fields. The key fields therefore form a directory, comparable with the table of contents in a book, which enables you to quickly find the information you need.

Key fields

> **Using Key Fields in Table Joins**
>
> If possible, always use key fields for your table links because they will improve the performance of your reports. Frequently, the key field is also known as a primary index. If your data query is not based on key fields, you can use a secondary index to improve performance. In Chapter 14, Data Retrieval and Function Modules, you will learn how to create a secondary index, which is comparable with an index in a book, and thus improve performance.

[+]

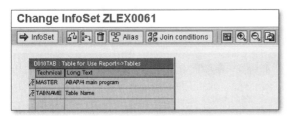

Figure 6.5   Table Join Before Inserting Additional Tables

Now you need to link the table D010TAB with the table TSTC (Transaction Code). To do this, choose [icon] to insert tables. The system now displays an ADD TABLE window. In the dialog box, you enter the table name TSTC in the TABLE field (see Figure 6.6).

Figure 6.6   Adding the Table TSTC to a Table Join

In the graphical join editor, the new table TSTC is added to the existing table D010TAB. A line is used to graphically link both tables with each other. In this case, the MASTER field (ABAP/4 MAIN PROGRAM) in the table D010TAB is linked with the field PGMNA (PROGRAM NAME) in the table TSTC (see Figure 6.7).

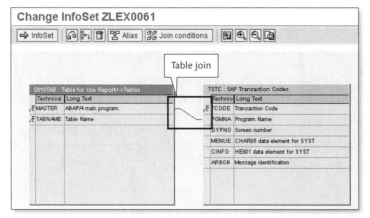

Figure 6.7 Field Link Between Two Tables

The system automatically suggests a link for the two table fields D010TAB-MASTER (ABAP/4 MAIN PROGRAM) and TSTC-PGMNA (PROGRAM NAME). For the link between these two table fields, the system checked whether both fields are of the same data type and whether they have the same number of characters, and, if necessary, the same number of decimal places.

Click the table field D010TAB-MASTER so that you can take a look at its technical attributes. When the field with the long text ABAP/4 MAIN PROGRAM is highlighted, choose the menu path EXTRAS • FIELD DOCUMENTATION (see Figure 6.8).

You then see a technical description for the field D010TAB-MASTER. The ABAP/4 MAIN PROGRAM field has the data type CHAR, and a data length of 40 characters (see Figure 6.9). The field PGMNA (PROGRAM NAME) in the table TSTC has the same data type and the same number of characters.

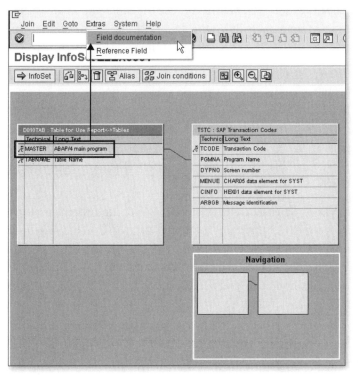

Figure 6.8 Displaying Field Information About a Table Field

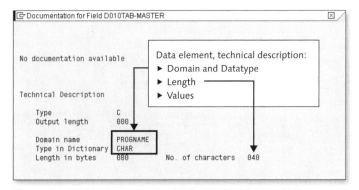

Figure 6.9 Field Information for the Field D010TAB-MASTER

Because the two data fields have the same technical attributes (data type and number of characters), the system creates the table link.

Technical field attributes

Table link

Be sure to check the table link before you use the table join as a basis for your analyses. For some table links, the data fields have the same technical attributes, but the link is not the one you need.

For your table links, the linked table field in the table on the left-hand side may not have a related entry in the table on the right hand-side. For example, if you query the number of ABAP programs for the table VBAK (Sales Document: Header Data) directly in the Data Browser, you get approximately 5,100 hits. If, on the other hand, you use our current InfoSet to query the table VBAK (Sales Document: Header Data), you get approximately 1,500 hits.

Left inner join

For the table VBAK (Sales Document: Header Data), the system currently displays only those ABAP programs for which a transaction has also been created. The system only outputs a report if the ABAP PROGRAM data field in both tables contains data records. If you want to only query data records for which there is an entry in the table D010TAB and an entry in the table TSTC, the current setting is correct (also known as the *left inner join*).

Left outer join

If you also want to display ABAP programs for which there is no transaction, you must change the table link so that you also get a result if the ABAP program only exists in the table D010TAB. To do this, right-click the link arrow between the two tables D010TAB and TSTC (also known as a *left outer join*; see Figure 6.10).

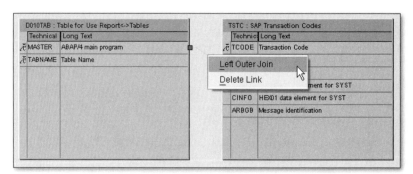

Figure 6.10 Using a Left Outer Join to Link Tables

Now you can choose 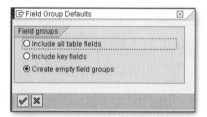 (BACK) to exit the graphical interface in which you edit your table join. In the next section, you will learn how to structure your table fields into field groups.

6.4 Field Groups

You can use field groups to group table fields according to your own criteria. You can also decide which table fields you want to make available to the query as a data basis.

When you exit the join definition in the InfoSet (as described in the previous section), the system displays the FIELD GROUP DEFAULTS dialog box. For each table used in the table join, the system now automatically creates a field group with the same name as the respective table. You can now fill the fields contained in the automatically created field groups (see Figure 6.11).

Field group defaults

Figure 6.11 Field Group Defaults

For the field group defaults, you can choose from the following three options:

- ▶ INCLUDE ALL TABLE FIELDS
- ▶ INCLUDE KEY FIELDS
- ▶ CREATE EMPTY FIELD GROUPS

The first option inserts all table fields in a table into a field group. The second option inserts only key fields (see the descriptions at the start of Section 6.3, Table Join) into the field groups. Alternatively, you can add all nonkey fields in a table to a field group.

Including all table fields in the field groups

For our example, follow these steps:

1. Choose the third option, CREATE EMPTY FIELD GROUPS, and create the field groups without adding any fields. Choose ✅ to confirm your selection. You then return to InfoSet design mode (see Figure 6.12).

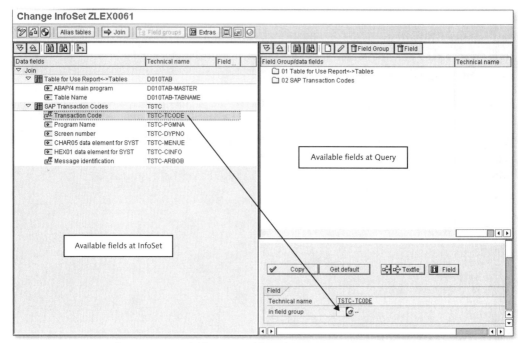

Figure 6.12 Available Data Fields and Assignment to a Field Group

<table>
<tr><td>Expanding and
collapsing data
fields in a table</td><td>2. On the left-hand side of the screen, you now see the two tables that you inserted into the table join: D010TAB and TSTC. You can choose 🔳 to expand and collapse the tables. When the table is expanded, the system displays all of the fields related to the table below the table itself.</td></tr>
<tr><td>Field groups
without fields</td><td>Two field groups are now inserted on the right hand-side of the screen. The first field group (Number 01) has assumed the original table name TABLE FOR USE REPORT ↔ TABLES. A field group was also created for</td></tr>
</table>

the second table used in the table join. So far, no fields have been assigned to these two field groups, and because the InfoSet represents the data basis for the query, there are still no fields available for selection in the query.

3. Double-click the first table field (Transaction Code) in the table TSTC (SAP Transaction Codes). On the lower-right side of the screen, the system displays additional information about the field TSTC-TCODE. For example, the technical name of the field TSTC-TCODE is displayed again as well as its assignment to a field group. Because the field is not assigned to any field group at the moment, the IN FIELD GROUP field has not been filled yet. Take a look at the complete explanation provided for the table field TSTC-TCODE (Transaction Code) (see Figure 6.13).

Detailed information about a data field

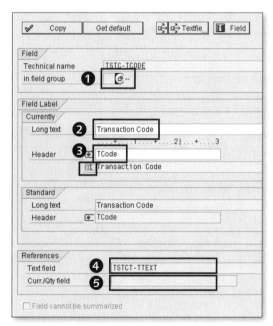

Figure 6.13 Explanations for the Table Field TSTC-TCODE

The following information is available for the field TSTC-TCODE:

- You can see the field group to which the field is assigned (❶).

- You can change the field long text, which will also be displayed on the query selection screen (❷).

- You can enter a name for the field header, which will be displayed as the column header in your report output (❸).

- If the system automatically generates another text field for your field, the original table for the text field is displayed here (❹).

- The associated currency or quantity field for currency and quantity fields is displayed here (❺). In addition to the amount and/or quantity field, for example, you can add the related currency or unit field to your field group.

Assigning fields to a field group

4. Add the field TSTC-TCODE (TRANSACTION CODE) to field group 02 SAP TRANSACTION CODES by dragging the field from the left-hand side of the screen to field group 02 on the right-hand side of the screen. The field TSTC-TCODE is then assigned to field group 02 (see Figure 6.14).

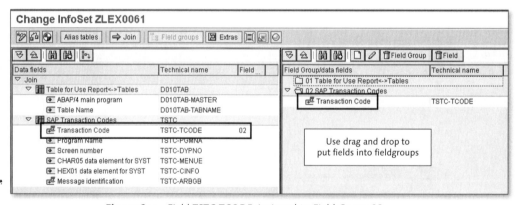

Figure 6.14 Field TSTC-TCODE Assigned to Field Group 02

Assigning multiple fields to a field group simultaneously

5. Drag and drop the field TSTC-PGMNA (PROGRAM NAME) to field group 02. You can also select multiple fields simultaneously. The selection functions available in Windows programs are also available here. If

you hold down ‎⌐Ctrl⌐‎, you can select multiple entries. Alternatively, you can use the arrow key on your keyboard to select multiple fields.

6. Add the two table fields MASTER (ABAP/4 MAIN PROGRAM) and TAB-NAME (TABLE NAME) to field group 01 TABLE FOR USE REPORT ↔ TABLES.

Two field groups and the corresponding two table fields are available for the query. Furthermore, the query contains an automatically created field group with the additional field TSTCT-TTEXT (TRANSACTION CODE TEXT). The usual functions are also available (e.g., changing field group names, deleting field groups, or removing fields from field groups). In the next section, you will learn how to create a new field group and add an individual additional field to the field group.

6.5 Individual Additional Fields

Now that you have read the earlier sections in this chapter, you must be thinking that InfoSets are pretty cool! However, even more flexibility can be achieved by implementing additional fields, which were considered almost impossible, for potential analyses and making reports more user-friendly so that users can display the information they require.

You can use additional fields to add more field information from any table to the InfoSet. Alternatively, you can use existing data fields to perform arithmetic operations and then display the result of such arithmetic operations in an additional field.

In our example, the InfoSet automatically provided the associated transaction text for the TRANSACTION field in the background. After you have called the report, you always get such information in your logon language. The transaction texts are maintained in the table TSTCT in all languages installed on the system. If, for example, you have installed eight languages, you get eight hits for each transaction in the table TSTCT in the Data Browser (see Figure 6.15).

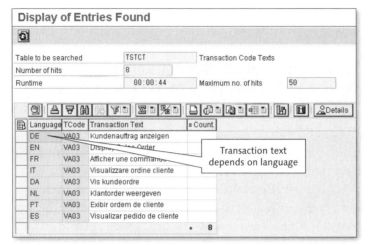

Figure 6.15 Language-Dependent Transaction Code Texts

You could now also add the table TSTCT (Transaction Code Texts) to your table join. However, each transaction would then be displayed eight times in your report output. Consequently, it makes more sense to display the English text in an additional column next to the German text.

[»] | **Multiple Data Records**

Multiple data records exist for all language-dependent information. Whenever you link an existing table field with another table that has multiple data records in your table join, the hit list multiplies. This constellation frequently exists in real-life situations (e.g., if you link sales documents with customer information). The customer information for the sales documents is managed in a separate table. For each sales document or sales document item, the customer is managed in multiple partner roles. For example, the standard system already has four partner roles for sales documents (sold-to party, ship-to party, payer, and bill-to party). You will want to see the sales document in the report once and the various partner roles in separate columns.

In the InfoSet, using additional fields helps avoid having numerous data records as a result of language-dependent tables. Follow these steps to use additional fields:

1. In the menu bar, click [🗟 Extras] (see Figure 6.16).

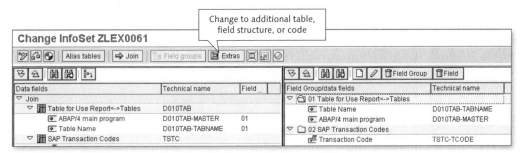

Figure 6.16 Click the Extras Button

2. The right-hand side of the screen contains the EXTRAS tab. Choose ☐ (CREATE) to display the view shown in Figure 6.17.

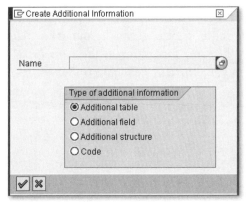

Figure 6.17 Selecting the Button for Creating Additional Information

3. You can now add further additional information to the InfoSet. Enter the text "ZTEXT" in the NAME field. Select the ADDITIONAL FIELD option (see Figure 6.18). We will discuss all other options in Chapter 11, ABAP Fundamentals in the InfoSet.

4. The system now displays an additional dialog box in which you define the name and technical attributes of the additional field. In the LONG TEXT field, enter the text "Transaction Text", which will be displayed on the selection screen for your report. Then, enter the text "TTEXT" in the HEADER field. The text TTEXT will be displayed as a column header in the list output.

Defining an additional field

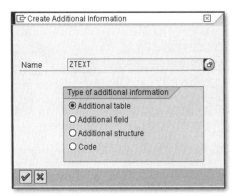

Figure 6.18 Creating an Additional Field

5. Define the technical format, including the type, length, output length, and number of decimal places. The easiest option is to enter the existing field TSTCT-TTEXT in the LIKE REFERENCE field. Your new additional field TTEXT now gets the same formatting as the field TSTCT-TTEXT. Choose ✔ to confirm your entries (see Figure 6.19).

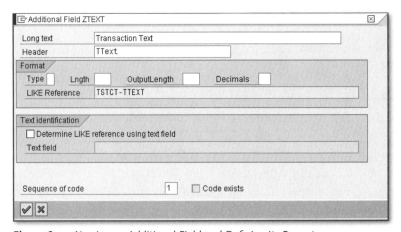

Figure 6.19 Naming an Additional Field and Defining Its Format

Adding ABAP code to the additional field

6. You have now created your new additional field, which will be displayed on the EXTRAS tab. If you want your additional field to also display content in the report, you must define ABAP code for the new field TTEXT. To do this, select the field TTEXT, and choose 🔳 (INSERT CODE) (see Figure 6.20).

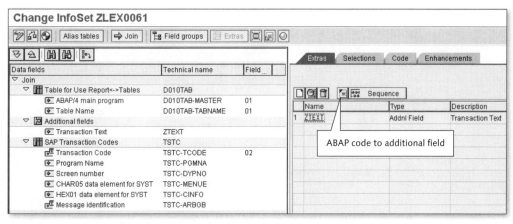

Figure 6.20 Switching from the Additional Fields Overview to the Code Screen

7. An editor screen appears in which you can insert your own individual code. From the table TSTCT (Transaction Code Texts), select the English text in your additional field. You have used the statement SPRSL = 'EN' to fix the content of your additional field to English. Now transfer the code from Figure 6.21. The meaning of this code will be explained in further detail in Chapter 11, ABAP Fundamentals in the InfoSet.

Selecting transaction code text in an additional field

8. Check whether your code is syntactically correct by choosing 🔲 (CHECK), and then choose the disk icon 🔲 to save your lines of program code.

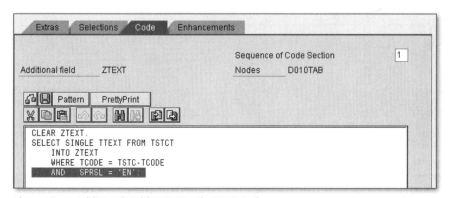

Figure 6.21 Additional Field ZTEXT with ABAP Code

9. Now choose ⊕ (BACK) to exit the editing screen for the additional field. The system then issues an onscreen warning message indicating that you have not yet assigned your additional field to a field group (see Figure 6.22). Consequently, your additional field is available in the InfoSet but not in your query.

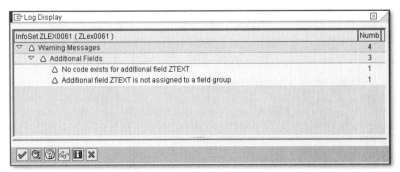

Figure 6.22 Warning Message: "Additional field ZTEXT is not assigned to a field group"

Creating a new field group

Now you can create a new field group for your additional field ZTEXT by following these steps:

1. Choose ☐ (CREATE NEW FIELD GROUP) (see Figure 6.23).

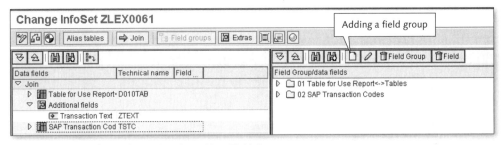

Figure 6.23 Creating a New Field Group

Naming a new field group

2. The system now displays the CREATE FIELD GROUPS screen. In the FG column on the left, enter the field group number "91" and, in the DESCRIPTION column on the right, enter "Additional fields" (see Figure 6.24).

Figure 6.24 Creating a New Field Group and Entering a Description

3. Your new field group is now displayed on the right-hand side of the screen. On the left-hand side, you see a new grouping with the header ADDITIONAL FIELDS and your additional field ZTEXT. Drag the additional field ZTEXT to the new field group 91. The system displays the assignment of the field ZTEXT to the field group 91 in the FIELD GROUP column on the left-hand side of the screen (see Figure 6.25).

Assigning the additional field to a new field group

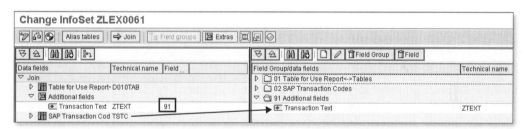

Figure 6.25 Assigning the Additional Field ZTEXT to Field Group 91 Additional Fields

In addition to the transaction code text in the logon language, the system also displays the English text for your query in an additional report column. If you now want to display the Spanish text in the report, you can define another additional field in the same way. You must define a new additional field for each language and show and hide the columns in the report as required. However, you can also give the user the option of selecting the text language of the second language, so that only one additional field is required. Therefore, use a selection to enhance the selection screen in a flexible manner.

6.6   Selection

Selections are comparable to additional fields. The selection functions are available to you when you choose ⊞ Extras . You can create two types of selections, namely selection criterion and parameters. If you want to use an interval as a selection, you can achieve this by using a selection criterion. To select a value (e.g., a language), you use parameters. You create a new selection in the same way as you created the additional field. To do so, follow these steps:

1. Choose ☐ (CREATE). The system now displays a CREATE SELECTION dialog box (see Figure 6.26).

Figure 6.26 Creating a Selection for the Language Selection

Creating selection parameters

2. Enter the text "ZSPRL" for the language key in the NAME field. Select the PARAMETERS option, and confirm your entry. The system then displays a dialog box in which you define a name and technical attributes for your selection (see Figure 6.27).

Defining selection parameters

3. Enter the text "Language" in the DESCRIPTION and SELECTION TEXT fields. Format the selection by copying the technical attributes of the field TSTCT-SPRSL. To do this, enter the text "TSTCT-SPRSL" in the LIKE field. Now change the code for the additional field ZTEXT from Section 6.5, Individual Additional Fields.

Parameter ZSPRSL ⊠

Sequence on selection screen   1

Definition

Description	Language
Selection text	Language

Format   Type   Lngth

LIKE   TSTCT-SPRSL

Extras

Error Message

✓ ✗

Figure 6.27   Naming the Language Key and Defining the Format

4. Until now, you have used the program statement SPRSL = 'EN' to fill your additional field ZTEXT with English text. Now use the text SPRSL = ZSPRL to change the code for the additional field ZTEXT (see Figure 6.28).

Assigning the content of the selection parameter to the additional field

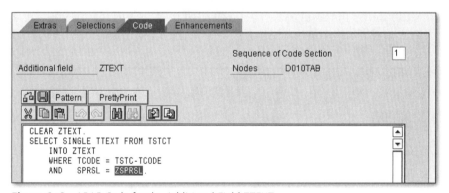

Figure 6.28   ABAP Code for the Additional Field ZTEXT

It is no longer necessary for you to create another additional field for each language. If you execute your report now, you can define the language in which you want to view the transaction text. On the selection screen, you can therefore determine the language in which you want the transaction text to be displayed in the list output (see Figure 6.29).

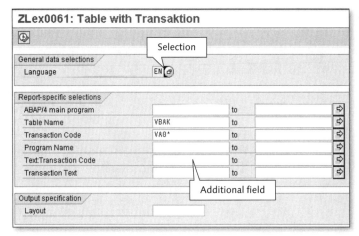

Figure 6.29 Selection and Additional Field on the Selection Screen

Selection and additional field on the selection screen
Your individual selection is displayed on the upper half of the selection screen. The transaction text in the logon language was automatically provided in the InfoSet and is also available on the query selection screen. Your additional field is also displayed on the selection screen. Here, it has the name TRANSACTION TEXT. You now have the flexibility to search for transactions on the basis of tables or language-dependent texts. Figure 6.30 shows the result when you select all transactions that use the table VBAK (Sales Document: Header Data) and start with VA0.

ZLex0061: Table with Transaktion

ZLex0061: Table with Transaktion

Table Name	Main prg	TCode	Transaction Code	TText
VBAK	SAPMV45A	VA01	Create Sales Order	Create Sales Order
VBAK	SAPMV45A	VA02	Change Sales Order	Change Sales Order
VBAK	SAPMV45A	VA03	Display Sales Order	Display Sales Order
VBAK	SAPMV75A	VA05	List of Sales Orders	List of Sales Orders
VBAK	SDBANF02	VA07	Compare Sales - Purchasing (Order)	Compare Sales - Purchasing (Order)
VBAK	SDBANF01	VA08	Compare Sales - Purchasing (Org.Dt.)	Compare Sales - Purchasing (Org.Dt.)

Figure 6.30 Selection Result with an Additional Field and Selection

The transaction text automatically generated in the InfoSet is displayed in the fourth column, TRANSACTION CODE, while the transaction text translated into English is displayed in the last column, TTEXT.

6.7 Summary

The InfoSet provides you with numerous options for a flexible data basis for your query. For example, you can select different sources (table join, table, logical database, and data retrieval program) as a data source. In addition, text fields are automatically provided for a large number of characteristics.

The tables are automatically linked with each other in a graphical interface, and you can adjust table relationships. For example, you can link table fields with each other, or you can choose a left outer join instead of a left inner join. You have the flexibility to structure the fields in selected tables into separate field groups. For example, you can create additional field groups or provide only those fields that are relevant for your query.

You can provide additional information or calculations in additional fields in the InfoSet. Finally, in an InfoSet, you have the flexibility to design the selection screen for your query. In the next chapter, you will use the InfoSet to create your query. You will also learn about other options associated with designing a query.

In this chapter, you will learn how to convert a QuickViewer report into a query, use your own field names or additional local fields to optimize your query, and use the graphical design and formatting options. In addition, you will become familiar with statistics, ranked lists, and the report/report interface.

7 SAP Query in Detail

This chapter provides a detailed description of Transaction SQ01 (SAP Query). We will provide a practical example to explain how to execute the functions available within Transaction SQ01. First, we will explain the functions available to you on the initial screen. Then, you will name a query and define the output format on the creation screen. In a further step, you will change the field headers for the list output.

In the query, you also have the option of inserting local fields as additional columns. In the local fields, you can store the results of arithmetic operations that use other fields, or you can display graphical icons. Finally, you will learn how to adjust the selection screen and select selection and layout fields.

7.1 Fundamentals

With just a few simple clicks, you can quickly create a query. The main task associated with creating a query is to provide the correct tables and table fields in an InfoSet. Before we provide you with a detailed description of the query functions, let's discuss the importance of SAP Query (see Figure 7.1).

Your query objects are stored for a particular query area in the system. You have created your InfoSet ZLEX0061 (Tables with Transactions) in the standard area. In the standard area, there are separate user groups for authorization management and user management. Here, you have used

User group

the user group ZLEX (Special Reports). On one hand, the user group comprises several users. On the other, the InfoSets are assigned to the user group. Therefore, when you create your query, you must be assigned to the correct user group in the standard area so that you can use your InfoSet as a data basis for your query.

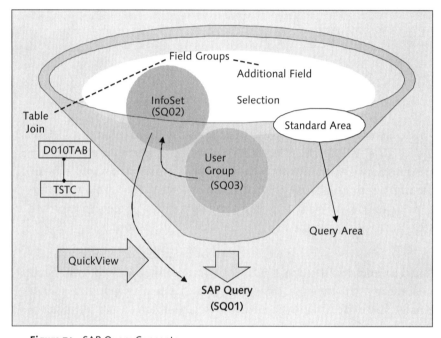

Figure 7.1 SAP Query Concepts

InfoSet Your InfoSet is based on a table join in which the PROGRAM NAME data field is used to link the two tables D010TAB (SAP Tables) and TSTC (Transaction Code) with each other. For each table used in the table join, the system creates a field group in the InfoSet by default.

Additional field An additional field has been created in the InfoSet. We assigned this additional field to a newly created field group 91 (Zlex: Special Fields). We also created a selection in the InfoSet so that you could restrict your data in a more flexible manner.

We will also introduce you to some other report design options:

- Initial screen, with the function for converting a QuickView into a query
- Creation screen with editing options (in particular, output formats)
- Changing field names and adding local fields
- Graphical formatting options
- Additional functions (statistics, report/report interface)

You will change your user group on the initial screen and convert a QuickView into a query. Any reports created using QuickViewer are only available to the person who created the report. However, you can convert your QuickViewer report into a query so that all users can use this report.

Converting QuickView into a query

On the creation screen for query editing, you can enter a long text and some editing comments for your query. You can also influence the list format and table format. In addition, you can change the print output. On the initial screen, you can also define or fix a variant for report execution as a proposal. So far, you have used the known output format SAP List Viewer. However, a total of nine different output formats are available to you. For example, statistics in a format other than SAP List Viewer can be output as an ABAP list.

Output formats

You can make the query more user friendly by adjusting the field name or supplementing the query output with additional column information.

Field names

In addition to some graphical formatting options, two highly user-friendly additional functions are available to you: *statistics* and the *report/report interface*. You can use the statistics function to display a summary of your data volume, while the report/report interface enables you to navigate from your query to other reports or to drill down directly to the SAP application transactions.

Formatting options

The use of Transaction SQ01 by a user also corresponds to the SAP concept. Consequently, query creation occurs in several transactions. SAP Query only enables you to access the data available in the InfoSet. Therefore, it is not regarded as critical. Rather, SAP Query supports the user department in the creation of suitable reports. SAP Query is therefore a tool for all SAP users. In the next section, we will show you how to convert a QuickView into a query.

Use of a query by an (end) user

7.2   Initial Screen

Before you convert a QuickView into a query, you should select the correct user group in the standard area. Queries located in another query area or another user group are frequently missed in real-life scenarios.

7.2.1   Changing User Group

Call Transaction SQ01 (SAP Query) to edit the query. Your screen should have the name QUERY FROM USER GROUP ZLEX: INITIAL SCREEN (see Figure 7.2). In other words, when you work in Transaction SQ01, your editing steps should be performed on the basis of the user group.

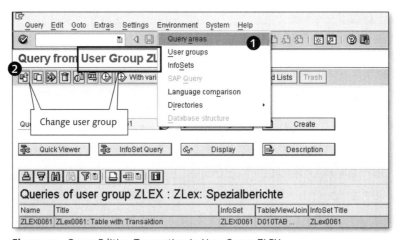

Figure 7.2 Query Editing Transaction in User Group ZLEX

Changing the query area
If the user group ZLEX is not displayed on your screen header, there may be two reasons for this:

▶ You are in the global area, not the standard area.

▶ You are in the standard area, but another user group is preconfigured.

In the first scenario, choose the menu path ENVIRONMENT • QUERY AREAS (❶, in Figure 7.2) to switch from the global query area to the standard area.

In the second scenario, choose 🔲 (CHANGE USER GROUP) to change your current user group to the user group ZLEX (❷). If you are already in the user group ZLEX, change the query area and user group to see the different effects and results. You will see that different queries are displayed, depending on the query area and user group.

Change user group

If, as in this book, you always work with the standard area and primarily in one user group, you can define the parameters for the query area and your user group in your user master. You can use Transaction SU3 (Maintain Own User Profiles) to call your user data. For the standard area, leave the PARAMETER ID AQW blank. If you generally work in the global area, enter a "G" as the parameter. On the PARAMETERS tab, enter the following values (see Figure 7.3):

Using the standard area

▸ AQB: ZLEX   (user group)

▸ AQW: blank   (query area)

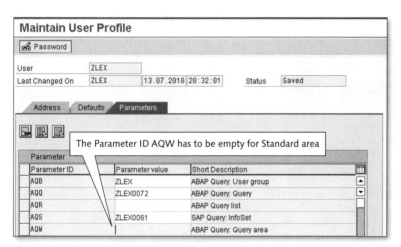

Figure 7.3 Users with Default Parameters

7.2.2   Converting QuickView into a Query

You will now learn how to convert a query. All of the QuickViews created so far are stored on the basis of your user. In other words, you are the only person who can use all of the QuickViewer reports that you have created. Therefore, nobody other than the person who created the

QuickView can use this report or view it in the application. You will now learn how you can make your QuickViewer reports accessible to all users. In the SAP system, changing a QuickViewer report into a query report is known as a *conversion*. To convert a QuickView into a query, follow these steps:

1. Choose the menu path QUERY • CONVERT QUICKVIEW as shown in Figure 7.4.

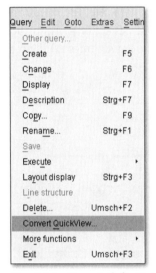

Figure 7.4 Menu Path for Converting a QuickView

2. After you have made your selection, the system displays the CONVERT QUICKVIEW dialog box (see Figure 7.5).

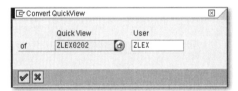

Figure 7.5 Entering a QuickView for Conversion into a Query

3. In the QUICKVIEW field, enter the QuickView that you created in Chapter 3, QuickViewer. Then, enter your user name in the USER field.

Choose 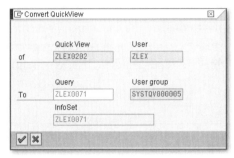 to confirm your entries. The system then adds another input area to your CONVERT QUICKVIEW window (see Figure 7.6).

Figure 7.6 Naming a Query Converted from a QuickView

4. In the QUERY field, enter the name of the newly created query, and choose ✓ to confirm your entry. You now return to the SAP Query initial screen (see Figure 7.7).

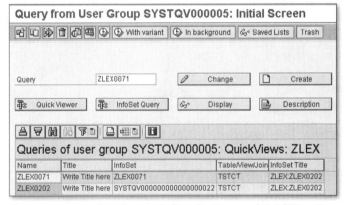

Figure 7.7 Query Overview, Including the Converted QuickView Query

The new query ZLEX0071 is now available for report execution or further editing. For example, you can now rename the query text or make the query available to your users.

7.2.3 Additional Functions on the Initial Screen

On the query initial screen, the menu environment contains additional functions. If you receive a notification indicating that your query has

Query report name

not been updated for the InfoSet, you can reconcile the query with the InfoSet. Similarly, you can regenerate the ABAP program created by the query. Because the query is a utility for creating an ABAP program, the system automatically creates an ABAP report name. You can choose the menu path QUERY • MORE FUNCTIONS to display the functions for reconciling the InfoSet with the query (ADJUST), generating the query program (GENERATE PROGRAM), and displaying the report name (DISPLAY REPORT NAME) (see Figure 7.8).

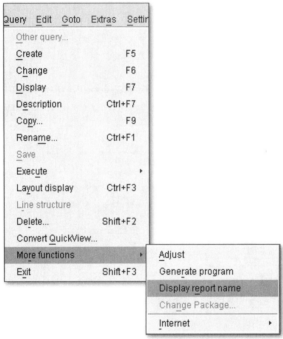

Figure 7.8 Displaying the ABAP Report Name for the Query

Display the report name for the query that we have just created (see Figure 7.9).

Figure 7.9 ABAP Report Name Automatically Generated for a Query

The ABAP report name has 30 characters, structured as follows:

Logic for query report name

- **Characters 01 and 02:** Permanently AQ for ABAP Query (before Release 4.6, SAP Query was known as ABAP Query).
- **Characters 03 and 04:** Encoding for client. If you create queries in the global area, the third and fourth characters are permanently ZZ.
- **Characters 05 and 06:** User group name with a maximum of 12 characters.
- **Characters 17 to 30:** Query name. A query name can comprise a maximum of 14 characters. If the query name is shorter than 14 characters, the ABAP report name is filled with "=".

[+]

Displaying Queries

You are now familiar with the logic used to assign an ABAP report name to a query. Armed with this knowledge, you can now use the Data Browser to query your system queries in the table REPOSRC (Report Sources). The table REPOSRC also contains additional interesting information (e.g., the creator, creation date, last changed by, change date, and version).

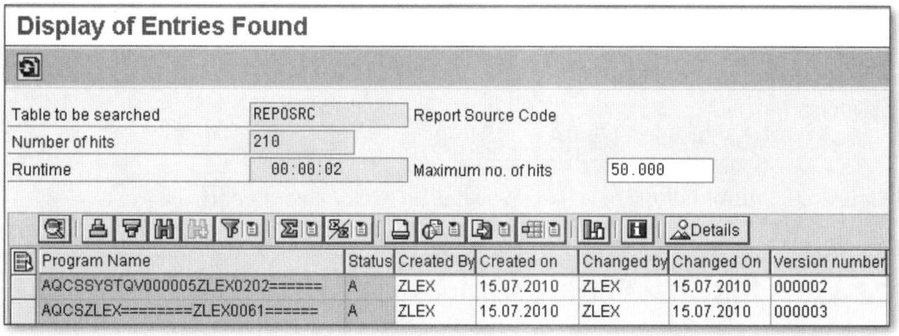
Display of Entries Found
Table to be searched
REPOSRC
Report Source Code
Number of hits
210
Runtime
00:00:02
Maximum no. of hits
50.000
Details
Program Name
Status
Created By
Created on
Changed by
Changed On
Version number
AQCSSYSTQV000005ZLEX0202======
A
ZLEX
15.07.2010
ZLEX
15.07.2010
000002
AQCSZLEX========ZLEX0061======
A
ZLEX
15.07.2010
ZLEX
15.07.2010
000003

Figure 7.10 Data Browser with ABAP Program Names

Displaying QuickViews

For reports created using QuickViewer, the system automatically creates a user group (that starts with the letters SYSTQV) in the background. In the ABAP program, the user group is coded as of the fifth character (see Figure 7.10). You can therefore see which QuickViews exist in your system. In the table D010TAB (Table for Use Report ↔ Tables), you see which tables are queried. This identifies a security risk in your system, namely that data content not intended for a particular group of users could be queried. Many tables contain personal data (e.g., order confirmations in the table AFRV). On the other hand, it may make sense to convert QuickViewer reports into a query so that other users can query very useful information.

Displaying a query in the ABAP Editor

If you now want to use queried tables to easily determine the queries in your system, it is best to create a new InfoSet and use it as a basis for your query.

After you have called your query, the system displays the name of the ABAP program if you navigate to Transaction SE38 (ABAP Editor: Initial Screen). The system transfers the program name to Transaction SE38 as a set/get parameter (see Figure 7.11).

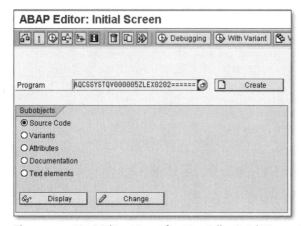

Figure 7.11 ABAP Editor View After You Call a QuickViewer Report

7.2.4 Additional Editing Options

The initial screen for the query (Transaction SQ01) contains numerous icons that represent very useful functions (see Table 7.1).

No.	Icon	Shortcut	Description
1	🔲	Shift + F7	Change user group
2	🔲	F9	Copy
3	🔲	Ctrl + F1	Rename

Table 7.1 Query Functions on the Initial Screen

No.	Icon	Shortcut	Description
4	🗑	`Shift` + `F2`	Delete
5	📑	`Ctrl` + `F3`	Layout display
6	📰	`Ctrl` + `F8`	Test
7	📰	`F8`	Execute
8	With Variant	`Shift` + `F5`	Execute with a variant
9	In background	`Shift` + `F6`	Execute in the background
10	Saved Lists	`Shift` + `F4`	Saved lists
11	Trash	`Ctrl` + `F6`	Trash
12	Change	–	Change
13	Create	–	Create
14	Quick Viewer	–	QuickViewer
15	InfoSet Query	–	InfoSet Query
16	Display	–	Display
17	Description	–	Description

Table 7.1 Query Functions on the Initial Screen (Cont.)

At the start of this section, we explained how to change user groups. If you want to copy existing queries, you can choose 🗔. You can also copy queries from other user groups if the associated InfoSet is assigned to your current user group. If you want to rename queries, you can choose 🗔. If you rename queries, you should inform your colleagues so that they do not search for existing queries in vain. If necessary, inform your colleagues if you use of the 🗑 button to delete queries. The queries are not deleted immediately. Instead, they are moved to the trash folder. You can therefore retrieve your query, if necessary. Additional information about the trash folder is available in Section 5.5.2, Trash Folder, in Chapter 5. The other functions are self-explanatory.

Copying, renaming, and deleting a query

The next step is to choose [☐   Create   ] to create your own query.

7.3   Query Creation Screen

In this section, you will learn how to work with the query creation screen:

1. In the QUERY field, enter the text "ZLEX0072", and choose the CREATE button as shown in Figure 7.12.

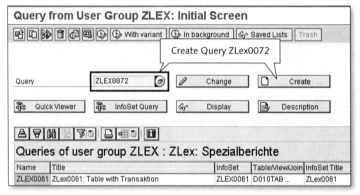

Figure 7.12   Creating the Query ZLex0072

2. The system displays another window, which contains all of the Info-Sets in the user group ZLEX. Double-click the InfoSet ZLEX0061 (TABLES WITH TRANSACTIONS) (see Figure 7.13).

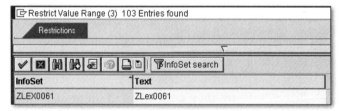

Figure 7.13   Selecting an InfoSet for Creating a Query

The system displays a screen in which you can name and format the query (as shown in the next section).

7.3.1 Query Title and Formatting

You can give your query a title and apply various formatting options (see Figure 7.14).

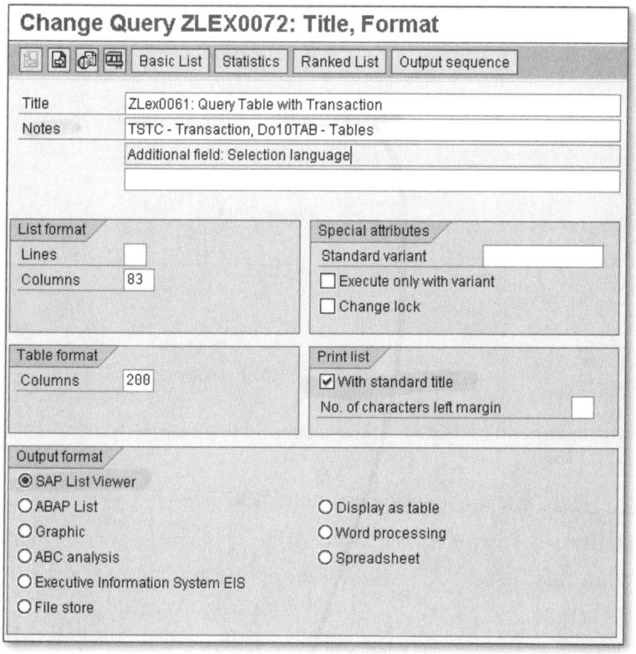

Figure 7.14 Specifying a Title and Formats for a Query

In real-life situations, the query title is frequently the same as the query itself (e.g., the query is called Zlex0072 and the name also begins with Zlex0072). The text in the TITLE field is displayed on the selection screen. Furthermore, in the NOTES area, the data source (e.g., the InfoSet) is explained in further detail. The menu bar contains eight other buttons (see Table 7.2).

Naming a query

You can use the first two buttons to navigate between the various screen templates, while the Test button (button 4 in the preceding table) enables you to test the current query settings before you permanently save the new settings. You can use the BASIC LIST button (button 5) to navigate directly to the selection screen for list and selection fields. The other buttons represent jumps to other functions, namely statistics, the ranked

Query navigation

list, and output sequence, which will be explained separately in Chapter 10, Summarized Data Output with Statistics and Ranked Lists.

No.	Icon	Shortcut	Description
1		F5	Last screen
2		F6	Next screen
3		Ctrl + F3	Layout display
4		Ctrl + F8	Test
5	Basic List	Shift + F4	Basic list
6	Statistics	Shift + F5	Statistics
7	Ranked List	Shift + F7	Ranked list
8	Output sequence	Ctrl + F4	Output sequence

Table 7.2 Navigation and Function Buttons on the Query Editing Screen

Assigning a variant   In the LIST FORMAT and TABLE FORMAT areas, you can influence the number of lines and columns in the output and printout. These formats do not affect the frequently used SAP List Viewer, but they do affect the ABAP List output format.

You can assign a standard variant to your query as well, which is explained in Chapter 8, Selection and Layout Variants.

Change lock   A change lock can be assigned to the query. If you want to adjust an existing query that has a change lock, copy the query, delete the query that has the change lock, and then copy the query back to the original query. However, you should apply this method with caution because existing selection and layout variants may be lost during the copy and delete actions. Instead, we recommend that you call the query directory as described in Section 5.3.2, Query Overview, and choose CANCEL EDIT LOCK as shown in Figure 5.9 of Chapter 5.

The most important part of this screen is the output format. Alternatively, you can use the report query directory to cancel the change lock (see Section 5.3.2, Query Overview, in Chapter 5).

7.3.2 Output Format

You can choose from the output formats for SAP Query listed in Table 7.3. Since Release 4.6C, the new SAP transactions use SAP List Viewer.

No.	Output Format
1	SAP List Viewer
2	ABAP List
3	Display as table
4	Graphic
5	Word processing
6	ABC analysis
7	Spreadsheet
8	Executive Information System EIS
9	File store

Table 7.3 Output Formats for an SAP Query

The predecessor to SAP List Viewer was the ABAP list. The ABAP list continues to be used with statistics and ranked lists. Statistics summarize your data in accordance with certain characteristics, and they require an ABAP list to output the report. File store saves the result lists with their current statuses. You can use the SAVED LISTS function to display these lists.

ABAP list

7.4 Field Name

When you create a query, the SAP system guides you through several settings screens, so that you can configure reports to your requirements. You will pass through the following screen templates:

▶ Initial Screen: Specify a query name.

▶ Title, Format: Assign a title and specify formats.

▶ Select Field Group: Select the field groups.

▶ Select Field: Select fields.

▶ Selection: Design the selection screen.

▶ Basic List: Define list and selection fields.

You can use the two navigation buttons 🔲 🔲 (BACKWARD and FORWARD) in the toolbar to move back and forth between the screen templates. Choose the navigation button 🔲 (FORWARD) to navigate to the next screen template. The system now displays the SELECT FIELD GROUP screen (see Figure 7.15).

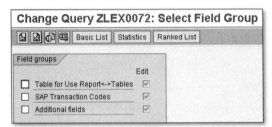

Figure 7.15 Selecting the Field Group on the Query Editing Screen

Field groups   The system displays the known field groups from the InfoSet. The field group you select here determines which fields are displayed on the next screen template. Because our data basis is manageable, you can select all field groups and choose 🔲 to navigate to the next screen (see Figure 7.16).

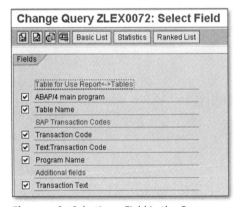

Figure 7.16 Selecting a Field in the Query

The system now displays the field groups of the InfoSet in a structured form. The table fields that you have assigned to the field groups in the InfoSet are displayed below the field groups. You can see the effects of designing field groups in the InfoSet. Our field group for the additional fields, which was created in the InfoSet, is also displayed. Therefore, if you have numerous data fields, you can structure your data into field groups.

7.4.1 Changing the Column Header of Query Fields

On this screen, you can optimize the column headers of data fields for your query. Select the TEXT: TRANSACTION CODE field, and choose the menu path EDIT • COLUMN HEADER • MAINTAIN (see Figure 7.17).

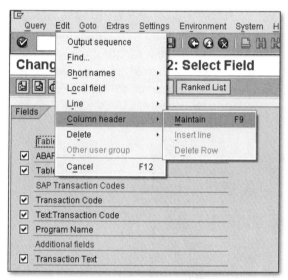

Figure 7.17 Changing the Column Header of a Field

The system now displays a COLUMN HEADER OF A FIELD dialog box (see Figure 7.18). Here, you change the text in the HEADING field from TCODE to TRANSACTION CODE.

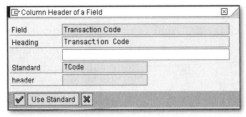

Figure 7.18 Changing the Column Header of a Query Field

You can therefore design even more descriptive report fields by using suitable text fields for your enterprise. You can also add additional columns with additional information to your report.

7.4.2 Local Fields

Let's assume that, in your report, you want to use icons to indicate whether the transaction text has been translated into a foreign language. If the transaction text in your logon language is identical to the transaction text in the second language, this is indicated by a red icon. If the content of both transaction text fields is different, this is indicated by a green icon. Choose the menu path EDIT • SHORT NAMES • SWITCH ON/OFF (see Figure 7.19).

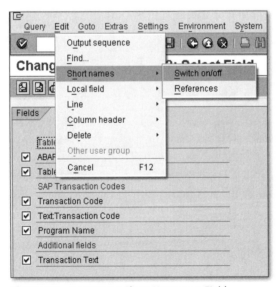

Figure 7.19 Assigning a Short Name to a Field

On your screen, the system displays free input fields to the right of the data fields in the SHORT NAME column. Enter the short name "LAN-GUAGE1" for the TEXT: TRANSACTION CODE field. Then, enter the short name "LANGUAGE2" for the TRANSACTION TEXT field (see Figure 7.20).

Displaying a short name for fields

Change Query ZLEX0072: Select Field

| | | Basic List | Statistics | Ranked List |

Fields

		Short name	Local
Table for Use Report<->Tables			
☑ ABAP/4 main program			
☑ Table Name			
SAP Transaction Codes			
☑ Transaction Code			
☑ Text:Transaction Code		LANGUAGE1	
☑ Program Name			
Additional fields			
☑ Transaction Text		LANGUAGE2	

Figure 7.20 Assigning a Short Name to Transaction Text Fields

The other field name has the purpose of indicating the fields that you require for an additional field. Furthermore, it is easier to work with meaningful names if you create new fields in your query. To create a new local field, choose the menu path EDIT • LOCAL FIELD • CREATE (see Figure 7.21).

Naming a local field

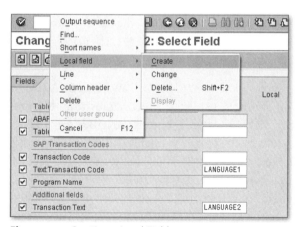

Figure 7.21 Creating a Local Field

On the next screen, define your local field (see Figure 7.22).

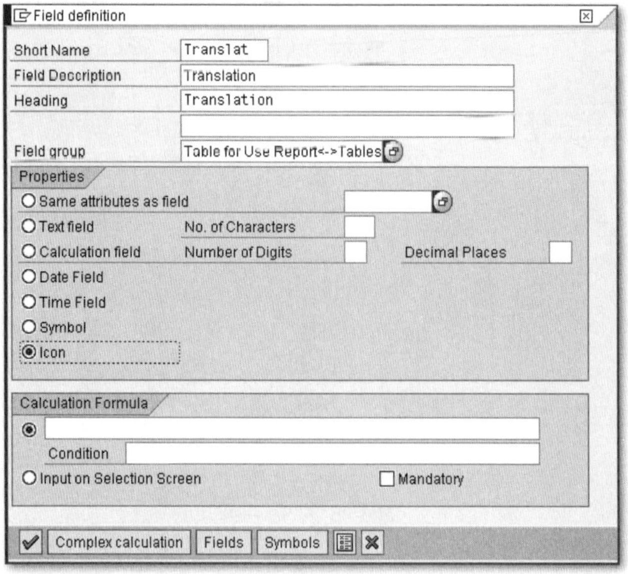

Figure 7.22 Defining a Local Field

Defining a
local field

In the SHORT NAME field, enter the text "TRANSLAT". Then, enter "Translation" in the FIELD DESCRIPTION and HEADING fields. Because you want the system to display an icon in your local field (report column), choose the ICON option in the PROPERTIES area. For further editing, choose COMPLEX CALCULATION, so that you can enter the conditions for displaying colored icons. The system then displays the DEFINE FIELD: COMPLEX CALCULATION window (see Figure 7.23).

Complex
calculation

You have assigned the short names LANGUAGE1 and LANGUAGE2 to the two data fields. You can now use both short names to determine the content of your local field. Therefore, enter "LANGUAGE1 = LANGUAGE1" as the CONDITION in the complex calculation. In the FORMULA area, you must enter the text for displaying the icon. If the LANGUAGE1 = LANGUAGE1 condition is not fulfilled, you can enter text for another icon in the OTHERWISE field. To display the existing icons and associated text, choose 🔲 (ICONS) on the lower-right side of the screen. The system then displays a screen in which you can select SAP system icons (see Figure 7.24).

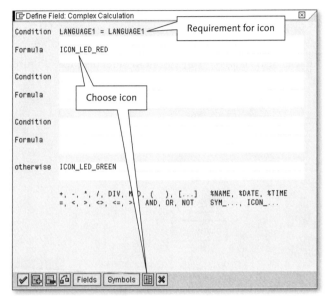

Figure 7.23 Defining a Complex Calculation for a Local Field

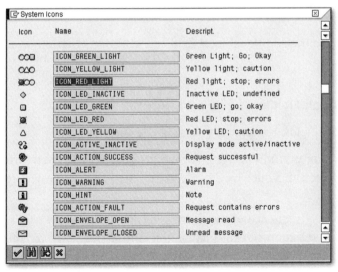

Figure 7.24 Selecting SAP System Icons

Selecting an icon
More than 1,000 different icons are available in the system. The text relating to the system icon is displayed to the right of the icon. Select the system icon ICON_RED_LIGHT, and choose ✅ to confirm your entry. You now return to the DEFINE FIELD: COMPLEX CALCULATION field. Once again, choose ✅ to confirm your entry. You now return to the FIELD DEFINITION screen. Choose ✅ to confirm your entry. You have now defined the local field, which is also displayed in the field selection (see Figure 7.25).

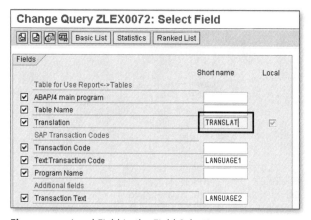

Figure 7.25 Local Field in the Field Selection

You can now use the additional local field as a selection criterion or as a list field.

7.4.3 Selection Fields

To edit selection fields, proceed as follows:

1. Choose 📄 (FORWARD) to navigate to the next screen. The system displays the screen in which you can edit selection fields (see Figure 7.26).

Defining a
sequence for
selection fields
You can define the sequence in which the selection fields are to be displayed on your selection screen. Change the current sequence for the selection fields by entering the relevant number in the No column. For

example, you can display the table name in first position on your selection screen. You can also adjust the texts on the selection screen to your requirements. To do this, simply change the proposed text in the SELECTION TEXT column, and the original SAP text will continue to be displayed on the left-hand side of the screen. In the next step, choose BASIC LIST, which we will describe in the next section.

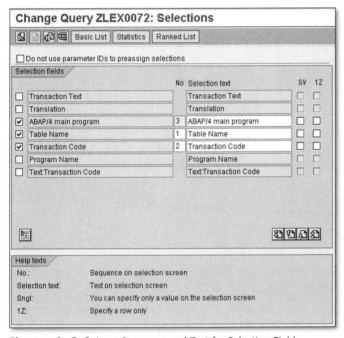

Figure 7.26 Defining a Sequence and Text for Selection Fields

7.5 Basic List

The structure of the basic list is identical to the structure of the basic list in QuickViewer. The functions available in QuickViewer are also available here (see Chapter 3, QuickViewer). Compared to QuickViewer, your additional fields from the InfoSet and the local fields created in the query are also displayed in the basic list. The text fields generated for a field are also available (see Figure 7.27).

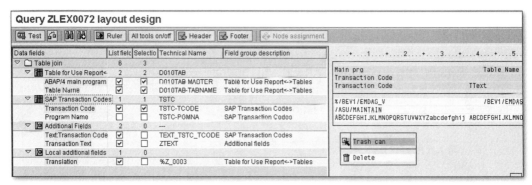

Figure 7.27 Basic List with the Option to Select List and Selection Fields

Selecting layout fields

A total of four field groups with a total of seven data fields are now available to you. Select all seven fields as list fields and selection fields. Now choose 🖫 to save your query design. You can now choose 🖳 Test to view the result of your query. In Chapter 8, you will learn about the options available to you when selecting and designing selection and layout variants.

7.6   Additional Functions

Report/report interface

In addition to the options just outlined, two highly user-friendly additional functions are also available to you: *statistics* and the *report/report interface*. You can use statistics to display a summary of your data volume, while the report/report interface enables you to navigate from your query to other reports or to drill down directly to the SAP application transactions. These two functions (statistics and the report/report interface) are used frequently in real-life situations. Both functions offer you considerable added value and will be discussed in detail in the following chapters. We will devote Chapter 9, Traffic Light Icons, Drilldown, Graphics, and ABC Analyses, to the report/report interface, and Chapter 10, Summarized Data Output with Statistics and Ranked Lists, to statistics.

7.7   Summary

The InfoSet provides many options, especially in the area of data retrieval. With just a few clicks, you can create a query or add individual functions. You can assign any name to your query. Furthermore, numerous formatting options are available to you. In addition to choosing the output format, you can assign names to individual columns. You can also adjust the sequence of the selection fields and their names to your requirements. You can add additional columns to your query as well. For example, you can use colored icons to highlight actual column values or you can perform additional calculations in another column. Finally, you can use statistics to display a summary of your data, and you can use drilldown to navigate to individual data records.

In this chapter, you will learn how to select and display your data and create selection variants for consistent query criteria. You will also explore the layout variant functions that are available.

8 Selection and Layout Variants

Many reporting requirements can be fulfilled on the basis of a specific data selection. In such cases, you don't have to change the data basis or adjust the query. Rather, you can select the relevant data when you execute the report. The SAP Query selection screen, which you already know from other transactions, gives you great flexibility in terms of querying different types of data.

For example, you can select not only single values but also multiple value intervals. Unlike a single value, a lower value limit and an upper value limit are entered for a value interval. You can also select certain characteristic values or characteristic intervals.

Furthermore, when you create an InfoSet, you can add additional selection criteria to the selection screen, which you can then prepopulate with values. You can also exclude values in the background or hide the selection criteria for certain users. For example, you can indirectly exclude certain users from having access to a particular organizational unit (such as plant, sales organization, or company code).

For consistent queries, you can save the selection criteria in variants. Consequently, you do not have to reenter the characteristic values for every new query. You can also import the selection criteria into the selection screen. For example, if you get an Excel list of customer numbers from Sales, you can query the analysis on the basis of the data import.

Finally, very user-friendly data display options are available to you. You can sort, filter, total or display your data directly in Excel. Now let's explore the selection screen.

8.1   Selection Screen

Defining a
standard
selection variant
in the query

In your query definition, you can influence how your query is displayed on the selection screen. In the query Transaction SQ01, you can enter a selection variant in the SPECIAL ATTRIBUTES screen area (❶) (see Figure 8.1). You can also permit report execution with a variant only because preassignment with a variant simplifies the data selection when querying a report.

Specifying the
output format
in the query

When you create a query, you also specify a default value for the output format. If, for example, you choose the output format SAP LIST VIEWER (❷), this (unlike the output format ABAP LIST) works directly on the selection screen.

Figure 8.1   Query Criteria That Influence the Selection Screen

The output format SAP List Viewer not only provides you with additional data display options, but it also simplifies the selection screen (see Figure 8.2).

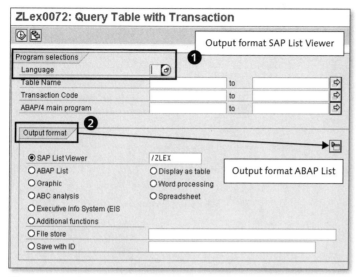

Figure 8.2 Selection Screen with Different Output Formats

If you choose the output format SAP LIST VIEWER in the query (Transaction SQ01), the system displays an additional GENERAL SELECTIONS screen area (❶ in Figure 8.2). The general selections represent selections from the InfoSet, which you can use to make a better data selection. REPORT-SPECIFIC SELECTIONS, on the other hand, reflects the selection fields that you defined for your query.

Selection from the InfoSet

When you execute a report, you can only change the output format if you have already selected ABAP LIST as the output format in the query. In this case, the selection screen contains a selection box (❷ in Figure 8.2) in which you can specify the OUTPUT FORMAT. The query then transfers the preassigned output format to the selection screen.

Output format ABAP List

The selection characteristics also differ in terms of their input options. For example, only one input field exists for the LANGUAGE OF THE TRANSACTION TEXT characteristic. However, two input fields are available for the other characteristics (e.g., TRANSACTION CODE). If you can enter only one single value for a characteristic (❶ in Figure 8.3), SAP uses the term "parameter." If, on the other hand, two input fields are available for a characteristic (❷), SAP uses the term "selection criterion" (see Figure 8.3). A selection criterion also enables you to make a multiple selection.

Parameter versus selection criterion

A button ⇨ for defining the multiple selection is displayed to the right of the two input fields for the relevant characteristic.

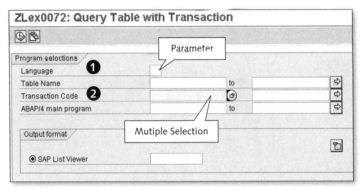

Figure 8.3 Selection Screen with One Parameter and Multiple Selection Criteria

Options for multiple selection

When specifying the characteristic values for a data selection, you can choose from the following four multiple selection options (see Figure 8.4):

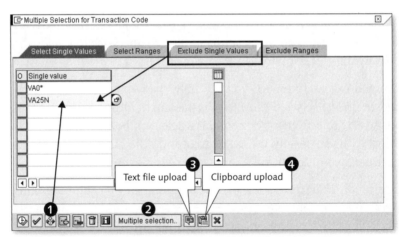

Figure 8.4 Data Selection on the Multiple Selection Screen

▸ Manual input, possibly involving the use of selection options (❶)

▸ A multiple selection on the basis of a search screen for a characteristic (❷)

- Import from a text file (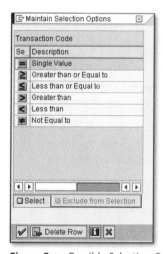❸)
- Upload from the clipboard (❹)

If you use a manageable number of characteristic values for the data selection (❶ in Figure 8.4), you can use manual input here. For manual input, you can enter any number of single values or intervals. You can enter the characteristic values to be selected as well as exclude individual characteristic values or intervals. You can use placeholders in your selection. For example, the placeholder * is used to represent any number of characters, while the placeholder + is used to represent a single character. For example, you can select all transactions that start with VA0, including Transaction VA25N (List of Quotations). The additional selection options shown in Figure 8.5 are also available to you when you choose ⬥.

Manual input on the multiple selection screen

Figure 8.5 Possible Selection Options Within Multiple Selection

In our example, we chose the selection option ▬ (SINGLE VALUE) to display all transactions that start with VA0. We recommend that you use comparison selection options for amount and quantity fields. For example, you can use the selection option ▷ (GREATER THAN) to select all data as of a particular value or date. By doing so, you can improve performance and, for example, exclude documents whose creation date lies in the past. If you select only a few characteristic values, it is preferable to select single values in an interval selection for performance reasons. In real-life situations, the ≠ option (NOT EQUAL TO) is frequently used

Selection options within a multiple selection

to exclude initial or null values from the selection to reduce the number of hits displayed in the hit list.

Matchcode search as a utility for a multiple selection

If, as a result of a particular criterion, you want to use characteristic values from another SAP transaction (❷ in Figure 8.4, shown earlier), however, you can select the data directly in the multiple selection. To do this, simply choose MULTIPLE SELECTION... The system now displays the general search screen for your analysis characteristic (see Figure 8.6). In contrast to the usual F4 help, this screen contains an additional column to the left of the TCODE column. You can now select your characteristic values, either by choosing ☷ (SELECT ALL) to select all entries found or by manually selecting only those individual characteristic values you require.

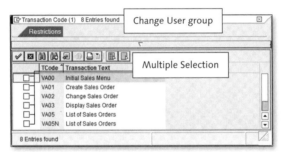

Figure 8.6 Characteristic Values as a Result of the Matchcode in the Multiple Selection

After you have selected the characteristic values, the system displays a green success message on the lower-left side of the screen, indicating that the values you selected have been transferred. You do not yet see the values at this time in the multiple selection. However, the characteristic values are already taken into account during the selection and displayed the next time you call the multiple selection. You can, for example, select customers from a particular country so that the system displays a summary of particular information at country level.

Import the .txt file into the multiple selection

If there are numerous selection values, you should import these into the multiple selection (❸ in Figure 8.4, shown earlier). If you already have a manually edited list of characteristics (e.g., material numbers or customer numbers), you can transfer these to the multiple selection. To do this, choose 🖻 (IMPORT FROM TEXT FILE), and select your file path and corresponding file. The file that you want to import must be available in the .txt file format.

An even easier way is to transfer the characteristic values within the SAP system into the multiple selection (❹ in Figure 8.4, shown earlier). In the SAP system, use [Ctrl] + [Y] to select and [Ctrl] + [C] to copy, which are the same shortcuts used in Microsoft Office. You can use the command [Ctrl] + [V] or choose 🖺 (UPLOAD FROM CLIPBOARD) to transfer the values from the clipboard to the multiple selection.

Upload from clipboard to multiple selection

After you have selected the characteristic values for your selection criterion, choose ⊕ to transfer them to the selection screen. The first characteristic value from the multiple selection is now displayed directly on the selection screen. Furthermore, the 🖻 button for multiple selection is now grayed out (see Figure 8.7).

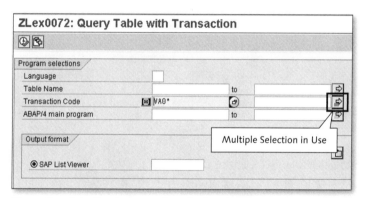

Figure 8.7 Selection Screen with Multiple Selection

You can now save this new data selection with a multiple selection so that you can use it again as a selection variant.

8.2   Selection Variants

Selection variant
for recurring
queries You can use the selection variant specifically to select the data that you want to select. For recurring entries, the selection variant makes your work easier because you can use it to transfer consistent characteristic values to the selection screen.

To use a selection variant, follow these steps:

1. Enter the relevant selection criteria in the selection screen.

2. Choose 🖫 (SAVE) to access the screen in which you can preassign values. Now save these preassigned values in a selection variant.

3. You then access the VARIANT ATTRIBUTES screen (see Figure 8.8).

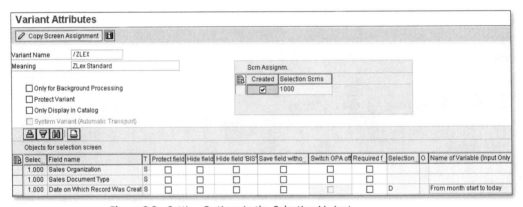

Figure 8.8   Setting Options in the Selection Variant

Variant attributes
within a selection
variant 4. In the VARIANT NAME field, enter a short text for your variant and, in the MEANING field, enter a descriptive name. For the selection variant, you can also specify whether you want it to be used in background processing only, whether you want it to be protected against changes by other users, and whether you want other users to be able to view or select it.

Setting options
within a selection
variant 5. The lower screen area contains six additional setting options for selection fields, which you can also save in a selection variant (see Table 8.1). You specify the selection characteristic in the third column, TYPE. P stands for parameter and S for selection criterion.

No.	Function	Meaning
1	PROTECT Field	This field is grayed out on the selection screen and therefore not ready for input.
2	HIDE Field/ HIDE FIELD 'BIS'	This field can contain a default value. The field and its contents are not displayed on the selection screen.
3	SAVE FIELD WITHOUT VALUES	When you start the variant, previously entered values are not changed.
4	Switch off GPA	GPA stands for get/set parameter. An entry is no longer proposed.
5	REQUIRED FIELD	This field is marked as a required field. You must make an entry here before the execution.
6	SELECTION VARIABLE / Option/Variable name	Characteristic value proposed on the basis of a variable.

Table 8.1 Setting Options in the Selection Variant

You can use these setting options to simplify the selection variant, influence the preassignment or control the selection criteria. For example, you can use selection variables and control a field as a required entry to improve your data display, increase user friendliness, and improve performance.

For a date field, you can preassign characteristic values dynamically. You can therefore use a selection variable to perform a dynamic date calculation. The functions described in this chapter apply not only to the query but also to many standard SAP analyses. Let's take a closer look at the variant attributes for a date field: You can define the SELECTION VARIABLE in the latter columns (see Figure 8.9).

Dynamic date variable

1. For a date field, select the ⌑F4⌑ help (matchcode) in the SELECTION VARIABLE column.

2. Select a date variable D for your date field (see Figure 8.10). You must use the ⌑F4⌑ help to select the selection variables. You cannot enter, for example, the letter "D" for date variable directly.

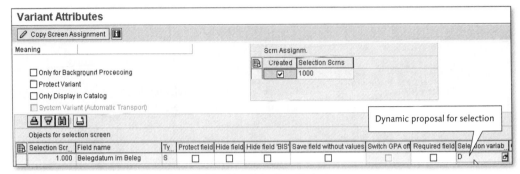

Figure 8.9 Date Field with a Selection Variant

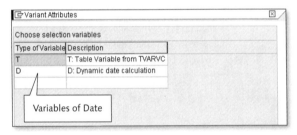

Figure 8.10 Figure 8.10 Selecting a Date Variable in the Selection Variant

3. Position your cursor for your date field on the VARIABLE NAME (INPUT VIA F4 ONLY) column (refer to Figure 8.9), which we explained earlier. After you have called the F4 help, the system displays a screen in which you can select more selection variables (see Figure 8.11).

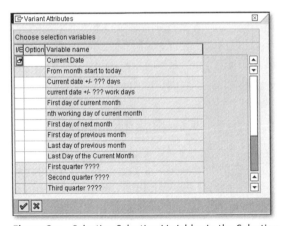

Figure 8.11 Selecting Selection Variables in the Selection Variant

4. Use the ⌨F4 help to select the CURRENT DATE +/- ??? WORK DAYS option. The system now displays a screen with six relational operands (*see* Figure 8.12).

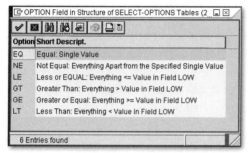

Figure 8.12 Relational Operands for Dynamic Date Variables

5. The relational operands help you restrict data further without having to change the input values in the selection screen. Select the GT — GREATER THAN: EVERYTHING > VALUE IN FIELD LOW option. The system then displays a dialog box in which you can enter parameters for the date calculation (*see* Figure 8.13).

Relational operands for dynamic date variables

Figure 8.13 Dynamically Preassigning a Selection Variable with a Date Based on the Factory Calendar

6. You can now determine when you want the data selection to take place. In real-life scenarios, the selection variables FROM THE START OF THE MONTH TO THE CURRENT DATE or LAST DATE IN THE PREVIOUS MONTH are used. Now choose 🖫 to save your settings in the selection variant.

7. Choose ⬅ (BACK = ⌨F3 key) to return to the selection screen. On the selection screen, you also have the option of entering a layout variant for the data display.

8.3   Layout Variant

Functions in the layout variant

The system displays selected data in a modern list (SAP List Viewer). Numerous functions are available for adjusting the list display. For example, you can sort the data in ascending or descending order. A filter function is also available in the layout variant. For the amount and quantity fields, you can create the total and subtotal according to a characteristic. If there are numerous columns, it may be helpful to use the function for fixing the column. You can call this function from the menu path SETTINGS • COLUMNS • FIX TO COLUMN.

To work with layout variants, follow these steps:

1. Call your report, and use SAP List Viewer to display the data. The SAP List Viewer editing functions are displayed above the data display as icons (see Figure 8.14).

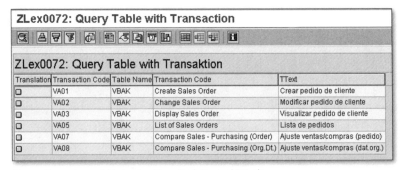

Figure 8.14 Layout Variant with a Grid Control Display

Excel Inplace

2. You can display the result in Excel, so that you can edit it further within the SAP system (Excel Inplace). To switch from the grid control display to the Excel interface, choose EXCEL INPLACE as shown in Figure 8.15.

3. The report result is now displayed in the Excel interface within the SAP system. If you want to analyze the data further, you can use pivot functions or the Excel data filter, for example (see Figure 8.16).

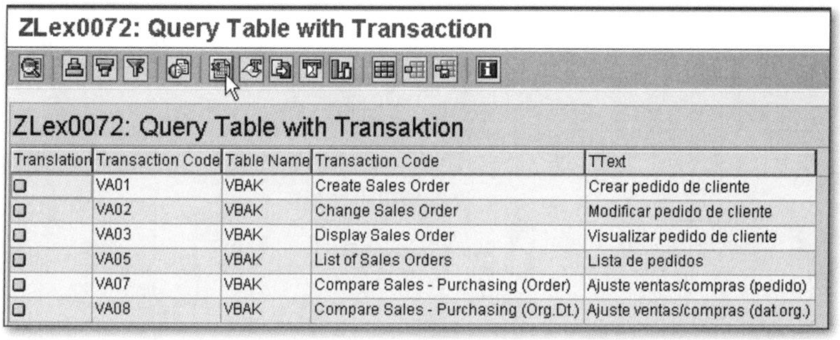
ZLex0072: Query Table with Transaction
ZLex0072: Query Table with Transaktion
Translation | Transaction Code | Table Name | Transaction Code | TText
VA01 | VBAK | Create Sales Order | Crear pedido de cliente
VA02 | VBAK | Change Sales Order | Modificar pedido de cliente
VA03 | VBAK | Display Sales Order | Visualizar pedido de cliente
VA05 | VBAK | List of Sales Orders | Lista de pedidos
VA07 | VBAK | Compare Sales - Purchasing (Order) | Ajuste ventas/compras (pedido)
VA08 | VBAK | Compare Sales - Purchasing (Org.Dt.) | Ajuste ventas/compras (dat.org.)

Figure 8.15 Switching to the Excel Interface in the Data Display

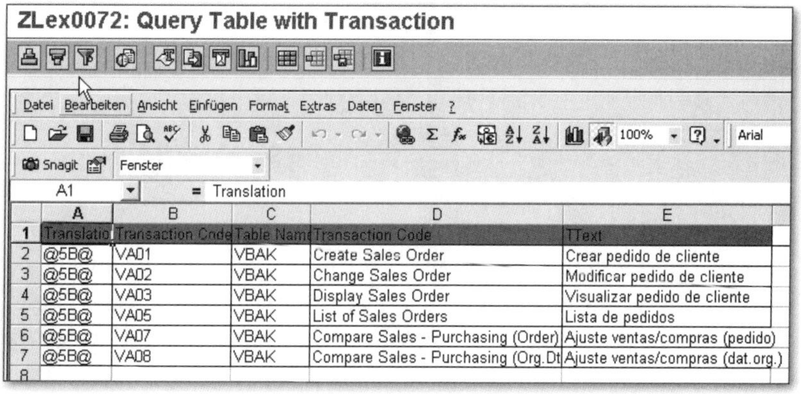
ZLex0072: Query Table with Transaction
Datei Bearbeiten Ansicht Einfügen Format Extras Daten Fenster ?
100%
Arial
Snagit
Fenster
A1
= Translation
A B C D E
1 Translatio Transaction Code Table Name Transaction Code TText
2 @5B@ VA01 VBAK Create Sales Order Crear pedido de cliente
3 @5B@ VA02 VBAK Change Sales Order Modificar pedido de cliente
4 @5B@ VA03 VBAK Display Sales Order Visualizar pedido de cliente
5 @5B@ VA05 VBAK List of Sales Orders Lista de pedidos
6 @5B@ VA07 VBAK Compare Sales - Purchasing (Order) Ajuste ventas/compras (pedido)
7 @5B@ VA08 VBAK Compare Sales - Purchasing (Org.Dt Ajuste ventas/compras (dat.org.)
8

Figure 8.16 Layout Variant Displayed in Excel

Control break in print preview

In real-life situations, it is advisable to configure a control break for the printout. Sometimes, for example, a new page is printed for each subtotal with a single data row. To prevent this, you can define when you want a printed page break.

You configure this setting in the print preview for the layout variant:

1. Choose [ALV] or press [Ctrl] + [Shift] + [F10] for the print preview. Alternatively, choose the list output display instead of the Excel Inplace display, as shown earlier in Figure 8.15. In the print preview, choose [ALV] to display the subtotals. The system now displays the DEFINE SORT ORDER screen (see Figure 8.17).

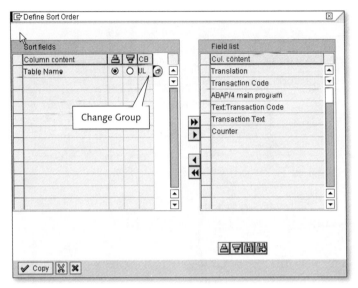

Figure 8.17 Control Break in Print Preview

2. In this setting, you define the control break (CB) in addition to the sort order and subtotal. If you enter an asterisk (*) in the CB column, the printout starts on a new page for each new subtotal. If you enter "UL" for a characteristic in the CB column, the control break is indicated by a border in the printout. If you leave the column blank, neither a border nor page break appears.

8.4   Summary

You are now familiar with the data selection options. In particular, you know how to use a multiple selection to select the data to be analyzed. For your reporting requirements, you can use selection variants for recurring queries. In the selection variants, you can hide fields, control characteristics as a required field, or use dynamic date variables to preassign date fields.

In the selection variant, you can also save the layout variant required for the data display. The layout variants provide you with additional data formatting functions. You can therefore display the data in Excel within the SAP system. You can also use the Excel functions directly.

Useful symbols, user-friendly report jumps (drilldown functions), and graphics, as well as ABC analyses, increase the acceptance of reports among users, especially management. In this chapter, you will learn the best way to use these options.

9 Traffic Light Icons, Drilldown, Graphics, and ABC Analyses

When you use various visualization and drawing utilities, you can design reports that are more manageable and more user friendly. In real-life scenarios, the use of *multicolored icons* (e.g., traffic light icons) offers considerable added value. You can easily integrate more than 1,000 different icons into a report table and highlight certain data in this way. For example, you can configure a threshold value for a column so that the relevant line whose value exceeds or falls below the threshold value is highlighted. You can choose suitable symbols from an extensive catalog and define column values for the different symbol displays.

The report recipient can then select those data records of interest and double-click them to navigate directly to other report displays or transactions. For example, the report recipient can comfortably navigate from your defined *drilldown* to individual documents. For example, a jump to master data is frequently used to improve data quality.

SAP Query enables you to display the selected data in a simple graphic as well. However, you can also perform an *ABC analysis* for your data, in which the values are structured according to freely definable percentages.

For the functions shown in this chapter, you do not need any ABAP calculations or any knowledge of ABAP. The only prerequisite is that you release Transaction SQ01.

9.1 Symbols

You can use symbols and icons to highlight certain rows or columns of data. In the context of query editing, you can use up to 55 different symbols and more than 1,000 icons. We will use an open item list to illustrate the use of icons and symbols (see Figure 9.1).

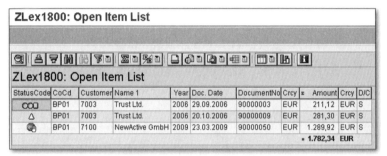

Figure 9.1 Symbols and Icons — Based on the Amount Column

Symbol In the open item list, we have inserted a traffic light icon in column 1, an index finger (SYM_RIGHT_HAND) in column 5, and a telephone (SYM_PHONE) in column 7.

[»] **Symbols and Icons**

Symbols are monochromatic graphical elements, while icons are multicolored graphical elements. SAP provides an extensive catalog of icons for selection in addition to icons that exist by default in all SAP applications. You can enter the command ICON in the command window to display potential icons.

Next, you will learn about potential symbols and icons in greater detail. You will also learn how to add them to your report.

ABAP report You can use the ABAP program SHOWSYMB in Transaction SA38 to call
SHOWSYMB an overview of the symbols available (see Figure 9.2). We also recommend that you use this transaction to select symbols for a report. If you do not have any authorization for this transaction, you can ask an administrator to print out the list of symbols for you (see Figure 9.3).

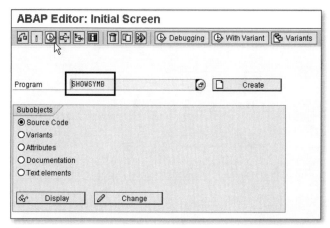

ABAP Editor: Initial Screen

| | | | | | | ⊕ Debugging | ⊕ With Variant | ⊡ Variants |

Program   [SHOWSYMB]   ⊡   ◻   Create

Subobjects

◉ Source Code
○ Variants
○ Attributes
○ Documentation
○ Text elements

   Display   ✎   Change

Figure 9.2   Transaction SA38 — Calling the Program SHOWSYM

Display Symbols in Lists

Symbol	Name of symbol	Comment	Lngth
✔	SYM_CHECK_MARK	check mark	1
✎	SYM_PENCIL	pencil	1
👓	SYM_GLASSES	glasses	2
🔒	SYM_LOCKED	closed padlock	1
🔓	SYM_UNLOCKED	open padlock	1
☎	SYM_PHONE	telephone	2
🖨	SYM_PRINTER	printer	2
📠	SYM_FAX	fax machine	2
✴	SYM_ASTERISK	asterisk, *	1
☞	SYM_RIGHT_HAND	hand pointing right	2

Figure 9.3   Extract from the List of Standard SAP Symbols

To insert a symbol into your report, go to Transaction SQ01, and choose the CHANGE button to change the query ZLex1800 (see Figure 9.4). If the query Zlex1800 is not in your system, you can also perform the following steps using any other query.

Inserting symbols into a report

1. Double-click the right arrow 🔲 (see Figure 9.5) so that the system displays the CHANGE QUERY ZLex1800: SELECT FIELD screen (see Figure 9.6).

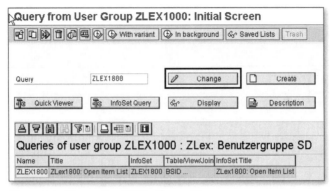

Figure 9.4 Transaction SQ01: Change Query

Figure 9.5 Navigate to the Next Screen

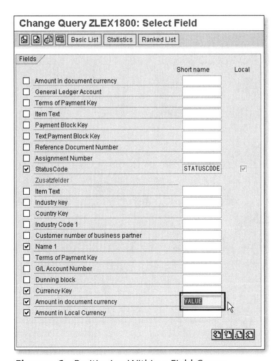

Figure 9.6 Positioning Within a Field Group

2. Position your cursor on the field ZKNA1_TELF1, for example. If you want to edit another query, you can simply position your cursor on that query. Your cursor position determines the field group to which the local field is assigned.

Inserting a local field into a query

3. Choose the menu path EDIT • LOCAL FIELD • CREATE to display the FIELD DEFINITION screen (see Figure 9.7). Here, you can define allowed entries for the local field.

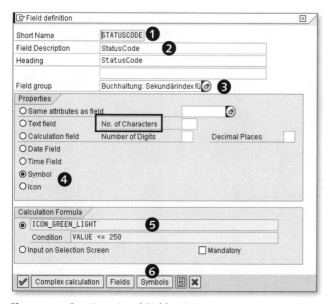

Figure 9.7 Creating a Local Field — Icon

To define the entries, follow these steps:

Naming an icon

1. Enter a short name in the SHORT NAME field (❶) (in our example, "STA-TUSCODE"). This text is only displayed within the query definition and is helpful if you want to use this field for further calculations.

2. Assign a FIELD DESCRIPTION (❷) (in our example, "StatusCode"). This field description is displayed in the basic list and in the column set after the query selection. To select the local field in the query, select it as a list field in the basic list. You can also define the local field as a selection field. For example, you can select data records according to the status.

Selecting an icon

The new local fields are assigned to the field group ACCOUNTING: SECONDARY INDEX FOR (❸). (In earlier releases, a FIELD GROUP was known as a FUNCTIONAL GROUP — this change has not been applied to this screen yet.)

3. Mark the local field in the PROPERTIES area as an ICON (❹).

4. Insert the text for the icon in the CALCULATION FORMULA area (❺) (here, "ICON_GREEN_LIGHT"). You can obtain the relevant text from the list output for the ABAP report SHOWSYMB, or you can choose SYMBOLS (❻). The system then displays a window in which you can select the symbols you want to use (see Figure 9.8).

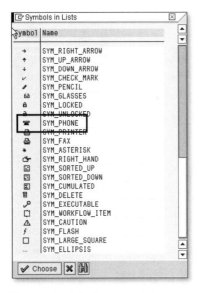

Figure 9.8 Selecting a Symbol

5. Double-click a symbol to select it, and the symbol's name is then transferred to the calculation formula.

6. Save the local field.

7. Create another symbol field. Insert the SYM_PHONE symbol into the local field.

8. Go to the basic list and select the new symbol as a list field, and call the report again.

9. Select a layout variant. For the available columns, you can select the new symbol for your report. Consequently, column 7 in the report ZLEx1800: OPEN ITEM LIST is also displayed in your report.

9.2 Icons

In this section, you will learn how you can insert different icons into a column. We will use the preceding example to explain how you can use green, yellow, and red traffic lights to mark different rows. Icons are comparable with symbols, with the only difference being the color of symbols, which are displayed in monochrome. The report recipient can therefore easily identify icons.

In this example, we will select different icons on the basis of an item amount. If an open item (AMOUNT column) exceeds a certain amount, the system displays a predefined icon. You can query and highlight various characteristics or events. In real-life scenarios, the sales order status, for example, is displayed in this way. Another icon is displayed, depending on whether a goods issue or billing document is created, for example.

The following example illustrates the basic function of traffic light icons:

Conditions for traffic light icons

▸ AMOUNT =< EUR 250: Green icon displayed

▸ AMOUNT > EUR 250 and AMOUNT < EUR 1,000: Yellow icon displayed

▸ AMOUNT > EUR 1,000: Red icon displayed

In the standard system, you can choose from 1,000 different icons. To also involve the report recipient, you can execute the ABAP program SHOWICON (*see* Figure 9.9) and print out a list of icons.

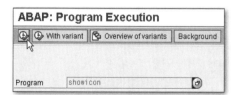

Figure 9.9 SA38 — ABAP Report for Displaying Icons

The extract shown in Figure 9.10 demonstrates that the list of icons is extensive. To display an icon in your report, enter the name of the icon in the local field (see Figure 9.11).

Display Icons in Lists

Icon	Icon name	Comment	Lngth	Printab.	internal	B
	ICON_GRAPHICS	Graphic	2	✓	0N B_GRAF	1
	ICON_INFORMATION	Information	2	✓	0S B_INFO	1
	ICON_CALCULATION	Costing	2	✓	0M B_CALC	2
	ICON_SET_STATE	Set Status	2	✓	3J B_STAT	1
	ICON_VARIANTS	Variants	2	✓	0R B_VARI	2
	ICON_CHECKED	Checked; OK	2	✓	01 S_OKAY	1
	ICON_INCOMPLETE	Incomplete; critical	2	✓	02 S_NONO	2
	ICON_FAILURE	Failed	2	✓	03 S_ERRO	2
	ICON_POSITIVE	Positive; Good	2	✓	04 S_POSI	2
	ICON_NEGATIVE	Negative; Bad	2	✓	05 S_NEGA	2
	ICON_LOCKED	Locked; Lock	2	✓	06 S_LOCL	2
	ICON_UNLOCKED	Free; unlock	2	✓	07 S_LOOP	2
	ICON_GREEN_LIGHT	Green Light; Go; Okay	4	✓	08 S_TL_G	1
	ICON_YELLOW_LIGHT	Yellow light; caution	4	✓	09 S_TL_Y	1
	ICON_RED_LIGHT	Red light; stop; errors	4	✓	0A S_TL_R	1
	ICON_ACTIVATE	Activate	2	✓	3C B_ACTI	2
	ICON_GENERATE	Generate	2	✓	39 B_GENR	2
	ICON_CHECK	Check	2	✓	38 B_CHCK	2

Figure 9.10   Extract from More Than 1,000 Icons

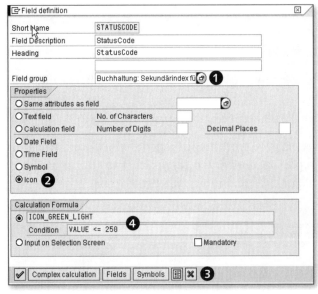

Figure 9.11   Defining a Colored Icon

To define an icon, follow these steps:

1. Enter a SHORT NAME, FIELD DESCRIPTION, and HEADING and then assign the icon to a FIELD GROUP (❶ in Figure 9.11).

2. Select the ICON option in the PROPERTIES area (❷).

3. Enter the icon name in the CALCULATION FORMULA field. Alternatively, you can choose 🔢 to the right of the SYMBOLS button (❸).

   Calculation formula

4. A condition determines which icon is displayed. If only one condition is required, you can enter this directly in the CALCULATION FORMULA screen area. In our example, we entered "Amount <= 250" in the CONDITION field (❹). Because we want to create a scaled condition, choose COMPLEX CALCULATION. The system then displays the DEFINE FIELD: COMPLEX CALCULATION window (see Figure 9.12).

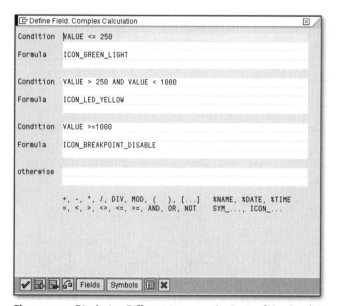

Figure 9.12 Displaying Different Icons on the Basis of the Conditions

You can enter several conditions in this window. The SHORT NAME of the corresponding field is relevant when formulating the condition (refer to Figure 9.6). Because the short name of our field is AMOUNT, we will query this field content.

5. Our condition is scaled, in other words, a yellow traffic light is displayed for an amount between EUR 250 and EUR 1,000. The query is performed using the `AND` command. It is important that the field to be queried is listed again. Instead of `AMOUNT >= 250 AND < 1000`, enter `AMOUNT >= 250 AND AMOUNT > 1000`.

You have now added additional code to an ABAP program without having any ABAP knowledge whatsoever. Your icons are now displayed in the report output (see Figure 9.13).

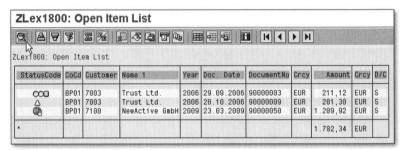

Figure 9.13 Displaying Symbols/Icons in the Print Preview

Icon as a filter criterion The inserted icons are also displayed in the print preview. Furthermore, you can filter according to the icons, or you can create a subtotal (see Figure 9.14).

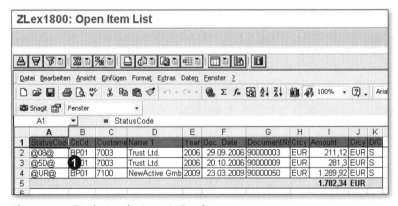

Figure 9.14 Displaying the Icons in Excel

To display an icon in Excel, choose the PRINT PREVIEW icon to switch to Excel. The icons are displayed as a character string in the standard Excel display integrated into the SAP system (❶ of Figure 9.14). This display is very helpful in terms of selecting data according to the character string of an icon (see Figure 9.15).

Displaying an icon in Excel

ZLex1800: Open Item List			

Report-specific selections

StatusCode	@08@	to		⇨
Geschäftsjahr		to		⇨
Debitorennummer 1	7003	to	7100	⇨
Belegdatum im Beleg		to		⇨

Output specification

| Layout | |

Figure 9.15 Selection — Depending on the Icon

Now that we know the value of an icon in Excel, we can also use this value directly in the selection screen for the purposes of querying data. Consequently, you can select and display only those data records that have a green icon, for example.

Selection according to an icon

9.3 Drilldown Options

In the previous two sections, you learned how to use symbols and icons to mark and/or highlight data for the report recipient. The user can now double-click to call other reports or navigate to the transactions for data maintenance.

To use drilldown for reports or data maintenance, follow these steps:

Report assignment

1. Call Transaction SQ01 to change your query. Then choose the menu path GOTO • REPORT ASSIGNMENT to access the screen shown in Figure 9.16.

2. In this window, you can display the current report/report links. Then choose the green plus icon ⊞ to include other reports. The system then displays another window called ADD ABAP/4 QUERY (see Figure 9.17).

Calling the report/ report interface

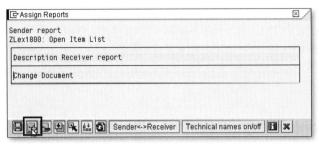

Figure 9.16 Calling the Report/Report Interface (RRI)

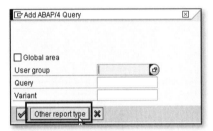

Figure 9.17 Selecting the Report Type

Changing the report type This window contains the option to navigate to another query. In our case, however, we want to call an SAP transaction or ABAP report:

1. Choose OTHER REPORT TYPE (see Figure 9.17). The system now displays another window called REPORT TYPE FOR THE REPORT/REPORT INTERFACE (see Figure 9.18).

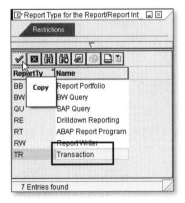

Figure 9.18 Selecting the "Transaction" Report Type

2. To jump to a transaction, select the Transaction report type. The system then displays an Add transaction window (see Figure 9.19).

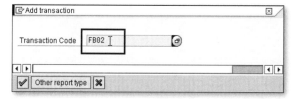

Figure 9.19 Entering Transaction FB02

3. In the Transaction Code field, enter the transaction you require (e.g., "FB02" for changing a document). In addition, enter Transaction "VD02" for changing the customer master. The text for the transaction you have inserted is now displayed in the Assign Reports window (see Figure 9.20).

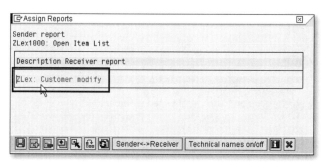

Figure 9.20 Individual Text for the Drilldown

4. To change the name of the selected reports, double-click the data. Execute the report again, and double-click the data row. The system now displays the Assign Reports window (see Figure 9.21).

5. In this window, you can choose the transaction to which you want to navigate. For example, you can display details about a document and add a comment to this information, if required. Alternatively, you can navigate to the customer master. Here, you can enter additional information or display other details (see Figure 9.22).

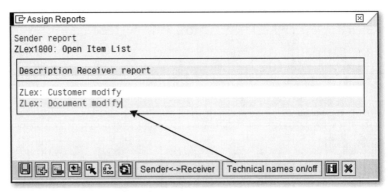

Figure 9.21 Drilldown from the Report

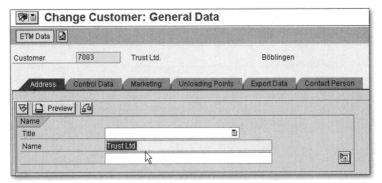

Figure 9.22 Drilldown to Transaction XD02 — Change Customer

[»] **Drilldown to Transaction**

In some cases, the drilldown to a transaction does not work in the report/report interface. In these cases, you can use a small ABAP program to perform a drilldown. The ABAP program for a drilldown to the material master display (Transaction MM03) is as follows:

```
REPORT z_call mm03.
PARAMETERS p_matnr LIKE mara-matnr. "dd ref. as in mm03
SET PARAMETER ID 'mat' FIELD p_matnr. "id for mara-matnr
CALL TRANSACTION 'mm03' AND SKIP FIRST SCREEN.
```

For more information, refer to SAP Note 383077 — RRI: Transaction call fails.

9.4 Using Graphics and the ABC Analysis

SAP Query enables you to create simple graphics. You can pre-assign GRAPHIC as the output format. If you then call the report, the system displays another query window called GRAPHICAL DISPLAY (see Figure 9.23).

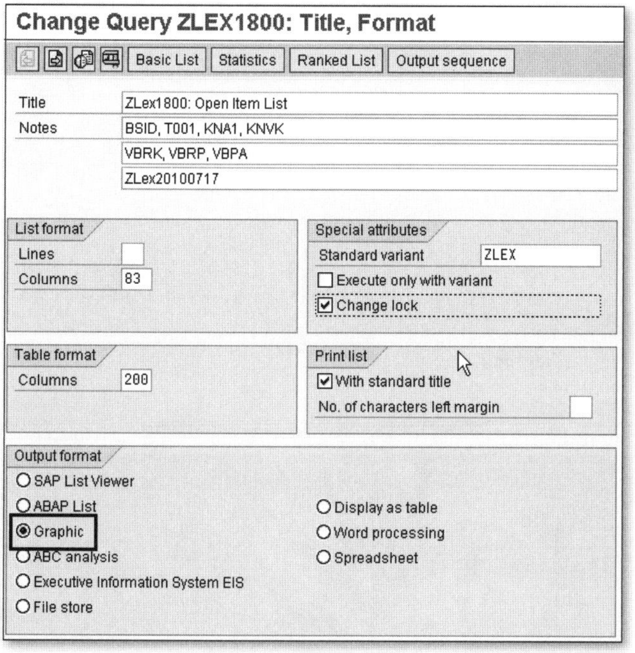

Figure 9.23 Output Format: Graphic

To create a graphic, follow these steps:

1. In the GRAPHICAL DISPLAY window, select the required graphic type (see Figure 9.24).

2. The data is frequently displayed in Excel, and the graphics are created in the Excel environment. Select the column that you want to display as a graphic (see Figure 9.25).

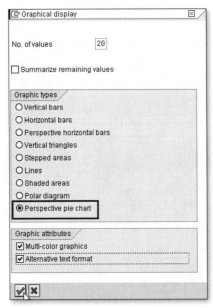

Figure 9.24 Specifying a Graphic Type

ZLex1800: Open Item List

StatusCode	CoCd	Customer	Name 1	Crcy	DocumentNo	Amount	Year	Doc. Date	Crcy	Crcy	D/C
☾☾☾	BP01	7003	Trust Ltd.	EUR	90000003	211,12	2006	29.09.2006	EUR	EUR	S
△	BP01	7003	Trust Ltd.	EUR	90000009	281,30	2006	20.10.2006	EUR	EUR	S
	BP01	7100	NewActive GmbH	EUR	90000050	1.289,92	2009	23.03.2009	EUR	EUR	S
						▪ 1.782,34			EUR		

Figure 9.25 Selecting the Customer for the Graphical Display

3. Our example contains three open items (data records). Customer 7003 has two open invoices (90000003 and 90000009), while customer 7100 has one open invoice (90000050). Now choose the graphic icon ▨. The system creates an SAP presentation graphic, which visualizes the three selected data records (see Figure 9.26).

The label contains the company BP01, customer numbers 7003 and 7100, and the invoice numbers.

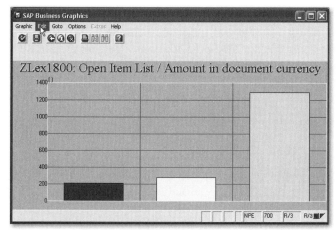

Figure 9.26 Graphic with Two Customers and Three Invoices

Even clearer than the graphical data display is the ABC analysis. To use ABC analysis, select a key figure column (e.g., Amount) and then choose ABC. The system then displays the ABC ANALYSIS window (see Figure 9.27).

ABC analysis

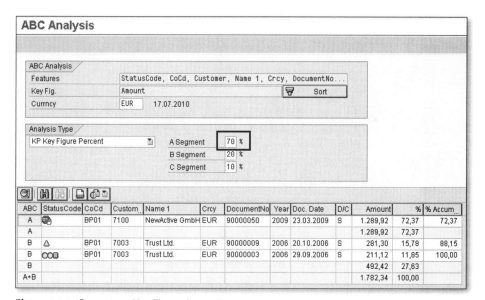

Figure 9.27 Percentage Key Figure Amount

If you select the analysis type KP KEY FIGURE PERCENT for the ABC analysis, you must enter percentages for segments A, B, and C. If, for example, you enter 70% for segment A, all of the data records in the selected key figure column are summarized until the cumulated percentage 70 is reached. In addition to this ABC classification, a percentage for each individual data row is also displayed in the second last column.

9.5   Summary

You can now use monochromatic symbols or multicolored icons to highlight specific information in your report. In real-life situations, colored icons are frequently used to display the status of documents.

For example, you can display the status of the sales document. In the SAP tables VBUK (Sales Document: Header Status and Administrative Data) and VBUP (Sales Document: Item Status), the system displays various statuses at the header and item level. In this way, the information concerning a delivery or billing document is also displayed graphically.

The sales employee can therefore use graphical symbols to inform users about the status of the respective sales orders. Furthermore, shipping can indicate which goods deliveries have already taken place and which are still outstanding.

Icons are also used in data selection. In an order confirmation report, for example, the cost center from the HR master record and the cost center from the confirmed work center are displayed. If the cost centers are identical, a green icon is displayed. If they differ, a red icon is displayed. A selection is made for data records that have a red icon (relief work — these employees do not work in your master cost center). All data records that have a red icon are selected and displayed in Excel. The Excel file is saved and then imported into Transaction KB21N (for internal activity allocation) via the SAP import tool known as the Legacy System Migration Workbench (LSMW).

Furthermore, you can navigate from your own reports to other reports to display information in a different format or to select individual items. You can also call application transactions and master data transactions via a drilldown and adjust the data content, if necessary. Finally, you learned how easy it is to create graphics in the SAP system.

PART III
Designing User-Friendly Reports

In this chapter, you will learn how to display data at the aggregated level in the basic list. You will also learn how to use statistics to display a summary of your data. Finally, we will show you how to use ranked lists to list top key figure values.

10 Summarized Data Output with Statistics and Ranked Lists

In SAP Query reports, all data records are displayed individually in a basic list. You can then use SAP List Viewer to process this data further. For example, you can use filter functions to filter out irrelevant data, or you can use summation functions to display one total figure for a key figure column (e.g., amount or quantity). You can also calculate subtotals for any number of characteristics. Furthermore, you can use summation levels to display only the summarized total for each characteristic. Alternatively, you can use the Excel display within the SAP system to summarize the data according to grouping levels.

There are many occasions in business when you will want to output summarized data. In addition to the basic list, two other output types are available in the SAP system: the *statistic* output type, which you can use to display a summary of selected single values for characteristics, and the *ranked list* output type, which you can use to display a number of ranked list positions that you have predefined in a selection. In addition to the *basic list*, you can create up to nine statistics and nine ranked lists in a query. In the standard system, the basic list is always displayed first. However, you can change the output sequence of the basic list, statistics, and ranked lists so that, for example, a statistic is displayed first.

10.1 Example: Open Item List

To help you follow and reproduce the example provided here for summarizing individual data records in your SAP system, it would help to already be familiar with Chapter 6, InfoSet in Detail, and Chapter 7, Query in Detail.

You will create a new InfoSet and SAP query from the area of Financial Accounting (FI). You will then summarize the data records in a basic list and in a statistic. Because we use a simple numerical example to explain the summarization functions, you will create an InfoSet that analyzes the open items in your system. The InfoSet uses the table BSID (Accounting: Secondary Index for Customers) as its basis (see Figure 10.1).

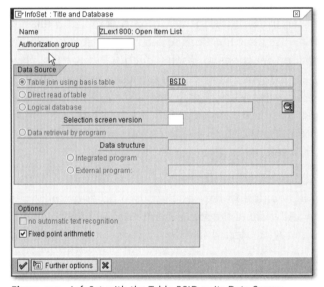

Figure 10.1 InfoSet with the Table BSID as its Data Source

Document status of FI documents FI documents can have the status *cleared* or *open*. FI documents in accounts receivable (AR) accounting are cleared if the customer no longer has any outstanding receivables. Usually, an FI customer document is cleared when an incoming payment from the customer is recorded in the system. Cleared customer documents can be analyzed in the table

BSAD (Accounting: Secondary Index for Customers (Cleared Items)), while open documents are stored in the table BSID (Accounting: Secondary Index for Customers). Because only part of the FI documents is usually open, you only need to select a few data records from the table BSID (thanks to the two-part storage of data contained in FI customer documents). Add the following table fields to your InfoSet:

- Company Code (BSID-BUKRS)
- Customer Number (BSID-KUNNR)
- Posting Date in the Document (BSID-BUDAT)
- Amount in Local Currency (BSID-DMBTR)

Your InfoSet therefore contains one field group with four fields (see Figure 10.2).

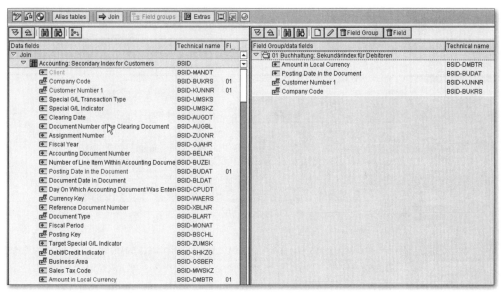

Figure 10.2 InfoSet Based on the Table BSID with One Field Group and Four Fields

In Transaction SQ02 (InfoSet), assign your InfoSet to the user group ZLEX (see Figure 10.3).

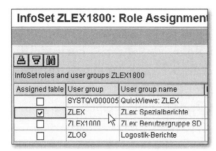

Figure 10.3 Assigning the InfoSet ZLEX1800 to the User Group ZLEX

In the next step, you will create a new query in Transaction SQ01 (SAP Query):

1. Select the user group ZLEX, and create the query ZLEX1800 (see Figure 10.4).

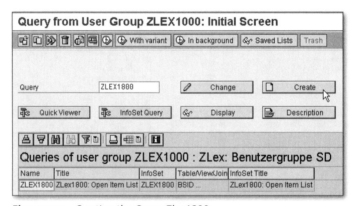

Figure 10.4 Creating the Query Zlex1800

Basic list   2. You now access the first of four navigation screens in SAP Query (see Figure 10.5). From each of these four screens, you can navigate to the BASIC LIST, STATISTICS, and RANKED LIST. From the first screen, you can also navigate to the OUTPUT SEQUENCE. Furthermore, you can navigate to the basic list at any time. The basic list is intended for displaying single values. However, you can also create a query without a basic list. In addition to the optional basic list, you can create a total of nine statistics and nine ranked lists. Choose the OUTPUT SEQUENCE button to determine the sequence in which you want to view the basic list, statistics, and ranked lists.

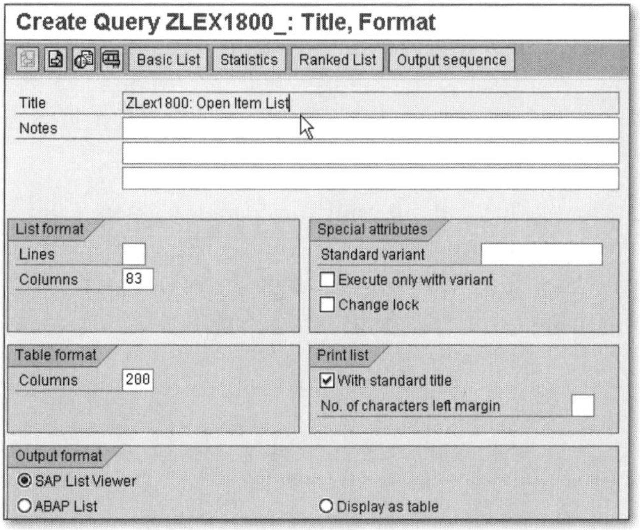

Figure 10.5 First Navigation Screen for the Query Zlex1800

3. Use the navigation arrows ⊞ ⊞ to navigate between the following four windows:

▶ TITLE, FORMAT

▶ SELECT FIELD GROUP

▶ SELECT FIELD

▶ SELECTIONS

All four windows have a jump button for creating statistics and/or ranked lists. You can even create a ranked list/statistic without having previously created a basic list. The SELECT FIELD GROUP and SELECT FIELD navigation windows are only partially redundant. In these two windows, you can configure settings such as the field selection for statistics and ranked lists. The screen templates also contain additional functions such as ADJUST COLUMN NAME, CREATE LOCAL FIELDS, or CHANGE SELECTION TEXTS. Before you create a statistic, take a moment to read the next section, which takes a look at the grouping options and other settings options available to you when using a basic list.

Selecting the list and selection fields

229

10.2 Basic List Without a Graphical Query Painter

Basic list for
displaying
data records

In a basic list, data is displayed in nonsummarized form. Here, you specify the display and selection fields for a query in graphical layout mode. Layout mode provides you with a very simple editing option, especially when it comes to selecting selection and list fields. After you have created the query, you can use numerous options in the SAP List Viewer output format.

Graphical Query
Painter

You can also create a basic list without using the Graphical Query Painter (layout mode). You can then use other functions to edit your query in Transaction SQ01. To do this, deselect the GRAPHICAL QUERY PAINTER under the menu path SETTINGS • SETTINGS (see Figure 10.6).

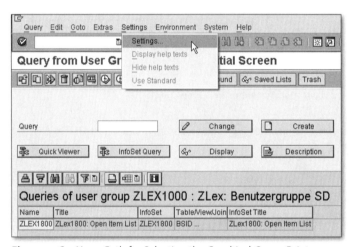

Figure 10.6 Menu Path for Selecting the Graphical Query Painter

Deactivating
the Graphical
Query Painter

After you have deselected the Graphical Query Painter, other functions for creating the basic list and the SAP List Viewer list display are available to you on several settings screens. Because these settings screens contain numerous options, it is useful to display the help texts provided for each option. Such help texts are displayed in the lower screen area. If you do not see a field area entitled HELP TEXTS, choose 🛈 (with help texts). You can also preview the settings you configure. To do this, deselect the flag for the GRAPHICAL QUERY PAINTER, and select the DISPLAY HELP TEXTS display variant (see Figure 10.7).

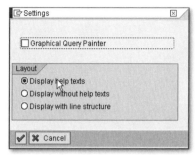

Figure 10.7 Query Editing Without the Graphical Query Painter

Figure 10.8 Navigating to the Settings Screens for the Query Basic List

After you have deactivated the Graphical Query Painter, additional navigation windows for configuring the basic list are available to you. You can select the menu path GOTO • BASIC LIST to navigate to the eight new settings screens for the basic list (see Figure 10.8).

Settings screens without the Graphical Query Painter

- ▶ STRUCTURE

- ▶ CONTROL LEVELS

- ▶ CONTROL LEVEL TEXTS

- ▶ LINE OUTPUT OPTIONS

- ▶ FIELD OUTPUT OPTIONS

- ▶ TEMPLATES

- ▶ HEADERS

- ▶ GRAPHIC

Formatting
output lists

These settings options enable you to output data in a more targeted manner in a defined output format. You therefore no longer have to configure the setting in a layout variant. For example, you can predefine the sequence in which you want to output the fields. You can also specify how you want the data to be sorted and totaled. Of course, you can continue to use these functions in SAP List Viewer, or you can adjust the settings in SAP List Viewer as necessary.

In addition to the SAP List Viewer functions, other functions are available to you. For example, you can highlight the lines and columns separately in 16 different colors. Such functions affect the ABAP List output format, in particular. Here, the data is displayed at the grouping level. Additional help texts (e.g., an individual page header and footer) can be assigned to lists.

Now navigate to the BASIC LIST. The system displays a settings screen in which you can specify the line structure for your basic list (see Figure 10.9). If you enter the command "TECH" in the command field, you can display the technical names of each field so that you know exactly which field you are editing.

Line structure in
the basic list

If you have selected a large amount of data, you can perform a multiline output. This will not affect the output in SAP List Viewer. For the ABAP List output format, however, a multiline output can be displayed in the screen display and in the print output.

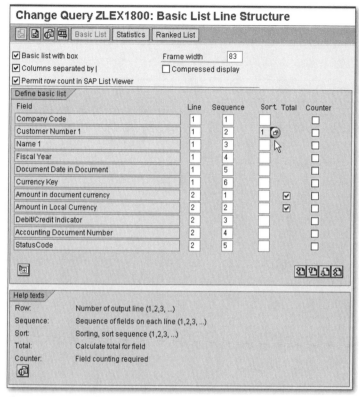

Figure 10.9 Specifying the Line Structure in the Basic List

Follow these steps for our example:

1. Select LINE 1 for the first six fields.

2. As the sorting characteristic (and therefore the summarization characteristic), enter "1" in the SORT column for the CUSTOMER NUMBER 1 field. Because you can only create totals for key figures, this function is available for the AMOUNT IN DOCUMENT CURRENCY and AMOUNT IN LOCAL CURRENCY fields only.

3. Select the TOTAL flag for the AMOUNT IN DOCUMENT CURRENCY and AMOUNT IN LOCAL CURRENCY fields.

4. Choose the navigation button 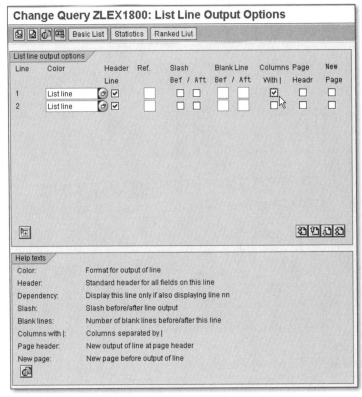 three times (NEXT SCREEN), or use the F6 key to access the LIST LINE OUTPUT OPTIONS screen (see Figure 10.10).

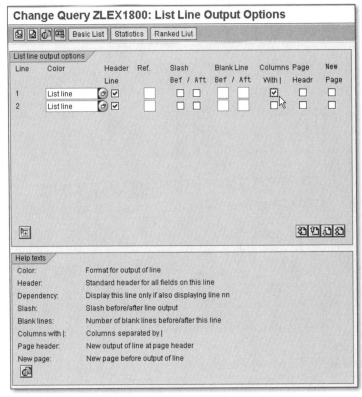

Figure 10.10 Specifying the Output Options for List Lines

Output options for list lines

5. Because you have decided to output all fields in two lines, only the formatting options for these two lines are available. Select the LIST LINE color for your two list lines. Help texts for the settings options are provided in the lower screen area of all navigation windows.

6. Select the HEADER flag, and choose the navigation button once (NEXT SCREEN), or use the F6 key to navigate to the CHANGE ZLEX1800: FIELD OUTPUT OPTIONS screen (see Figure 10.11).

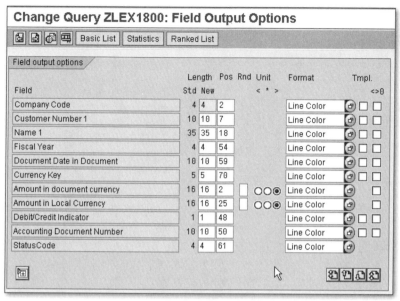

Figure 10.11 Output Options for Formatting Fields

7. On this settings screen, you can now specify the output length of the individual fields. In the RND column, you can scale key figure values. If, for example, you enter "3" in the RND field, the output values are displayed with a 1,000 scaling. In the UNIT column, you can specify whether the amount currency will be displayed before or after the amount, or whether you want to omit it completely. In the FORMAT column, you can specify which columns you want to highlight in color. In our example, select the LINE COLOR format for the AMOUNT IN DOCUMENT CURRENCY field.

> Output options for fields

8. In real-life situations, it is extremely helpful to only output key figure values if they are not null values. In our example, select the `<>0` column for the AMOUNT IN DOCUMENT CURRENCY field. Choose the navigation button 🔲 again (NEXT SCREEN) or press the `F6` key to access the CHANGE QUERY ZLEX1800: BASIC LIST HEADER screen (see Figure 10.12).

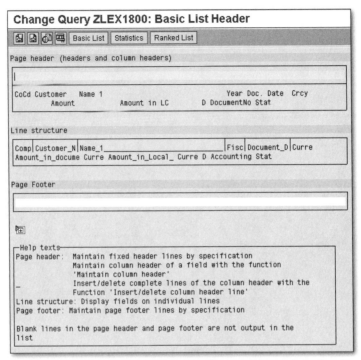

Figure 10.12 Specifying the Report and Column Headers and the Page Footer in the Basic List

Column header and page footer

9. You can now specify a header and page footer for your report. If you want to enter a header that contains more than one line, you can select the menu path EDIT • LINE • INSERT to add more lines. You can insert variables into the page header and page footer. In the list output, the variables are filled with actual values. The variables listed in Table 10.1 are available to you.

Variable	Explanation
&N	Name of the user who executes the query
&D	Current date when executing the query
&T	Current time when executing the query
&P	Current page number (three-character output)

Table 10.1 Variables in the Query Output

10. Enter text in both the page header and page footer. In addition to the text, add variables that will output the user, time, and page number. The column headers are displayed below the page header text.

Column name

11. Double-click the column header for the customer so that you access the window shown in Figure 10.13. Then change the column header from CUSTOMER NUMBER 1 to CUSTOMER.

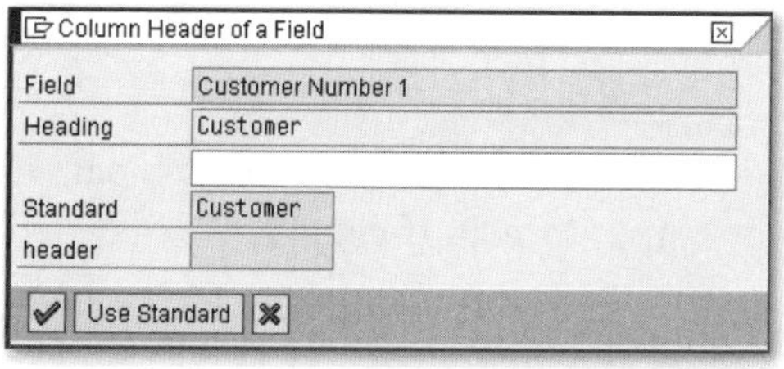

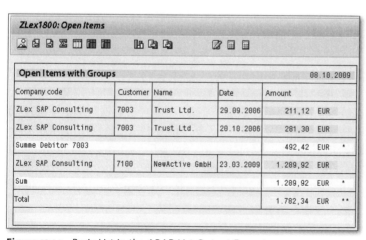

Figure 10.13 Adjusting the Column Header Text

12. On the next settings screen, you can select a default graphic for your report. Experiment with the individual functions in the respective settings screens and choose the simulation button ▦ (TEST) or press Ctrl + F8 to display the results of your settings. Select ABAP LIST as the output format. The list output result of the sample test is shown in Figure 10.14.

Graphic

Figure 10.14 Basic List in the ABAP List Output Format

Displaying a formatted list

The individual headers for your list output are now displayed. The current date of the list output is right-aligned in the list header. The standard column header for the customer is no longer CUSTOMER NAME 1 but CUSTOMER, and the individual list lines are colored. A color has also been assigned to the AMOUNT column. The output user and page number are displayed in the page footer. Here, the data is displayed in grouping level 1 for each customer. Under the menu path EDIT • BASIC LIST • DISPLAY TOTALS ONLY (⌈Shift⌋ + ⌈F4⌋), you can display data in summarized form for each customer.

Display in SAP List Viewer

To some extent, the settings made here affect the way in which data is displayed in the SAP List Viewer output format. If you have not created a layout variant yet, the system uses the summation levels of the basic list. The settings for displaying null values and assigning colors to lines and columns are also displayed (see Figure 10.15).

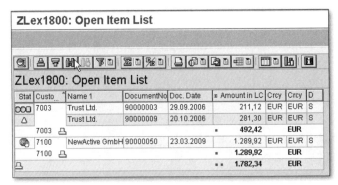

Figure 10.15 Basic List in SAP List Viewer Format

Summation levels in SAP List Viewer

Depending on the analysis, it may make sense to immediately display the total for a key figure column in summarized form according to different analysis characteristics. You could now reformat the data in SAP List Viewer in accordance with the required summarization characteristic, or you could create predefined statistics for the most important analysis characteristics (as shown in the next section).

10.3   Statistics

You can use a statistic to immediately display specific analysis characteristics for a key figure column as summarized data. In addition to the basic list, you can navigate between nine additional statistics. Follow these steps to create a statistic for open items (summarized for each customer):

1. Call the SAP Query transaction in change mode (see Figure 10.16).

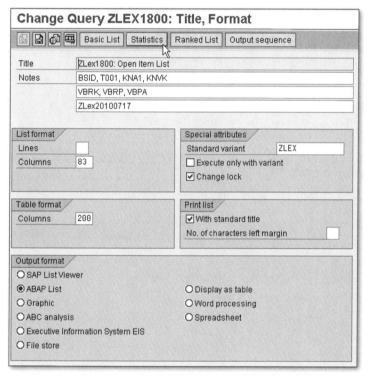

Change Query ZLEX1800: Title, Format

| Basic List | Statistics | Ranked List | Output sequence |

Title	ZLex1800: Open Item List
Notes	BSID, T001, KNA1, KNVK
	VBRK, VBRP, VBPA
	ZLex20100717

List format
Lines ☐
Columns 83

Special attributes
Standard variant ZLEX
☐ Execute only with variant
☑ Change lock

Table format
Columns 200

Print list
☑ With standard title
No. of characters left margin ☐

Output format
○ SAP List Viewer
◉ ABAP List
○ Graphic
○ ABC analysis
○ Executive Information System EIS
○ File store

○ Display as table
○ Word processing
○ Spreadsheet

Figure 10.16 Query Screen for Specifying the Title and Formats

2. For a statistics list display, you use the ABAP List output format. Choose the STATISTICS button to access the CHANGE ZLEX1800: STATISTIC 1 STRUCTURE screen (see Figure 10.17).

> ABAP List output format

3. Enter a title for your statistic. You can then specify how you want the system to display the fields in your statistic.

> Statistics structure

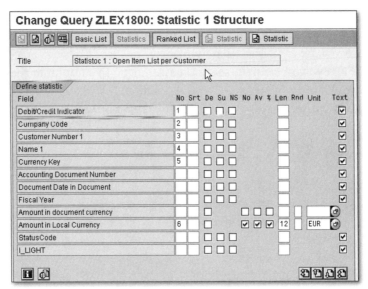

Figure 10.17 Settings Options for the Statistics Structure

4. Because you want summarized data for each customer, leave the No column blank for the Posting date in the document field. The functions listed in Table 10.2 are available in the statistic.

Function	Explanation
No	Column sequence for the individual fields
Srt	Sort data and summation level
De	Sort in descending order
Su	Subtotal
Ns	New page
No	Number of data records
Av	Average value
%	Percentage
Len	Field output length
Rnd	Scaling of the key figure value
Unit	Output unit
Text	Display text in the graphic

Table 10.2 Function Options Within a Statistic

In the statistic, you can now sort the summarized characteristics according to any characteristic. You can sort data records not only according to characteristics but also according to key figures. In our example, we want to sort according to the totaled amount for open items.

Sorting characteristics

5. Because we are generally most interested in customers who have the biggest open items, select the DE column field for the AMOUNT IN DOCUMENT CURRENCY key figure. As a result of selecting this column, the customers with the biggest amounts are displayed and sorted in descending order.

In real life, it frequently makes sense to display subtotals for data records with multiple characteristics. You can create subtotals for characteristic fields by selecting the flags in the SU column. If you select the characteristics flag in the NS column, a page break can be inserted for each characteristic.

Subtotals

The most popular functions within a statistic are those that enable you to display the number of data records, average value, and percentage in a statistic. Summarized data records are displayed in a statistic. If you activate the NO function, the system displays the number of individual data records for each summarized data line. If you select the AV function, the average value of an individual data record is displayed in the statistic.

Number of data records, average value, and percentage

As is the case in the basic list, you can also specify the output length for individual fields here. You can use the RND function to display scaled key figure values. If, for example, you enter "3" in the RND field, the values are displayed with a 1,000 scaling. In the statistic, you can also select other functions via the navigation button 🖹.

Output length and scaling

On the next settings screen, you can configure settings for the page header and page footer (in the same way as you do in the basic list). In other words, you must define statistic headers. To do so, follow these steps:

Headers

1. Choose the navigation button 🖹 twice to access the screen template in which you specify a presentation graphic for a statistic (see Figure 10.18).

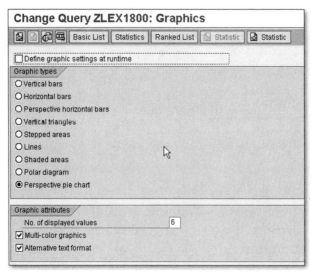

Figure 10.18 Specifying a Presentation Graphic for a Statistic

Default graphic
in a statistic

2. As is the case with the template for specifying headers, the graphic template has the same structure as the basic list. You can decide whether you want to select a graphic type from the report list or permanently define the graphic type for each statistic. Deactivate the DEFINE GRAPHIC SETTINGS AT RUNTIME button, and select the PERSPECTIVE PIE CHART graphic type.

3. Choose to test your settings in the ABAP List output format. In addition to the basic list, you now get your newly created statistic (see Figure 10.19).

Summarized
data display for
each customer

In our statistic, the individual data records are not displayed for each posting date. Instead, the data is summarized for each customer number. Furthermore, the sequence in which the customers are displayed has changed. In the basic list, the data is sorted according to the customer number. In the statistic, however, the summarized data records are sorted in descending order according to the AMOUNT field.

Number of
data records,
percentage

In contrast to the basic list, the statistic also displays the number of individual data records for each totals record. For the customer 7003 TRUST LTD., for example, it is clear that the amount EUR 492.42 refers to two individual data records. The summation line percentage in relation to the total is also displayed. The open item amounting to EUR 1,289.92 for the customer 7100 NEWACTIVE GMBH corresponds to 72.4% of the total. In the Av column, the value from the AMOUNT column is divided by the number of data records.

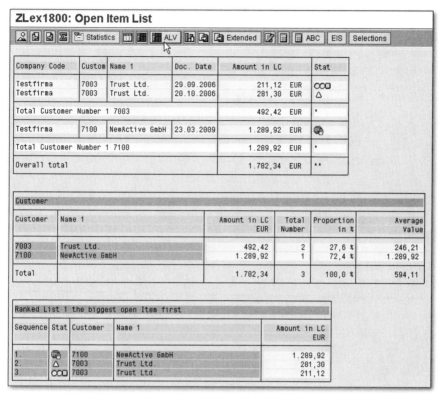

Figure 10.19 Displaying a Basic List and One Statistic

4. Position your cursor on the statistic, and choose ![ALV]. The system now displays the screen shown in Figure 10.20. The usual SAP List Viewer functions are available here.

5. Return to the query editing screen for statistics, and create another statistic. Also include the POSTING DATE field in the statistic, and create a subtotal for each company code. To create another statistic, choose ![Statistic] (ANOTHER STATISTIC).

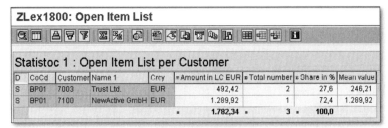

Figure 10.20 Displaying a Statistic in the ALV Layout

Subtotals in
statistics

6. To create a subtotal for a characteristic, you must sort the data according to this characteristic. The specifications for Statistic 1 could look as shown in Figure 10.21.

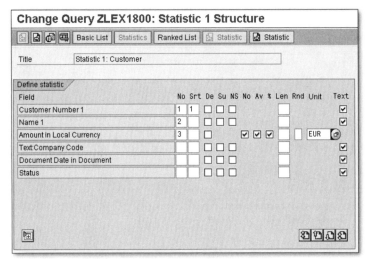

Figure 10.21 Statistic with a Subtotal

7. Because you want to obtain a subtotal for CUSTOMER NUMBER 1, mark this field as a sort field. You can only create a subtotal for the TEXT: COMPANY CODE field because CUSTOMER NUMBER 1 must be sorted first for the preceding field.

Output sequence

8. Your query now has a basic list and two statistics. If you want the system to display the data from Statistic 1 at the start of your analysis, you can change the output sequence. Choose OUTPUT SEQUENCE in the first navigation window, or press Ctrl + F4 to get the screen shown in Figure 10.22.

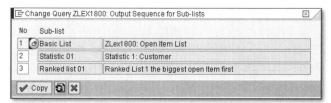

Figure 10.22 Specifying the Output Sequence for the Basic List, Statistics, and Ranked Lists

In the window for editing the output sequence, the system displays the basic list, statistics, and ranked lists. In the NO column, you can enter a number between 1 and 90. Enter output sequence number "1" for your BASIC LIST, "2" for STATISTIC 1, and "3" for RANKED LIST 1. The output list with the lowest number is displayed for the output in the SAP List Viewer output format. Following this change to the output sequence, CUSTOMER is displayed first in the ABAP List Viewer output format (see Figure 10.23).

Changing the output sequence

ZLex1800: Open Item List

Customer

Customer	Name 1	Doc. Date	Amount in LC EUR	Total Number	Proportion in %	Average Value
7003	Trust Ltd.	29.09.2006	211,12	1	11,8 %	211,12
7003	Trust Ltd.	20.10.2006	281,30	1	15,8 %	281,30
7003	*	*	492,42	2	27,6 %	246,21
7100	NewActive GmbH	23.03.2009	1.289,92	1	72,4 %	1.289,92
7100	*	*	1.289,92	1	72,4 %	1.289,92
Total			1.782,34	3	100,0 %	594,11

Statistic 2: Customer

Customer	Name 1	Amount in LC EUR	Total Number	Proportion in %	Average Value
7003	Trust Ltd.	492,42	2	27,6 %	246,21
7100	NewActive GmbH	1.289,92	1	72,4 %	1.289,92
Total		1.782,34	3	100,0 %	594,11

Figure 10.23 Statistic with Open Items Summarized for Customer and Posting Date, Subtotal for Each Company Code

Statistic with two characteristics

More lines are now displayed in CUSTOMER than in STATISTIC 2. As a result of adding the POSTING DATE analysis characteristic, the data is now summarized for the CUSTOMER/POSTING DATE combination. In addition, a subtotal is still displayed for each customer and company code. A summarized data display for two characteristics (customer and posting date) is frequently used in real-life situations. If, however, too many data records are displayed, the system can only display data relating to the biggest values. It uses a ranked list for this purpose, which we will discuss in the next section.

10.4 Ranked List

Function of a ranked list

The ranked list enables you to display the biggest key figure values for specific characteristics. For example, you can choose to display only the 10 highest ranked list positions for open items.

To use ranked lists, follow these steps:

1. Return to the query title screen, and choose RANKED LIST. The system then displays the screen shown in Figure 10.24.

Criterion for a ranked list

2. Select the characteristics that you want to see in your ranked list. Because the ranked list is based on a key figure value, only the AMOUNT IN DOCUMENT CURRENCY is available as a criterion for the ranked list. The ranked list is now also contained in the query and is displayed at the end of your output if you do not change the output sequence.

3. If you display the query in the ABAP List output format, you can navigate to an overview of the existing basic list, statistics, and ranked lists. To do this, choose ▨ (OVERVIEW) to display the screen shown in Figure 10.25.

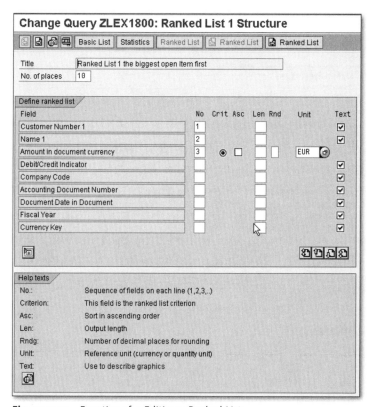

Figure 10.24 Functions for Editing a Ranked List

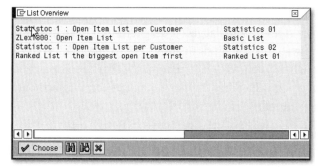

Figure 10.25 Overview of the Statistics, Basic List, and Ranked Lists

4. Double-click RANKED LIST 1. A ranked list appears of customers who have the biggest open items (see Figure 10.26).

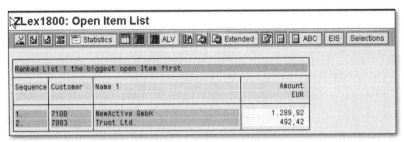

Figure 10.26 Ranked List of Customers Who Have the Biggest Open Items

5. Only the top entries for the AMOUNT field are displayed in the ranked list. In total, you can create up to nine ranked lists. You can also display the ranked lists by choosing ALV in SAP List Viewer.

10.5 Summary

You can use the Graphical Query Painter to edit the basic list for a query. If you display data in SAP List Viewer, you can total or filter this data. Additional functions for editing the basic list are available after you deactivate the Graphical Query Painter. For example, you can total or color the data in the report that you create.

If you want to display summarized data according to different characteristics, you can use the statistics function. In addition to a summarized data display, a statistic enables you to display the total number of summarized data records, the average value, and the percentage of summarized data lines in relation to the total.

You can use ranked lists to display a selection of top entries for each characteristic. In the ABAP List output format, you can display not only the basic list but also up to nine statistics and nine ranked lists. You also have the flexibility to navigate between analyses. Lastly, you can also display the relevant analysis in SAP List Viewer.

*In this chapter, you will learn more about SAP's data definition
and its data fields. You will also learn how to define your own
data fields and fill them with content. In particular, you will
learn about the following two ABAP statements:* IF *and* SELECT.

11   ABAP Fundamentals in the InfoSet

Each time you want to create a report, the system must read data from
the database and display it in a user-friendly list. It is therefore important
to know the descriptions of the data objects. As with all other languages,
a dictionary is available for the SAP language ABAP: the ABAP Dictionary. Tables, views, structures, and other data elements are defined in the
ABAP Dictionary. Unlike a structure, which stores data temporarily, data
is permanently saved in tables.

After you have taken a closer look at the ABAP Dictionary in the first
section in this chapter, you will delve further into the ABAP language.
How do entire records look in ABAP? Which specific commands enable
you to select data content, and which language elements are frequently
used in real-life scenarios? First, however, let's take a look at the ABAP
Dictionary.

11.1   ABAP Dictionary

The ABAP Dictionary (DDIC) is a data dictionary in which all data objects   **Table description**
(e.g., tables and views) are defined. The ABAP Dictionary contains table
descriptions as well. Here, a table comprises several rows, each of which
contains individual table fields. If you address a particular field, the
respective table/field name combination is always important.

Finally, you can find out whether one of the individual fields is a key
field that represents the "head of the family." Fields are described with
business and technical attributes. The business attributes (data element)

include a descriptive name and header, while the technical attributes (domain) are defined in a data element. In the domain itself, you specify the data type, field length, number of decimal places, and the output length.

To work with the ABAP Dictionary, follow these steps:

1. Access the ABAP Dictionary under the menu path TOOLS • ABAP WORKBENCH • DEVELOPMENT • ABAP DICTIONARY or by calling Transaction SE11 (ABAP Dictionary) (see Figure 11.1).

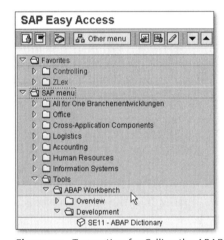

Figure 11.1 Transaction for Calling the ABAP Dictionary

The system displays the initial screen with seven different data objects. In this chapter, we will take a closer look at the database table, view, data type, and domain.

[»] **Comparing the Structure and Transparent Table in the DDIC**

After you end a program, the data continues to be stored in a table, while a structure, which represents a description of fields, is used only to temporarily store data within a program. Because data is only permanently stored in tables, only tables have key fields.

2. Select the DATABASE TABLE option, and enter the table "TSTCT" (see Figure 11.2).

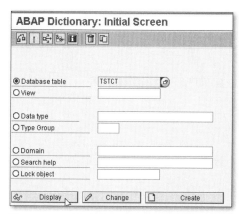

Figure 11.2 ABAP Dictionary — Initial Screen

3. Choose DISPLAY to display the table TSTCT (Transaction Code Texts) and its fields (see Figure 11.3).

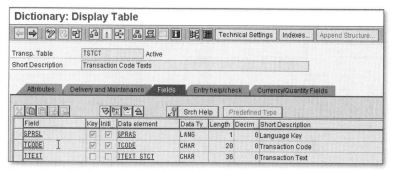

Figure 11.3 Displaying the Table TSTCT (Transaction Code Texts) in the ABAP Dictionary

On the FIELD tab, you obtain an overview of the three fields SPRSL, TCODE, and TTEXT in the table TSTCT (Transaction Code Texts). Most table fields comprise five letters. The field name for the language key SPRSL is also used in many other SAP tables. To ensure that a field is unique, you must always specify the name of the associated table (e.g., TSTCT-SPRSL).

Table fields

In the second column, the two table fields SPRSL and TCODE are defined as key fields. For key fields, the data is stored in the system with an index so that a search can be performed much more quickly. Here, you also specify whether a table field is predefined with an initial value. If

Key fields

no data content is found for a field, it does not remain empty. Instead, the initial value is output. In the case of a numeric field, for example, a zero is output.

The following information is also specified for each field:

▶ Data element

▶ Data type

▶ Length

▶ Decimal places

▶ Short description

To obtain an overview of all field attributes, you can double-click the individual field names in the FIELD column. If you double-click the field TCODE in the FIELD column, the system displays the screen shown in Figure 11.4.

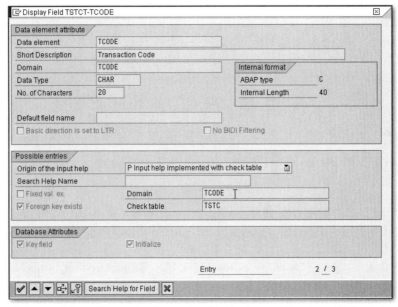

Figure 11.4 Data Element Attributes, Possible Entries, and Database Attributes for the Field TSTCT-TCODE

Check table   In addition to the information about the data element, the POSSIBLE ENTRIES (check table) and the DATABASE ATTRIBUTES are also displayed for the selected field. Let's first take a look at the DATA ELEMENT by double-clicking the field TCODE to display the screen shown in Figure 11.5.

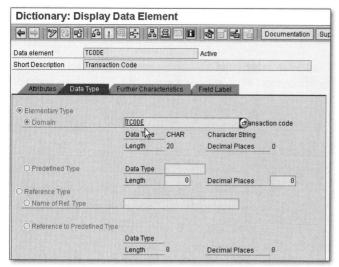

Figure 11.5 Data Type of the Data Element TCODE

The data element TCODE is assigned to the field TCODE in the table
TSTCT. In turn, the domain TCODE is assigned to the data element
TCODE. This is known as multilevel assignment. To see the exact format,
you can double-click the domain TCODE (see Figure 11.6).

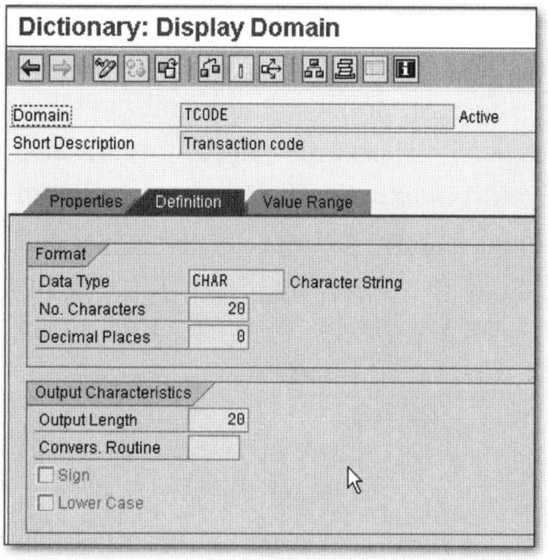

Domain

Figure 11.6 Domain TCODE with Format and Output Characteristics

Currency and
quantity fields

The field TCODE uses the data type CHAR (Character String). For the domain TCODE, 20 characters and 0 decimal places are defined.

[»]

Currency and Quantity Fields

A special logic applies to currency and quantity fields. A currency field is always of the type CURR and has a reference field of the type CUKY. The domain WAERS is permanently entered in the data element, and the table TCURC is automatically entered as a foreign key in the value range for the domain. A quantity field, on the other hand, is of the type QUAN and has a reference field of the type UNIT.

For available data objects, you can now take a look at the description in the ABAP Dictionary. You now know that the description of a data field is entered in the data element, that not only a business description but also a domain is entered in the data element, and that the domain contains the technical description of a data field. In particular, the data type (e.g., CHAR for character [Character String]) for the table field is specified in the domain. If you now create a new field that is not yet known in the SAP system, you must define the data type for this field. When specifying a type, you can use the LIKE command to refer to an existing field in the ABAP Dictionary, or you can enter the data type, and so on, in a new field.

11.2 Individual Data Objects in the InfoSet

Individual
data fields

The query reporting tools will help you create analyses in the fastest and easiest manner possible. You can therefore link existing database tables as a data basis for a report. If, however, report creation is more flexible, you can use query tools to easily add new data fields to your program. After you have defined an individual data field, you can read actual content from a particular table. Any table to be queried in the InfoSet must be made known to the query. Before you assign values to a new individual field, you must also define them in an InfoSet.

11.2.1 Data Fields

You use the ABAP command `DATA` to define new data fields. A data field **Data declaration** is characterized by a name that has no more than 30 characters, the data type, and the data length. The following data types are provided within an InfoSet (see Table 11.1).

Data Type	Description	Initial Value
C	Character	Blank character
CURR	CUKY	
QUAN	UNIT	
D	Date	YYYYMMDD '00000000'
I	Integer	0 Length 4
N	Numeric character	'00000…000'
P	Packed number	0 Length 8
T	Time	HHMMSS '000000'

Table 11.1 Data Types of Dictionary Fields

For example, you can assign a type to your new data field as follows:

```
DATA: field1 TYPE p DECIMALS 2.
```

This statement provides you with a new variable called FIELD1, which **Data type** uses the data type P and has two decimal places.

You can assign a type to every single field. However, it is much easier to **TYPE statement** simply refer to an existing field in the ABAP Dictionary. Instead of using the command `TYPE`, you can simply write: `field1` is the same as `field2`. In ABAP, this is formulated as follows:

```
DATA: field1 LIKE field2.
```

If you use this statement, `field1` obtains the same technical attributes as **Data type** `field2`. To determine the technical attributes of `field1`, the system looks at the output length and decimal places of the data type in the `field2` domain in the ABAP Dictionary.

You can use the equals sign (=) to assign data content to `field1`. In ABAP, you can write this as follows:

```
field1 = '5'.
```

Literals   It is important to always place the assigned value in quotation marks (literals). Furthermore, as a result of the data type, it is not possible to transfer all of the data content of one field to another field. If you transfer the field content from `field2` to `field1`, both fields use convertible data types. Take a look at the data definition for an additional field in an InfoSet, and then call Transaction SQ02 (InfoSet) in change mode (see Figure 11.7).

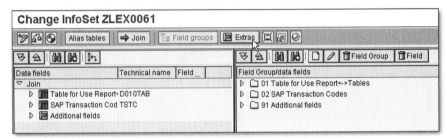

Figure 11.7 InfoSet in Change Mode — Field Group View

Switching from the field group view to the "Extras" view   To the right of the FIELD GROUPS button, which is grayed out, there are other buttons, which you can use to enhance the ABAP code in your InfoSet. You can add table fields, tables, structures, selections or your own code to your InfoSet. Follow these steps for our example:

1. Choose 🔲 Extras , or press the ⌷F5⌷ key. Instead of the field groups, the following four tabs are displayed on the right-hand side of the screen: EXTRAS, SELECTIONS, CODE, and ENHANCEMENTS (see Figure 11.8).

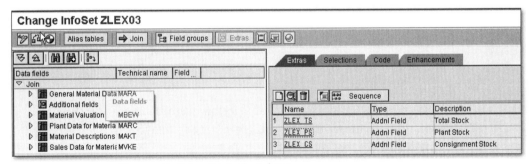

Figure 11.8 Extras Tab in the InfoSet

2. The first three buttons are used to create additional fields, tables, or structures. You can choose 🗋 (CREATE) to create extras in the InfoSet, 🔳 (DEFINITION) to display the long text and header for a field or the mapping for an additional table, 🔳 (DELETE) to delete extras that you no longer require, and 🔳 (CODE FOR EXTRA) to enter your own ABAP code on an editor screen for your additional field. Then choose 🗋 (CREATE) to display the dialog screen shown in Figure 11.9.

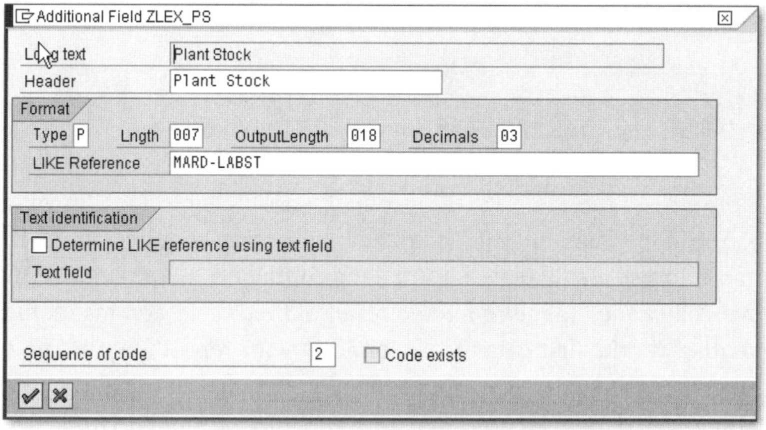

Creating, displaying, and deleting additional objects

Figure 11.9 Selection Screen for Creating Additional Information

3. As additional information, you can add an additional table, an additional field, or an additional structure to your InfoSet. If you add an additional table, this is different from adding a table in a graphical join editor because you must specify the actual conditions under which the information is to be read from the additional table. Furthermore, not all data records are read from the additional table. Instead, the first data record (SELECT SINGLE) is added to your list output (see Figure 11.10).

Selecting additional information

Adding an additional table helps you to add ABAP code to your query. The system proposes the following program lines to you:

Inserting an additional table

```
SELECT SINGLE * FROM tstct
   WHERE sprsl = sy-langu
      AND tcode = tstc-tcode
```

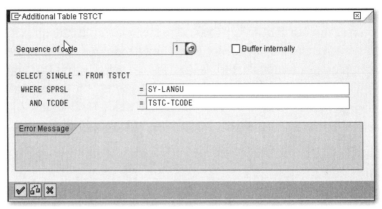

Figure 11.10 Adding a Data Record from an Additional Table to an InfoSet

SELECT SINGLE command for an additional table

Therefore, the entire table TSTCT is joined with the table TSTC in your query. You don't have to make the data declaration required in ABAP for a table yourself. In the background, the command TABLES: TSTCT. is automatically added to the code. As a result of the SINGLE command, the system displays the first data record found in your report output. The * character after the SELECT SINGLE command means that all of fields in the table are selected and can therefore be added to your query. Two WHERE conditions linked using AND are inserted as a condition for the transaction text. To add a data record, the table TSTCT must contain an entry for the correct language and for the transaction itself.

WHERE condition

The first WHERE condition refers to the logon language of the user. It is not always beneficial to add a table because the WHERE conditions are preassigned, and all of the fields in the table are read. Frequently, only individual table fields are required. Therefore, it is often more beneficial to add individual table fields.

To add the table, follow these steps:

1. Press ⌑Enter⌑ to add the additional table TSTCT to your query.

2. Choose ☐ (CREATE), and, this time, select ADDITIONAL FIELD as the type of additional information (see Figure 11.11).

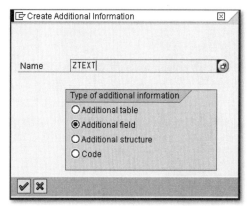

Figure 11.11 Creating an Additional Field in an InfoSet

3. Enter a long text and header for your additional field. When you define a query, the long text for an additional field is displayed on the selection screen, while the header of the additional field is displayed as a column name when the list is output. Now define the data format for your additional field. For a table field, the data declaration required in ABAP is also simplified for you. The command DATA ztext … is inserted in the background. However, the field ZTEXT requires a specific data type. You can insert the information for the data type below the FORMAT header line. This corresponds to the ABAP command TYPE. The code in an ABAP program looks as follows:

Creating an additional field

```
DATA: ztext TYPE c(36) DECIMALS 0.
```

4. It is even easier to define data by referring to a data field in the ABAP Dictionary. To ensure that your new field has the same technical attributes as a field in the ABAP Dictionary, you must make an entry in the LIKE REFERENCE field. In our example, enter "TSTCT-TTEXT" as a LIKE REFERENCE. As a result of this entry, the system searches the domain in the ABAP Dictionary for the field TSTCT-TTEXT and selects the data type in the same way (see Figure 11.12).

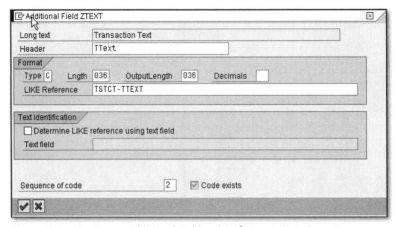

Figure 11.12 Naming an Additional Field and Defining Its Data Format

System fields   When defining data and entering code, you can make reference to system fields. For example, the WHERE condition shown earlier in Figure 11.10 already refers to the system field string. The SY-LANGU expression is always used to query the logon language. You can also permanently query the language E for English. Frequently, the system fields provide useful information that is available when the program is running.

11.2.2   System Fields

Program status   When the program is running, the system temporarily transfers program
SY-SUBRC   information to the structure SYST (ABAP System Fields). In real-life situations, a date field is frequently defined with reference to the system date. The relevant ABAP code looks as follows: DATA: field1 LIKE sy-date. Furthermore, the content of the system field SUBRC reflects whether or not the data was successfully accessed. Therefore, the field SY-SUBRC is frequently queried in real-life scenarios. If the field SY-SUBRC contains the number 0, data access was successful and, if the field SY-SUBRC contains the number 4, data access has failed. You can display the available system fields (171) in the ABAP Dictionary. Call Transaction SE11 and display the table SYST. The system then displays the screen shown in Figure 11.13.

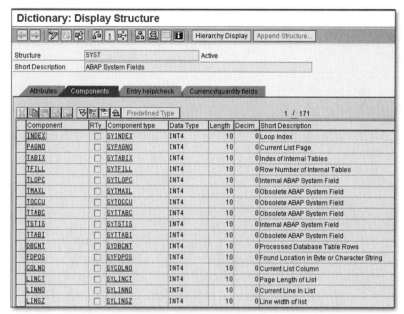

Figure 11.13 Displaying the System Fields in the ABAP Dictionary

The system fields are extremely beneficial because they are always available with the latest content. In the ABAP Dictionary, the structure of the ABAP system fields are defined with SYST and, in real life, the table is frequently shortened to SY. The names SYST and SY can be used synonymously. Frequently used ABAP system fields are listed in Table 11.2.

System fields

Command	Meaning
SY-DATE	Current date
SY-DBCNT	Data record in the database
SY-INDEX	Current loop counter
SY-LANGU	Logon language
SY-SUBRC	Return code
SY-UNAME	User logged on to the system
SY-TABIX	Line index for an internal table
SY-TIME	Current time

Table 11.2 System Fields

SY-SUBRC query

As already mentioned, the field SY-SUBRC (return code) is frequently queried in real life. The ABAP programs frequently contain the following code or similar:

```
IF sy-subrc <> 0
    variable1 = '4711'.
ENDIF.
```

You should now know which options are available for filling VARIABLE1 with content.

11.3 Helpful ABAP Code

Of course, you can create a query without having to enter your own ABAP code. You can simply link the relevant tables in an InfoSet with each other and define the selection and list fields in a query. Generally, a query analysis can be performed in just a few minutes. In an InfoSet, you can use ABAP code to design a more flexible data query. You can base your ABAP code on sample code.

11.3.1 Sample Code on the Editor Screen

Sample code

You can insert sample code into your additional field. To do this, choose the PATTERN button, and enter the relevant ABAP command. You will then get an example of a syntactically correct ABAP statement. In our example, we have inserted a table and an additional field (see Figure 11.14).

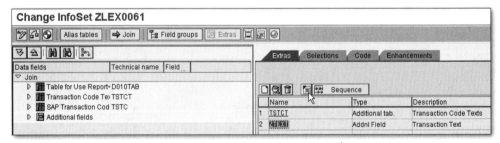

Figure 11.14 InfoSet with an Additional Table and Additional Field

The ABAP command SELECT SINGLE has already been used to link the additional table TSTCT (Transaction Code Text) with the join tables in the InfoSet. The additional field ZTEXT has been defined, but it does not have any code yet. Therefore, position your cursor on the additional field ZTEXT. Then choose ▤ (CODE FOR EXTRA). You then access the CODE tab. The additional field ZTEXT is displayed in the header line, while an empty input area in which you can enter ABAP code is displayed in the lower screen area (see Figure 11.15).

Additional field for transaction code text

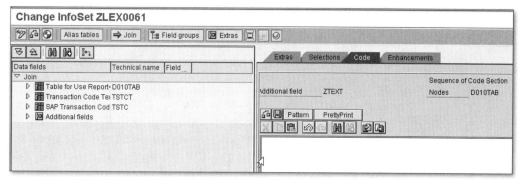

Figure 11.15   Editor Screen to Enter ABAP Code for an Additional Field

Extremely helpful function buttons are available on the editor screen. For example, you can check the syntactical accuracy of your ABAP code at any time. To do this, choose 🔲 (CHECK CODE). You can choose the well-known SAVE button to temporarily store your entries at any time. To the right of the disk icon for saving data, you will see a PATTERN button. If you choose this button, the system displays the dialog box shown in Figure 11.16.

Syntax check for code

The PATTERN button offers you various different ABAP commands. In real life, it is very helpful to use the PATTERN button and the ABAP command CALL FUNCTION to call a function module, for example. Function modules are finished ABAP programs that perform predefined arithmetic operations. You will get to know some helpful examples in Chapter 14, Data Retrieval and Function Modules.

Function modules

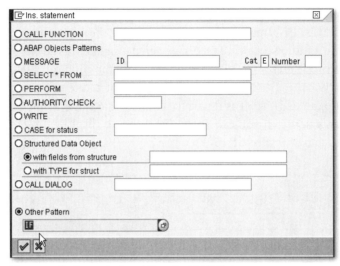

Figure 11.16 Screen to Insert Sample ABAP Code

Message output You can use the command MESSAGE to add an actual message from the message area to your InfoSet. The SELECT command is the most frequently used command in real life. You use the SELECT command to select data records from a source in a particular field. For the IF statement, you first insert ABAP code into your additional field. To do this, select the lower entry (OTHER PATTERN). In the field below the text, enter IF as the ABAP command, and press the Enter key to confirm your entry. The system then displays the screen shown in Figure 11.17.

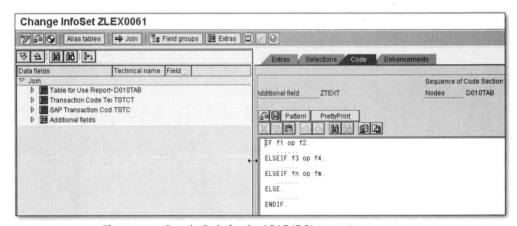

Figure 11.17 Sample Code for the ABAP IF Statement

11.3.2   IF Statement

The IF statement is very often used, for example, to query amount fields. The values are always stored in the database with a positive value, irrespective of the business transaction or, in the case of sales revenue, certain values are not considered for a particular billing document type. For example, the F5 and F8 billing document types in the standard SAP system are intended for pro forma transactions and therefore are not relevant for a sales evaluation. The IF statement does not calculate the values of the F5 and F8 billing document types for sales.

Data assignments based on the IF statement

Take a look at the sample code for the ABAP IF statement:

```
IF f1 OP f2.
   ......
   ELSEIF f3 OP f4.
      ......
   ELSEIF fN OP fm.
   ......
   ELSE.
   ......
ENDIF.
```

The sample code comprises nine lines. In the first line, the IF command is used to query the field content of the F1 variable. An operand is used to compare the field content of the F1 variable with the field content of the F2 variable. If the condition in line 1 is fulfilled, the statement in line 2 is executed. Frequently, a value is assigned to a variable in line 2. If the condition in line 1 is not fulfilled, another query can be performed in line 3 (e.g., the F3 variable). In the sample code, an operand is used to compare the content of the F3 variable with the content of the F4 variable. An actual value is frequently queried in real life. If a fixed value is queried, literals (e.g., 'x') are used to specify comparison variables.

Using the IF statement to query a field

For a sales query, the net values from the table VBRP (Billing Document: Item Data) are queried. A query can then refer to the field VBRP-NETWR (Net Value of Billing Document Item in Document Currency). The values in the field VBRP-NETWR are always displayed with a positive sign, irrespective of the associated billing document type. For certain billing document types (e.g., credit memos, cancellations, etc.), you could now assign a negative sign to the net value in the InfoSet. However, the billing document type is still in the table VBRK (Billing Document: Header Data), so you must query another table. The query also must be checked again when you create a new billing document type. In real life, the net value is therefore queried on the basis of the field SHKZG (Returns Item).

"Net value with the appropriate positive/ negative sign" additional field An additional field ZNETWR is created in the InfoSet. As a result of the LIKE statement, the new field ZNETWR obtains the same technical attributes as the field VBRP-NETWR. An IF statement then fills the new field with the appropriate positive/negative sign:

```
IF vbrp-shkzg = 'X'.
  znetwr = vbrp-netwr * ( -1 ).
ELSE.
  znetwr = vbrp-netwr.
ENDIF.
```

The IF statement now queries whether the field VBRP-SHKZG (Returns Item) contains an X, which would have the following significance for an accountant: If the debit/credit indicator (SHKZG) is filled, it concerns a credit item, and the value must be displayed with a negative sign. If the IF statement is filled, the value of the field NETWR (Net Value) is assigned with a negative sign to the new field ZNETWR. If the condition is not fulfilled, the value of the field NETWR is assigned with a positive sign to the field ZNETWR. The same logic also applies to Financial Accounting (FI) values. Once again, the query is performed on the basis of the field SHKZG. However, the value of the field SHKZG is filled with an S for a debit posting (= positive value) and an H for a credit posting.

```
IF bsid-shkzg = 'S'.
  zamount = bsid-wrbtr.
ELSE.
  zamount = bsid-wrbtr * ( -1 ).
ENDIF.
```

You can also formulate a shorter IF statement. For example, you can query whether field content has already been assigned to the Field1 variable.

```
IF field1 IS INITIAL.
    statement1
ENDIF.
```

Consequently, the IF statement can be nested differently. It may even make sense to insert an additional IF statement within an IF statement or to use the ELSEIF statement to query different case constellations. A comparison operator is used for all IF statements. In most cases, the equals sign (=) is used. However, you can also use other comparison operands. For example, the IF statement can look as follows:

ELSEIF statement

```
IF field1 BETWEEN 'A' AND 'B'.
      statement1
ENDIF.
```

The most important comparison operands are shown in Table 11.3. For example, you can use the comparison operand EQ or the equals sign.

Comparison operands

Operand	Character	Meaning
BT		Between
EQ	=	Equal to
NE	<>	Not equal to
LT	<	Less than
LE	<=	Less than or equal to
GT	>	Greater than
GE	>=	Greater than or equal to

Table 11.3 Comparison Operands for Querying Variable Values

The IF statement is also suitable for simple condition queries. With the IF statement, you can also use the AND command to query several conditions:

```
IF field1 = 'A' AND field1 = 'B'.
   field1 = field1 + field1.
ENDIF.
```

You can also add up the values of a variable within an IF query. If several data records are queried, you need a loop query. The SELECT statement also provides an easier option for adding up values.

Adding up variable values

11.3.3 SELECT Loop

You do not have to use a join to insert all tables into an InfoSet. Frequently, the table join comprises the central tables, which contain the core content of the query. If several tables are included in a join, this may have a negative impact on performance. When you use table links, multiple data records may exist as a result of an *n:n* relationship. Consequently, one data record is very often displayed because the joined tables contain several data records.

Generally only one or two fields from another table are required as additional information for the analysis. Therefore, the SELECT command reads the information for your program from another data source.

Loop selection   The SELECT-ENDSELECT command represents a loop and essentially reads the data records in the database, from the first line to the last. If the comparison criteria are fulfilled, another ABAP command can be inserted within the SELECT loop. The SELECT loop has the following structure:

```
SELECT * FROM table1
    INTO query area
    WHERE field1 OPERAND variable1 AND/OR
          field2 OPERAND variable2
    ORDER BY fieldx.
    ''Your own ABAP code''
ENDSELECT.
```

Line 1: Specifying the Fields and Table for the SELECT Command

As a result of the SELECT command, the data is read from the database. Furthermore, all fields are read if you specify an asterisk (*). The database table from which the data will be read is specified after the FROM command. TABLE1 must already be used in the InfoSet, or you must use the TABLES statement to define it. The SELECT command executes a loop around the complete TABLE1. This loop must be closed using the ENDSELECT command. The system now passes through all of the lines in the database.

Line 2: Transferring Field Values to Another Data Object

The query area can be an existing table, or you can temporarily define a new query area in this program.

Line 3: Condition Query

FIELD1 always refers to a field in TABLE1, which was specified in LINE1. The usual comparison signs (=, <>, >, >=, <, and >=) can be used as operands. Here, an existing table field from previous InfoSet fields can be used as a variable. Alternatively, you can permanently work with a previously defined variable. You can also insert a fixed value (e.g., 1,000) instead of the variable.

Line 4: Querying a Second Variable, Linked with And/Or

You can query several variables. You must then specify whether all variables (AND) or only one of the specified variables (OR) must be fulfilled.

Line 5: Optional Grouping

Lines 2 to 5 are optional. Line 5 is very rarely used in additional code for an InfoSet because SAP List Viewer can be used for sorting purposes. It is also important that line 5 ends with a period (.) so that the program recognizes that this is the end of the query. If you do not use line 5, you must set the period at the end of line 4 so that the program recognizes that no other conditions need to be fulfilled.

Line 6: Any ABAP Statement Within the Loop

You can insert any ABAP command in line 6. For example, you can perform a new SELECT.

Line 7: Closing the SELECT Loop

You must always close the SELECT command for selecting a complete table. You must therefore close a SELECT statement with an ENDSELECT statement.

The ABAP commands SELECT and ENDSELECT represent a loop statement. In particular, this form of SELECT command is used to display cumulated

Using the Stock additional field to enhance the material master analysis

values. For cumulated values, you must use conditions as the basis for querying all data records in a certain table. For example, you have created a join that uses the following material master tables (see Figure 11.18):

- ► MARA: General Material Data
- ► MBEW: Material Valuation
- ► MARC: Plant Data for Material
- ► MAKT: Material Descriptions
- ► MVKE: Sales Data for Material

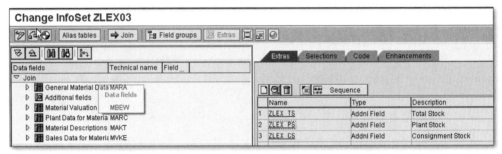

Figure 11.18 Table Join Using Material Master Data

Defining the Plant Stock additional field

The analysis of material master data is already very comprehensive. In real-life situations, it is interesting to display not only the material number but also the material stock in an additional field. The current material stock is in the table MARD (Storage Location Data for the Material). If you chose to add the table MARD to your join, a data row would be displayed for each material master and storage location. For the analysis, we are not interested in individual storage location stock but rather the sum of all stock across all storage locations. We therefore add a new additional field (e.g., ZLEX_PS for Plant Stock) to our InfoSet.

To create an additional field, follow these steps:

1. Go to the EXTRAS tab and create an additional field. The system then displays the dialog screen shown in Figure 11.19.

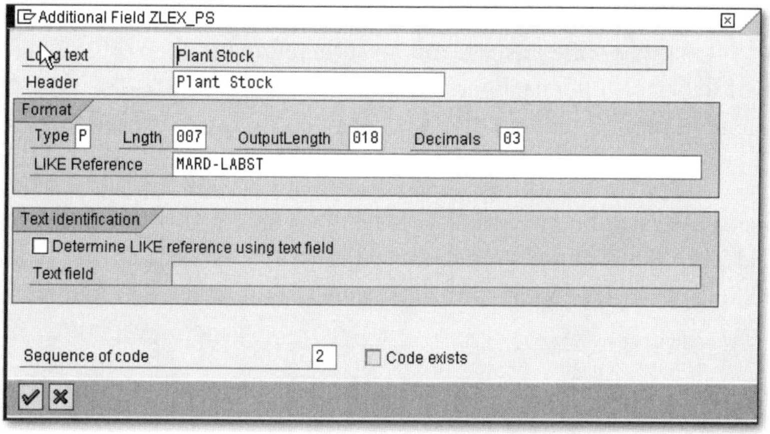

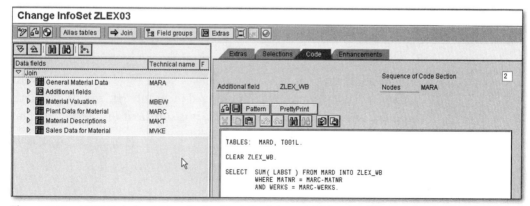

Figure 11.19 Additional Field for Determining the Plant Stock

2. Enter a long text and header for your additional field. When defining data, use the LIKE reference to refer to the field MARD-LABST. The unrestricted-use stock is stored in the field MARD-LABST. Because we want to use our additional field to add up the available stock across all storage locations, it makes sense for the additional field to have the same technical attributes as the SAP field MARD-LABST (valuated, unrestricted-use stock).

Code for the Plant Stock additional field

3. After you have defined the additional field, choose 📄 (CODE FOR EXTRA) to branch to the editor screen in which you can enter ABAP code.

Figure 11.20 ABAP Code for Adding Up the Plant Stock in an Additional Field

4. Up to now, the table MARD (Storage Location Data for the Material) was not yet known to the InfoSet. You must therefore use the TABLES statement to perform the data declaration for the table MARD. The TABLES statement is also used to define the table T001L (Storage Locations):

```
TABLES: MARD, T001L.
```

5. The CLEAR statement is used to clear the content of the additional field ZLEX_PS. The CLEAR statement therefore ensures that the field ZLEX_PS does not contain any data values from other program code:

```
CLEAR zlex_ps.
```

6. The SELECT loop is used to fill the additional field ZLEX_PS:

```
SELECT sum( labst )FROM mard
       INTO zlex_wb
       WHERE matnr = marc-matnr
       AND werks = marc-werks
       INTO  zlex_ps
ENDSELECT.
```

7. The table MARD (Storage Location Data) adds up all plant stock, thus fulfilling the WHERE condition. The SUM command is used to add up the plant stock. After the SUM command, you must insert an opening parenthesis, insert blank characters on either side of the relevant field, and then insert a closing parenthesis. In the WHERE condition, the material numbers are queried from the table MARC (Plant Data for Material). If the material has a plant-specific view, and the table MARD (Storage Location Data) contains data records for the respective plant, these values are added up. The sum total is then written to the field ZLEX_PS. All data records are selected by specifying the command ENDSELECT.

For amount and quantity fields, it makes sense to add up the relevant values. If, however, other fields are read in an InfoSet, you do not have to select all data records. In this case, it is sufficient to transfer the first data record found to the additional field.

11.3.4 SELECT SINGLE Statement

You can use the ABAP command SELECT SINGLE to import the first data record found into an additional field. As an example, create a new Info-Set with open items from FI by following these steps:

1. In the InfoSet, define a table join using the following tables:

   ▸ BSID (Accounting: Secondary Index for Customers)

   ▸ T001 (Company Codes)

2. Switch from the FIELD GROUPS display to the editing screen for extras for the InfoSet (see Figure 11.21).

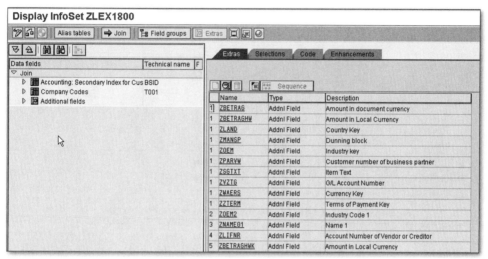

Display InfoSet ZLEX1800

Name	Type	Description
ZBETRAG	Addnl Field	Amount in document currency
ZBETRAGHW	Addnl Field	Amount in Local Currency
ZLAND	Addnl Field	Country Key
ZMANSP	Addnl Field	Dunning block
ZOEM	Addnl Field	Industry key
ZPARVW	Addnl Field	Customer number of business partner
ZSGTXT	Addnl Field	Item Text
ZVZTG	Addnl Field	G/L Account Number
ZWAERS	Addnl Field	Currency Key
ZZTERM	Addnl Field	Terms of Payment Key
ZOEM2	Addnl Field	Industry Code 1
ZNAME01	Addnl Field	Name 1
ZLIFNR	Addnl Field	Account Number of Vendor or Creditor
ZBETRAGHWK	Addnl Field	Amount in Local Currency

Figure 11.21 Table Join in the InfoSet with the Tables BSID and T001

3. The table BSID (Accounting: Secondary Index for Customers) displays all open items for the customers. Position your cursor on the EXTRAS tab, and choose ▢ (CREATE).

Additional field for the customer country

Figure 11.22 Additional Field for the Customer Country

Code for the
"Customer
Country"
additional field

4. When defining the additional field for the country, refer to an existing data field in the ABAP Dictionary. For the format definition with the LIKE reference KNA1-COUNTRY1 for the additional field ZCOUNTRY, create the field COUNTRY1 from the table KNA1 (Customers: General Data). Position your cursor on the additional field, and choose 📋 (CODE FOR EXTRA). The system then displays an editor screen in which you can enter ABAP code (see Figure 11.23).

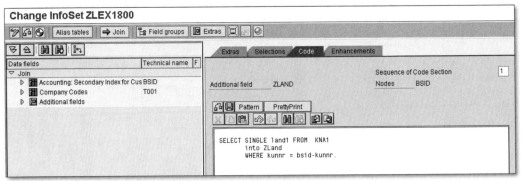

Figure 11.23 SELECT SINGLE for the Additional Field ZCOUNTRY

5. The InfoSet makes its selection from the table BSID (Accounting: Secondary Index for Customers). For the field BSID-KUNNR (Customer Number), now select the country for the customer from the table KNA1 (Customer: General Data).

```
SELECT SINGLE country1 FROM kna1
       INTO zcountry
       WHERE kunnr = bsid-kunnr.
```

When you use the SELECT SINGLE command, the system does not read the entire table KNA1. If the customer number is found in the table KNA1 (Customer: General Data), the selection ends. In contrast to the ABAP command SELECT–ENDSELECT, it is not necessary to read additional data records in the table KNA1. If only one data record is required in an additional field, the SELECT SINGLE command is more efficient than the SELECT-ENDSELECT command.

In many cases, you can use the IF or SELECT command to fill additional fields in the InfoSet. Sometimes, however, it is necessary to summarize the content of two fields in one field or to transfer only part of the content to a field.

11.3.5   Other Helpful ABAP Commands

You can use the usual arithmetic operations +, −, *, and / to assign content to an additional field. If you want to display the absolute or percentage variance in a field, this is very easy to do. For example, you can determine the price per unit in an additional field by dividing the billing document total by the billing document quantity:

```
zprnet = vbrp-kzwi2 / vbrp-fkimg.
```

Other helpful ABAP statements are listed in Table 11.4.

Command	Meaning	Explanation
cut	field1 = field2+3(5)	As of the third character, the field content is read with five characters.
DIV	field3 = field1 DIV field2	The integer resulting from a division is determined.
MOD	field3 = field1 MOD field2	The amount remaining after an integer division is transferred to a field.
REPLACE	REPLACE xyz in field1 by abc	One character string is replaced with another character string.
CONCATENATE	CONCATENATE field1 field2 into field3	The field content of several fields can be summarized in one field.
SPLIT SEPARATED BY	SPLIT field3 into field1 field2 SEPARATED BY blank.	The field content of one field is transferred to several individual fields.

Table 11.4 Important ABAP Commands

For selections, you define the additional fields and the code in the additional fields in the same way.

11.4 Using Your Own Code in the InfoSet

Events in the
ABAP program

For additional fields and selections, the query gives you the option to define your own code. You can also define your own code in an InfoSet. You can therefore execute the additional code in an InfoSet for a particular program event. An ABAP program has a lifecycle that passes through specific events in a fixed sequence.

When you call the program, the data is initialized; that is, you can enter start values in the selection fields after you have called the program. After the program initialization event, the Start-of-Selection event is activated as the next program event. The Start-of-Selection event occurs before the data selection starts.

You also access your own code by switching from the FIELD GROUPS display to the EXTRAS display. Now switch to the CODE tab. The system displays an editor screen in which you can insert ABAP code (see Figure 11.24).

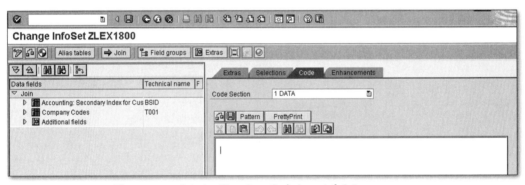

Figure 11.24 Entering Your Own Code in an InfoSet

The event is displayed in the CODE SECTION field. The code defined for the relevant event is valid until the next event. You can switch to the following code sections:

▶ 1 DATA
You define tables, variables, and data types (data declaration) in this part of the code section.

▶ **12 INITIALIZATION**

When the initialization event occurs, the parameters and selection criteria are preassigned default values.

▶ **2 START-OF-SELECTION**

The `Start-of-Selection` event occurs after the selection screen has been called. In this part of the program code, you can, for example, check the values that have been entered.

▶ **6 END-OF-SELECTION** (before the list)

This event occurs after you have entered the selection criteria but before the list is output.

▶ **7 END-OF-SELECTION** (after the list)

When this event occurs, programming is complete, and the list has been output.

▶ **8 TOP-OF-PAGE**

In this part of the code, you can use the ABAP List output format to output individual page headers.

Thanks to the flexible code sections, you have almost all of the options available in a normal ABAP program. You can also define your own code in your InfoSet. Note that your code must be called for the correct event.

11.5 Summary

To achieve the best analysis, it helps to have a basic knowledge of the ABAP Dictionary. You can display structures and tables in the ABAP Dictionary. Individual fields are displayed for the structures and tables. A data element and business description are defined for each field. You can enter a domain in the data element itself. The domain describes the technical attributes of a field (e.g., data type, output length, and number of decimal places).

InfoSets and therefore query analyses are highly valuable because of their flexibility in terms of displaying information. You can add tables from all applications to an InfoSet. You can enhance the InfoSet with additional fields, additional tables, selections, and your own code. To insert ABAP code, you can insert sample code for the relevant ABAP command into your InfoSet.

In real-life scenarios, it is often enough to assign content to a field (depending on the other field content). Here, the IF statement is a very simple way to query a condition. If you want to add up the values for an amount or quantity field in an additional field, you can use the SELECT-ENDSELECT loop for this purpose. If you want to select only one individual data record in an additional field, you can use the SELECT SINGLE command.

Displaying data in an ABAP list or in the ALV layout is extremely user friendly and functional. You can also display the data in an Excel interface within the SAP system. In this chapter, you will learn about the functions available to you as a result of integrating Excel into the SAP system.

12 Integration with Microsoft Excel

For many years now, SAP and Microsoft have worked together to integrate Microsoft Office and SAP products. Duet software is one such collaboration between these two organizations. Microsoft Excel can also be integrated into query analysis. For example, data in SAP planning screens can be entered in an SAP screen or an Excel screen. Report Painter reports can also be viewed in an Excel interface.

You can also use the Excel interface in the area of query reporting. Through the use of the Data Browser, you can display data in an Excel interface. Alternatively, you can use SAP List Viewer to call a list in Excel. Consequently, extensive Excel functions are available to you in the context of query analysis.

In this chapter, we will introduce you to the Excel interface, which is displayed when you call the Data Browser. Finally, we will explain the Excel integration (Excel Inplace) functions available to you when SAP List Viewer is used as an output format. In addition, we will show you how to integrate Excel into other query output formats.

12.1 Data Browser

To work with Excel and the Data Browser, follow these steps: Excel Inplace

1. Log on to the SAP system, or return to the SAP Easy Access menu. Use Transaction N or Transaction SE16N to call the Data Browser.

2. In the Data Browser, display the table BSID (Accounting: Secondary Index for Customers). Choose ⊞◢ (DISPLAY) to switch to the data display view.

3. Select the EXCEL INPLACE view, as shown in Figure 12.1.

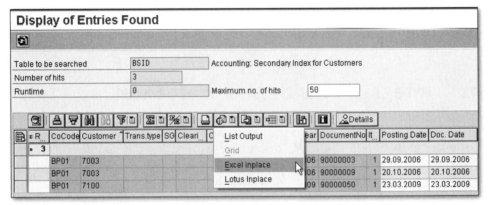

Figure 12.1 Switching from the Grid Display to the Excel Inplace Display in the Data Browser

Excel functions

Excel Inplace is used to display the data in an Excel interface within the SAP system. Almost all known Excel functions are available to you. However, the Excel Print Preview 🔍 is not available. As a result, this button is grayed out in the toolbar. If you want to work exclusively in Excel, you can choose 🖫 (SAVE AS), or you can press the F12 key to store the displayed data in a file. In addition to the Excel functions, you can continue to use the familiar SAP functions for filtering, sorting, and totaling (see Figure 12.2).

SAP Signature Design

The data display is based on settings made in SAP Signature Design. SAP expanded the SAP GUI display with a view to standardizing the visual representation of the SAP NetWeaver BW and SAP ERP interfaces. You will recognize the Signature display by its slightly indented screen components. In addition, small selection boxes ◢ are displayed to the right of the SAP buttons. To change the display, follow these steps:

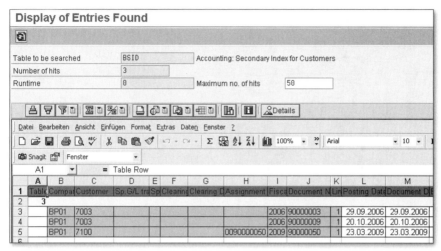

Figure 12.2 Using Excel Inplace to Display SAP Data Within the SAP System

1. Choose the following menu path in Windows: START • CONTROL PANEL (see Figure 12.3).

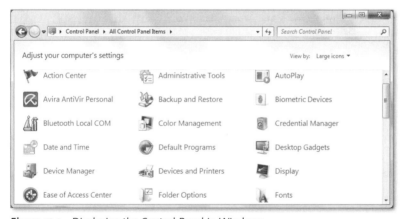

Figure 12.3 Displaying the Control Panel in Windows

2. A new icon called SAP GUI CONFIGURATION is displayed in the Control Panel. Here, you can choose from the CLASSIC DESIGN, ENJOY DESIGN, and SAP SIGNATURE DESIGN.

3. Double-click the GUI button, and choose the option USE SAP SIGNATURE DESIGN (see Figure 12.4).

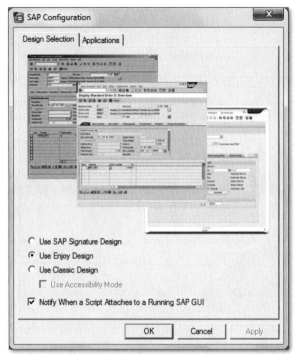

Figure 12.4 Selecting the SAP Signature Design in the Windows Control Panel

In the next section, you will use SAP List Viewer to display the data stored in the table BSID (Accounting: Secondary Index for Customers).

12.2 Excel Inplace in SAP List Viewer

To use Excel Inplace in SAP List Viewer, follow these steps:

1. Call Transaction SQ01 (SAP Query).

2. Select the query ZLEX1800 (OPEN ITEM LIST) in the user group ZLEX, or create a new query based on the table BSID. After you have called the data in SAP List Viewer, the system displays the screen shown in Figure 12.5.

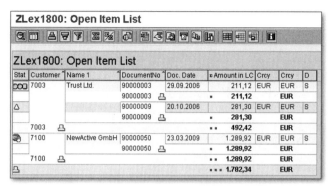

Figure 12.5 Displaying Statistical Data in SAP List Viewer

3. The statistical data displayed in SAP List Viewer can now also be dis-   Excel interface in
   played in the Excel interface. Choose (MICROSOFT EXCEL), or press   SAP List Viewer
   the key combination ⌈Ctrl⌉ + ⌈Shift⌉ + ⌈F7⌉ to display the screen
   shown in Figure 12.6.

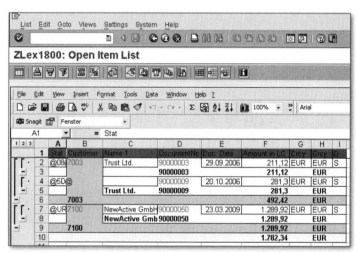

Figure 12.6 Excel Display in SAP List Viewer

4. To return to the SAP interface, choose the menu path VIEWS • SAP   Summation levels
   LIST VIEWER. To the left of the table, you see summarization options
   ⊟ from the Excel options. Depending on the number of summation
   levels, numbers 1 to n are displayed via the summarization options. If
   you click the number 1, the data in summarization level 1 is displayed
   (see Figure 12.7).

1 2 3		A	B	C	D	E	F	G	H	I
	1	Stat	Customer	Name 1	DocumentNo	Doc. Date	Amount in LC	Crcy	Crcy	D
✦	6		7003				492,42		EUR	
✦	9		7100				1.289,92		EUR	
	10						1.782,34		EUR	
	11									

Figure 12.7 SAP Data Display in Excel Summarization Level 1

Excel graphic   As is the case in the SAP interface, you can also call an SAP business graphic in the Excel interface:

1. Select the relevant data cells (e.g., several customers) and one key figure column. In our example, we selected customers 7100 and 7003 and the respective percentages.

2. Choose the SAP button 📊 to obtain a graphical display.

3. In the Excel interface, even more user-friendly Excel graphics options are available. Select the relevant data again, choose the Excel menu option INSERT, and select the diagram you require. An Excel graphic is now displayed within the SAP system (see Figure 12.8).

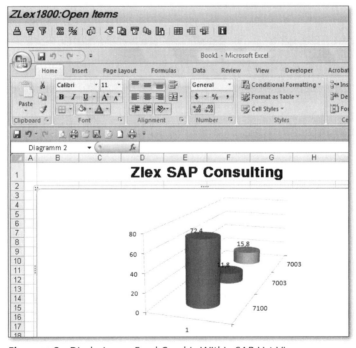

Figure 12.8 Displaying an Excel Graphic Within SAP List Viewer

You can now graphically format your data basis with relative ease. However, if you use fixed headers and formats, we recommend that you save these formats in a template. For example, follow these steps:

Excel worksheets

1. Insert a new Excel worksheet into your Excel folder.

2. Insert a header into your new Excel worksheet, as shown in Figure 12.8.

3. Select an Excel diagram.

4. For your data basis, you should refer to the RAWDATA tab. This tab is located to the right of the FORMAT, HEADER, PIVOT, and SUB1 – SUB10 tabs.

5. After you have applied all the necessary formats, save the Excel worksheet.

6. Choose ▦ (CHANGE LAYOUT), or press `Ctrl` + `F8`, and select the VIEW tab (see Figure 12.9).

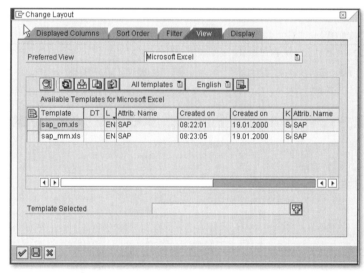

Figure 12.9 Template Management in the SAP Layout Display

7. Choose DOCUMENT VIA BDS (Business Document Service), and Windows Explorer opens.

Excel template

8. Select the file that you saved previously. The Excel file is now available in your own formats under template management. You can now

save the new template as a standard template for your data display. In future data selections, your data will be immediately displayed with your formats and a graphic.

9. If you require the data in a Word file, choose 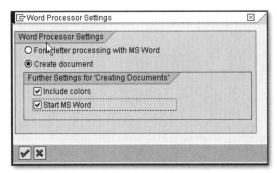 (WORD PROCESSOR), or press `Ctrl` + `Shift` + `F8` The dialog box shown in Figure 12.10 opens.

Figure 12.10 Exporting SAP Data to a Microsoft Word Document

SAP Word integration

10. You can now use the data for form letter processing. In our example, Windows Explorer is displayed with the command SAVE AS. Select a file path, and name the file. The data is then transferred from the SAP system to Microsoft Word (see Figure 12.11).

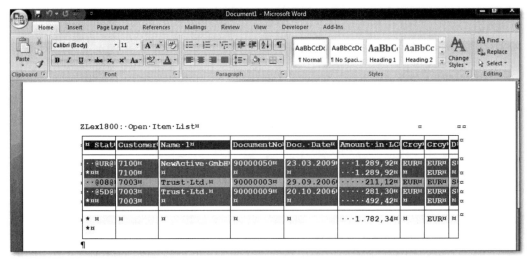

Figure 12.11 Microsoft Word Document with Data from the SAP System

The option to integrate Microsoft Office is also available for other query output formats.

12.3 Microsoft Excel Integration for Other Query Output Formats

You can call your analysis directly in the word processing or spreadsheet output format. For the word processing output format, the data is displayed in a Word document. Choose SPREADSHEET as the output format, and then select the PIVOT TABLE option in the EXPORT LIST OBJECT TO XXL window (see Figure 12.12).

Output format: spreadsheet

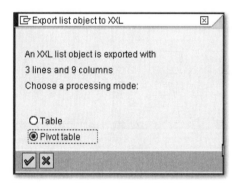

Figure 12.12 Selecting "Pivot Table" Processing in the Spreadsheet Output Format

After you have confirmed your entries, the system displays a dialog box with the Excel selection. Then confirm this selection to obtain the Excel pivot function within the SAP system (see Figure 12.13).

Pivot function

If you want to use the data further, save the data display as a file. The ABAP List output format contains numerous options for using Office Integration. Several export buttons are available in the toolbar (see Figure 12.14).

ABAP list

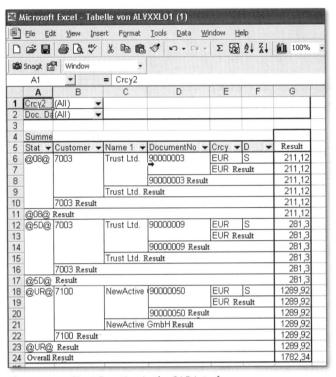

Figure 12.13 Pivot Function in the SAP Interface

Figure 12.14 Toolbar in SAP ABAP List

Microsoft Office Integration in SAP ABAP List

You can choose 🛠 ALV (SAP LIST VIEWER) or press Ctrl + Shift + F8 to switch to the Excel display within the SAP system. You can choose 📷 (FILE STORAGE) or press the F9 key to save the data in one of the following transfer formats: binary (BIN), ASCII (ASC), ASCII with a column tabulator (DAT), ASCII with an IBM code page (IBM), dBASE (DBF), or in the spreadsheet format (WK1). For an ABAP list, you can then choose 📊 (SPREADSHEET) or press the F7 key to call the pivot function. In real-life situations, the HTML data format is used for presentations or used by management. You can call this format under the following menu path: SYSTEM • LIST • SAVE • LOCAL FILE (see Figure 12.15).

Figure 12.15 Saving SAP Data in HTML Format

The HTML format is often very visually pleasing. In particular, the report   **HTML format**
is automatically displayed in color (see Figure 12.16).

	Stat	Customer	Name 1	DocumentNo	Doc. Date	Amount in LC	Crcy	Crcy	D
	@08@	7003	Trust Ltd.	90000003	29.09.2006	211,12	EUR	EUR	S
	@5D@	7003	Trust Ltd.	90000009	20.10.2006	281,30	EUR	EUR	S
*		7003				492,42		EUR	
	@UR@	7100	NewActive GmbH	90000050	23.03.2009	1.289,92	EUR	EUR	S
*		7100				1.289,92		EUR	
**						1.782,34		EUR	

17.07.2010   Dynamic List Display   1

ZLex1800: Open Item List

Figure 12.16 Displaying an SAP Report in HTML Format

Data export functions are available in almost all SAP transactions. If an   **Spool output**
export function is not available in an older transaction, print the displayed data in the spool output. The export function is then available in
the SAP spool itself via the button 🖫 (SAVE TO LOCAL FILE).

12.4 Summary

Integration of Microsoft Office into the SAP system is already at a very
advanced stage. You can already display data in an Excel interface within
the SAP system. You can use familiar Excel functions to display data not

only in the Data Browser but also in SAP List Viewer, ABAP List, and so on.

To use the Excel functions described in this chapter, you must first check the macro security settings in your version of Excel. The Excel functions may also depend on the trust relationship that exists with VBA objects.

You can also use your own template to display data within the SAP system. You can also export your data directly from the SAP system into Word. Consequently, you can call your data with an Excel graphic and with your own formats directly in the SAP system.

PART IV
Query Management

In this chapter, you will get to know which tables are used to store query objects, the user group, the InfoSet, and the query itself. You will also learn how to transfer query objects between systems and clients. Finally, you will explore the various transport options available to you.

13 Transport System

You can create query objects in the standard area or global area. The type of file storage and therefore the transport system used is different for both procedures. In the standard area, you create your query objects only in clients to which you are logged on. Furthermore, the data for the standard area is stored in different tables from those used to store data for the global area, and the data can be transferred to other clients by downloading and then uploading into the respective client. Alternatively, you can manually create transport requests for query objects in the standard area. If, on the other hand, you configure your settings in the global area of the Customizing client, the system automatically generates the transport requests for you.

Therefore, your choice of query area heavily influences the transport system used. If you are working in the global area, you should configure your settings in the Customizing client so that standard transport routes can be used. The advantage associated with automatically generated transport requests is accompanied by the disadvantage of needing more testing because you may have to generate suitable test data or perform a transport first. Even if you are working in the standard area of the production client, you need individual query objects to create query objects in the Customizing client. The reasoning behind this is that, in turn, you need the query objects in the Customizing client to create authorizations or transactions. "Body creation" can occur in the Customizing client, or you can make the query objects available by uploading them from a file.

In this chapter, you will get to know which tables are used to store query objects. We will then explain the SAP transport tool and introduce you to different transport options. At the end of the chapter, we will list the most important SAP Notes concerning the transport system.

13.1 Transport Dataset

In the database, the query objects are stored in the tables listed in Table 13.1, all of which start with AQ. The initial letters AQ refer to ABAP query, which was the former name for SAP Query before Release 4.6.

No.	Table	Description
1	AQLDB	Tables and Data (Local)
2	AQLQCAT	Query Catalog
3	AQLSCAT	Functional Area Catalog
4	AQLTQ	Texts for Queries
5	AQLTS	Texts for Functional Areas
6	AQTDB	Transport Datasets (Local)
7	AQSLDB	Tables and Data (Local, Trash)
8	AQLIDOC	Documentation for InfoSets (Key)
9	AQLQDOC	Documentation for Queries (Key)
10	AQRLASS	Role Assignment of InfoSet Query Call
11	AQGDB	Tables and Data (Global)
11	AQGIDOC	Documentation for InfoSets (Key)
12	AQGQDOC	Documentation for Queries (Key)

Table 13.1 Storing Query Objects in the Database

Database tables for query objects

The query area is always encoded in the table name. For example, the datasets for the global area are stored in the table AQ**G**DB (Tables and Data [Global]), while the datasets for the standard area are stored in the table AQ**L**DB (Tables and Data [Local]). For objects created in the global area, the contents of the table AQGDB are transferred to the transport system. If you export the query objects from the standard area, the table

AQTDB (Transport Datasets [Local]) is also filled for the manual transport system. A separate SAP Query transport tool has been developed for the transport processes.

13.2 Transport Tool

You can call the transport tool via the program RSAQR3TR, or you can choose the menu path ENVIRONMENT • TRANSPORTS in Transactions SQ03 (User Group) and SQ02 (InfoSet).

13.2.1 Transport Tool in the Standard Area

In the standard area, the transport tool offers you two ways to transport query objects. You can simply export the query objects and then import them, or you can transfer the query objects from the standard area to the global area and then use the standard SAP transport system. You can also display or delete the transport dataset (see Figure 13.1).

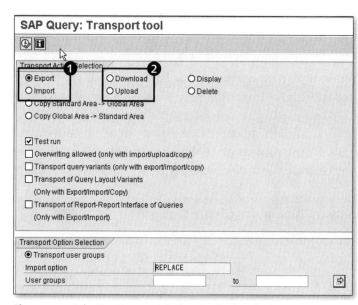

Figure 13.1 Selecting Transport Actions in the Standard Area

The query settings in the standard area are configured without a transport request and can be made in any client.

If you configure your settings in the Customizing client, you can use the EXPORT function (❶) to create a transport request for selected objects. The transport request must be released and transferred to other clients. You then import the data from a table into the target client (production client). So an additional table is used, which is filled using the EXPORT function in the target client. The table content is then transferred to other clients, and the IMPORT function is used to create query objects in the target client.

You can also transfer query objects from one client to another without the need for a transport request (❷). If you configure your query settings in a production client, for example, you can download the query objects to a local file and then upload them into another client. You can exchange queries among individual enterprises in this way.

You also have the option of using the download and upload function to transfer the real-life queries available for this book on the publisher's web site (*www.sap-press.com*) to any client in your system. However, no selection variants, layout variants, or report jumps are available to you during the download and subsequent upload process.

If you do not work in a production client but use numerous variants, the export and subsequent import process is more advantageous. If you configure your query settings in a production client, you do not necessarily have to use the variants immediately in a test client because the original settings for the production client are available via a copy of the production client in a test environment.

13.2.2 Transport Tool in the Global Query Area

The transport tool in the global query area contains a copy function, which you can use to transfer query objects from the global query area to the standard area (see Figure 13.2).

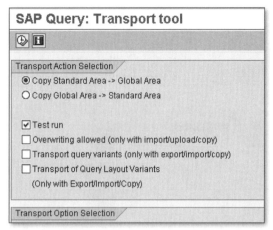

Figure 13.2 Selecting Transport Actions in the Global Query Area

As in the case for Customizing settings, automatically created transport requests are used to transfer data to other clients. You can also transfer individual objects to the standard area so that you can configure additional settings without the need for transport requests. You can also transfer query objects from the standard area to the global area.

Copying query objects into query areas

13.3   Transport Options

The transport tool offers you four ways to select data. The option of deleting a dataset after it has been successfully imported is available in the standard area only (see Figure 13.3).

The following options are available to you within the transport tool:

▶ Transport user groups (❶)

▶ Transport InfoSets (❷)

▶ Transport InfoSets and queries (❸)

▶ Transport queries (❹)

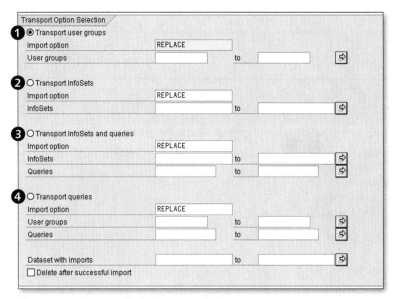

Figure 13.3 Transport Tool – Transport Options

In turn, the import options listed in Table 13.2 are available for each of these four options.

Transport Option	Replace	Merge	Group	Unassign
User groups	×	×	–	–
InfoSets	×	×	×	×
InfoSets and queries	×	×	–	–
Queries	×	–	×	–

Table 13.2 Import Options for Query Objects

Import options for the transport tool

The REPLACE function essentially overwrites the existing settings in the target client, while the MERGE import option enhances the existing settings. If, for example, only user B is assigned to the user group in the source client, other assigned users are not overwritten in the target client. Instead, they are enhanced. After the import, both user A and B are assigned to the user group in the target client. For the GROUP function, the query retains the assignment to the user group from the source client. For the UNASSIGN import option, the assignment of an InfoSet to a user group is essentially deleted.

As a result of the many functions available in the transport system, dependent objects may be missing for your query report. Therefore, in Transaction SQ02, you can perform a consistency check under the menu path GOTO • MORE FUNCTIONS • CONSISTENCY CHECK (see Figure 13.4).

Consistency check

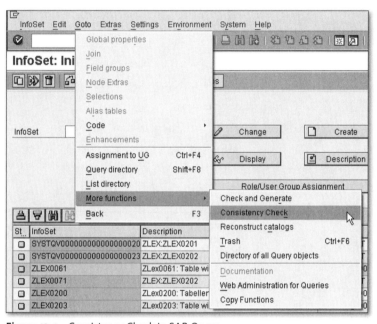

Figure 13.4 Consistency Check in SAP Query

If the consistency check fails, you can reconstruct the assignment between a query and InfoSet, for example. All assignments between the query objects are established again. This function is also available in Transaction SQ02 under the menu path GOTO • MORE FUNCTIONS • RECONSTRUCT CATALOGS.

Reconstructing
query catalogs

13.4 Additional SAP Notes

Both the standard transport system and the transport tool perform well in real-life scenarios. An overview of the most important SAP Notes with additional explanations about the transport system is provided in Table 13.3.

SAP Note	Description
119665	ABAP Query: Problems when transporting queries
127182	Transport in the global query area
127717	Creating system variants for queries
130316	ABAP Query: Transporting variants for queries
202839	SAP Query: Transporting functional areas/InfoSets
352617	SAP Query: Transport errors during download/upload
393044	SAP Query: Transporting objects in the standard area
393160	SAP Query: Using queries
412054	SAP Query: How do I transport variants?
431192	SAP Query: Transporting layout variants in the standard area
643330	ALV layout: Importing and exporting layouts

Table 13.3 SAP Notes on the Transport System

If you have created a large number of selection and layout variants, you will benefit from reading SAP Note 412054, "How do I transport variants?"

13.5 Summary

In total, there are three ways to transport query objects between clients/ systems. If you work in the global area, the query settings do not differ from other Customizing settings. Transport requests are automatically created in the background.

If you work in the standard area, you can transfer query objects by downloading them and subsequently uploading them into other clients. You can also create transport requests for query objects in the standard area. In this case, the process is as follows:

1. Export a query and all its dependent objects.

2. Release a transport request (Transaction SE09).

3. Import the transport request (Transaction STMS).

4. Import the query and all its dependent objects.

5. Consider your transport strategy in terms of a client copy or client deletion. Convert queries created using QuickViewer into queries so that you can also use the transport system for these queries.

In this chapter, you will learn how to use additional table indexes to improve the performance of your analyses. You will also learn how to create a table view for recurring data queries. Finally, you will learn how to use existing SAP system functions (function modules) for the purposes of data retrieval in your InfoSet.

14 Data Retrieval and Function Modules

Depending on your business requirements, data retrieval can be extremely challenging. You can therefore use the selection screen to restrict the data to be queried. If you frequently query a large number of data records, it may make more sense to run a separate ABAP program or to perform an analysis in SAP NetWeaver BW than to perform a query analysis. Always try to use key fields to restrict your query. If possible, check whether a secondary index would improve performance. In Section 14.1, Secondary Index, we will explain how to create a secondary index.

Frequently, certain tables are used repeatedly for the purposes of data retrieval. So, it may make sense to use a table join to link certain tables in the ABAP Dictionary with each other. On one hand, the table join makes it easier to create an InfoSet. On the other hand, the field selection in the InfoSet is clearer as a result of the fields previously determined in the ABAP Dictionary. In Section 14.2, Table View, we will use an example to demonstrate how to create a table view.

In many cases, you can access the program code in the SAP system (function modules) for the purposes of data retrieval. Therefore, you use standard function modules in your InfoSet. First, you fill a function module with preassigned field content. The function module processes the field content and then returns specific field content to you. In Section

14.3, Function Module, we will use an example to demonstrate how to use function modules.

14.1 Secondary Index

After you have entered data, it is stored in the database in the format defined in the ABAP Dictionary. The goal of data storage is to achieve fast data access. For practical use, it may make sense to display only part of the data from a table or only certain data from several tables. If you do not make a selection according to key fields, you can use an index to improve performance in some cases. The next section describes the table index.

You can look for information in primary data storage similar to how you search for information in a book via the table of contents and the keyword index.

Primary index
In the table of contents, the chapters are listed in sequence with their respective page numbers. You can therefore go directly to the page number that contains the information you require. This logic is also used for primary data storage. If you add a data record to a table, the data is stored on the basis of a primary index (key field).

Table of contents
It can take a very long time to search the table of contents if, for example, the information you require is at the end of the book or occurs in several places. If, for example, you search this book for the term *Index*, the keyword search will be much faster than the table of contents search. Therefore, it is useful to create an additional index (secondary index). In a book, it may even be helpful to create several keyword indexes. For example, this book could contain another index of tables used. However, note that each additional index requires space that must be managed. In individual cases, you must decide how many search indexes make sense for you.

An index is created with one to three characters. The primary index has   **Database utility**
the ID 0. Other indexes created in the customer namespace generally
start with the letter Y or Z.

1. Use Transaction SE11 to call the ABAP Dictionary.

2. Enter the table "TSTCT", and then display it (see Figure 14.1). A clear
   summary of all database fields and their indexes is available under
   the menu path UTILITIES • DATABASE OBJECT • DATABASE UTILITY. The
   ABAP/4 Dictionary is displayed with the name UTILITY FOR DATABASE
   TABLES. If you select the menu path EXTRAS • DATABASE OBJECT • DIS-
   PLAY, the system displays all table fields, the primary index, and all
   secondary indexes.

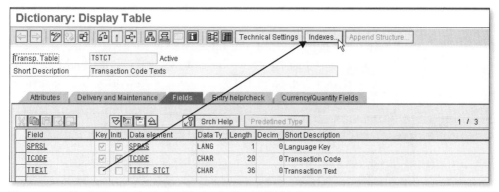

Figure 14.1   Navigating to the Index Display in the ABAP Dictionary

Two key fields are defined in the table TSTCT. The fields SPRSL (Language   **Displaying indexes**
Key) and TCODE (Transaction Code) represent the primary index. The
field TTEXT (Transaction Text) is not a key field. If you now search the
table TSTCT for transaction texts, this is more time-intensive than performing a search on the basis of the fields TCODE or TTEXT because the
field TTEXT is not indexed. Therefore, let's look at how we can create a
secondary index for the field TTEXT:

1. Click the INDEXES button in the table display. The system now displays a dialog box in which you get an overview of the secondary
   indexes (see Figure 14.2).

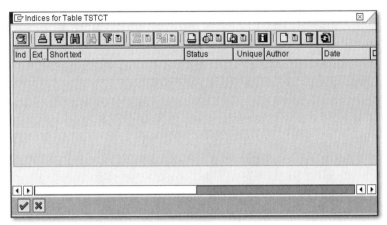

Figure 14.2 Table Indexes for the Table TSTCT

2. No secondary indexes exist for the table TSTCT. However, several indexes are delivered for the table MARA (General Material Data). You can also double-click each index to view the individual index. To create a new index, choose ☐◢ (CREATE A NEW INDEX). The system now displays the dialog box shown in Figure 14.3.

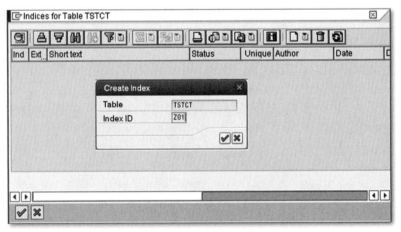

Figure 14.3 Assigning an Index ID to an Index

3. Enter "Z01" as the index ID, and choose ✔ to confirm your entry. The system now displays a screen in which you maintain the index (see Figure 14.4).

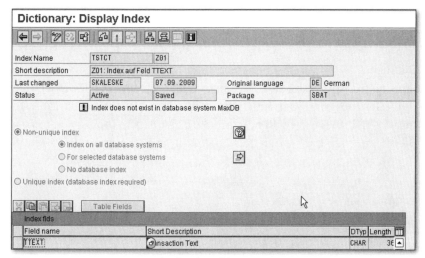

Figure 14.4 Maintaining an Index for the Table TSTCT

4. Enter a short description for your index. Select NON-UNIQUE INDEX. Maintaining
   Unique index means that there is only one data record for the index an index
   fields. The transaction text, however, can occur more than once (non-
   unique). Enter "TTEXT" (Transaction Text) as the index field, and
   choose 💾 to save your settings. To activate the index, choose 🔳
   (ACTIVATION). The following success message is now displayed on the
   lower half of the screen: "Object successfully saved and activated."

When you create an index, consider the following:

▶ Only create relevant indexes. It does not make sense to create an
  index of all fields (as is the case in this example).

▶ If you use several fields in the WHERE query, use the SELECT statement
  to structure your index in this sequence.

▶ Do not create two indexes for the same field.

14.2 Table View

You can use a table view to display a data view according to your own
criteria, irrespective of the tables defined there. You can therefore view
one or more tables in accordance with your requirements. For example,

you can use the Data Browser to display the billing document header data and item data in a table view. For billing documents, for example, you no longer have to call the tables VBRK (Billing Document: Header Data) and VBRP (Billing Document: Item Data) individually because the table view displays the data from both tables directly. In an InfoSet, you can insert not only individual tables as a data basis, but you can also insert a table view. We will now use the order data in production to take a look at the table view function. To do this, use Transaction SE11 to call the ABAP Dictionary (see Figure 14.5).

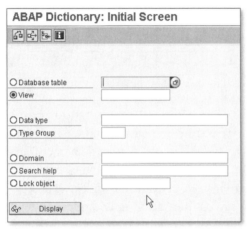

Figure 14.5   View Display in the ABAP Dictionary

Table view of header and item data

Let's assume that you want to analyze production orders. You have already found the table AFKO (Order Header Data for Production Planning and Control Orders), which contains relevant information about production orders. The table AFKO contains numerous relevant data fields, but it does not enable you to restrict your selection further according to order type or organizational unit (plant, company code, etc.). You can select the main order parameters in the Table AUFK (Order Master Data). If you now want to analyze the production orders, you need, at the very least, characteristics from the tables AFKO and AUFK. It makes sense then to obtain a view of both tables. You can now search the ABAP Dictionary for a view that accesses the table AFKO as its base table. To do this, position your cursor on the VIEW field, and call the F4 help (see Figure 14.6).

Figure 14.6 Input Help in the ABAP Dictionary

You can now search for a suitable view on the basis of your SAP applications. In our case, choose the REPOSITORY INFORMATION SYSTEM button, or press the ␣F5␣ key to call the repository information system (see Figure 14.7).

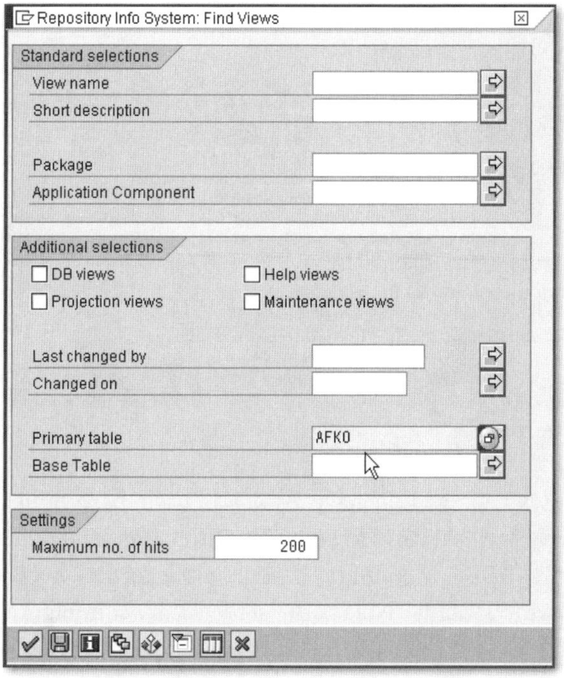

Figure 14.7 View Search Help in the ABAP Dictionary in the Repository Information System

You can now search for suitable views on the basis of the short descriptions, application components, change date, or primary table. To obtain additional selections, follow these steps:

Searching a table view

1. Choose ▣ (SELECTED SELECTIONS), or press ␣Shift␣ + ␣F8␣.

2. Enter "AFKO" as the primary table, as shown in Figure 14.7. Choose EXECUTE, or press ⌈Enter⌉ to confirm your selection. The system then displays the screen shown in Figure 14.8.

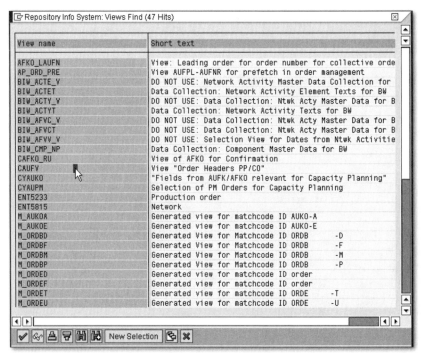

Figure 14.8 Displaying Table Views with AFKO as the Base Table

Join condition 3. The system now lists 45 views that have AFKO as their base table. Double-click the view CAUFV (View for PPS/RK Order Headers), and display the view in the ABAP Dictionary. If you switch to the TABLE/ JOIN CONDITIONS tab, the system displays the screen shown in Figure 14.9.

The database view is comparable with an InfoSet. You must enter the relevant tables, and, in the join condition, you must enter the table fields for the table link. The view CAUFV (View for PPS/RK Order Headers) links the following two tables: AFKO and AUFK. The table link is created using the table fields MANDT (Client) and AUFNR (Order Number). The fields available in the view are listed on the VIEW FIELDS tab (see Figure 14.10).

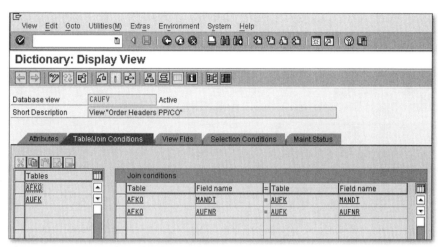

Figure 14.9 Join Condition for the Database View CAUFV

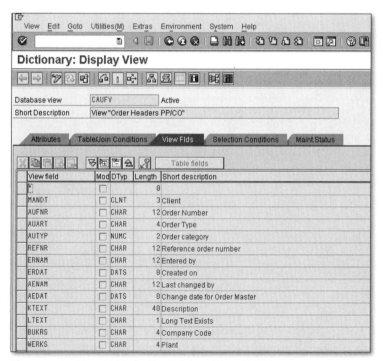

Figure 14.10 View Fields for the Database View CAUFV

4. In real life scenarios, additional information in the tables AFRU   View fields
   (Order Confirmations) and AFVV (DB Structure of the Quantities/

Dates/Values in the Operation) is frequently analyzed together. If you do not find a suitable database view, you can define a database view yourself. Use Transaction SE11 to call the ABAP Dictionary, and enter Zlex1644" in the VIEW field. Then choose the CREATE button (see Figure 14.11).

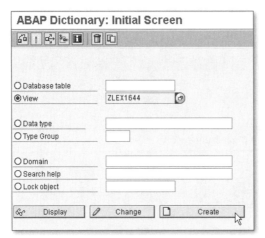

Figure 14.11 Creating the Database View Zlex1644 in the ABAP Dictionary

View type

5. The system displays the SELECT VIEW TYPE dialog screen. Here, select the DATABASE VIEW option (see Figure 14.12).

Figure 14.12 Selecting a Database View

6. On the next screen, you can now enter the tables and table link relevant for the view. In the TABLES area, enter the tables "AFRU" (Order Confirmations) and "AFVV" (DB Structure of the Quantities/Dates/Values in the Operation). Then enter the field "MANDT" (Client)

from the tables AFRU and AFVV as the first join condition (see Figure 14.13).

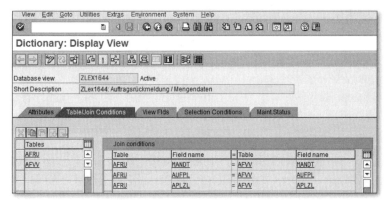

Figure 14.13 Table and Join Conditions in the Database View

7. Assign an appropriate short description to your view, and switch to the VIEW FIELDS tab. Then enter the table fields required for your query (see Figure 14.14).

View field	Table	Field	Key	Data elem.	Mod	DTyp	Length	Short description
MANDT	AFRU	MANDT	☑	MANDT	☐	CLNT	3	Client
RUECK	AFRU	RUECK	☑	CO_RUECK	☐	NUMC	10	Completion confirmation number for the operation
RMZHL	AFRU	RMZHL	☑	CO_RMZHL	☐	NUMC	8	Confirmation counter
AUFNR	AFRU	AUFNR	☐	AUFNR	☐	CHAR	12	Order Number
VORNR	AFRU	VORNR	☐	VORNR	☐	CHAR	4	Operation/Activity Number
PERNR	AFRU	PERNR	☐	CO_PERNR	☐	NUMC	8	Personnel number
ERSDA	AFRU	ERSDA	☐	RU_ERSDA	☐	DATS	8	Confirmation entry date
ERZET	AFRU	ERZET	☐	RU_ERZET	☐	TIMS	6	Confirmation entry time
STOKZ	AFRU	STOKZ	☐	CO_STOKZ	☐	CHAR	1	Indicator: Document Has Been Reversed
STLZHL	AFRU	STZHL	☐	CO_STZHL	☐	NUMC	8	Confirmation counter of cancelled confirmation
GMNGA	AFRU	GMNGA	☐	RU_GMNGA	☐	QUAN	13	Previously confirmed yield in order unit of measure
XMNGA	AFRU	XMNGA	☐	RU_XMNGA	☐	QUAN	13	Scrap to Be Confirmed
GRUND	AFRU	GRUND	☐	CO_AGRND	☐	CHAR	4	Reason for Variance
ISM02	AFRU	ISM02	☐	RU_ISMNG	☐	QUAN	13	Activity Currently to be Confirmed
ISM03	AFRU	ISM03	☐	RU_ISMNG	☐	QUAN	13	Activity Currently to be Confirmed
ISM05	AFRU	ISM05	☐	RU_ISMNG	☐	QUAN	13	Activity Currently to be Confirmed
ISM06	AFRU	ISM06	☐	RU_ISMNG	☐	QUAN	13	Activity Currently to be Confirmed
VGW02	AFVV	VGW02	☐	VGWRT	☐	QUAN	9	Standard Value

Figure 14.14 Tables Fields in the New Table View

Transport request 8. Choose 🖫 to save your entries. The system then displays a dialog box in which you can query the development package. Because this is a cross-client setting, this entry is mandatory. The development package is used to group your developments. Enter "Z001" (Customer Development Class) as a development package, or enter the development package preassigned to your enterprise.

9. On the next screen, create a workbench request. Choose ░ (ACTI-VATE), or press ⌈Ctrl⌋ + ⌈F3⌋ to activate your mini development. The table view is now available as another data retrieval option in the InfoSet.

In the next step, you will create an InfoSet with the new database view and you will use a function module to retrieve additional information.

14.3   Function Module

Standard SAP functions

As in the normal ABAP/4 program, you can also access function modules within an InfoSet. Function modules enable you to use standard SAP functions without any programming. You can populate your function module with data from your InfoSet. The data in the function module is then processed using a permanently preassigned programming logic. The function module corresponds to a subfunction within a transaction. The data processing result in the function module is then displayed as an actual result in your InfoSet.

14.3.1   Function Module for Converting the Time Dimension in the InfoSet

1. In Transaction SQ02 (InfoSet), create a new InfoSet called ZLEX1644: ORDER CONFIRMATIONS.

2. Enter your new database view Zlex1644 in the TABLE JOIN USING BASIS TABLE field or in the DIRECT READ OF TABLE field as shown in Figure 14.15.

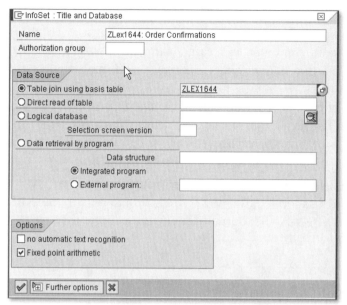

Figure 14.15 Database View as a Data Source in the InfoSet

3. You then see the database view Zlex1644 (ZLex1644: Order Confirmation/Quantity Data) on the left-hand side of your InfoSet screen. The system displays all fields contained in the tables AFRU (Order Confirmations) and AFVV (DB Structure of the Quantities/Dates/Values in the Operation) (see Figure 14.16).

Database view as a data source

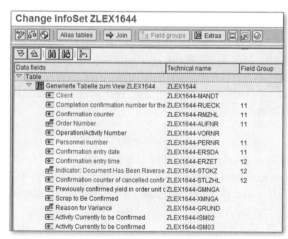

Figure 14.16 View Fields in the InfoSet

Creating an
additional field

4. You can use the database view to analyze, for example, the order number, confirmed yields, and confirmed times. You can confirm yields and times in different units of measure and time units. For example, you can confirm a time in hours, minutes, or seconds. If you want to analyze the time entered for your order, you must convert the time units of the different confirmations into one time unit. You must therefore create an additional field in which you can analyze the confirmations in minutes, irrespective of the time unit entered. Choose ⬚ Extras , and then choose 🗋 to create an additional field.

5. Name the field "MAC Actual (Machine Time)", for example. When defining the data format, use the LIKE reference to refer to the existing field ZLEX1644-ISM02 (Current Activity to Be Confirmed) (see Figure 14.17).

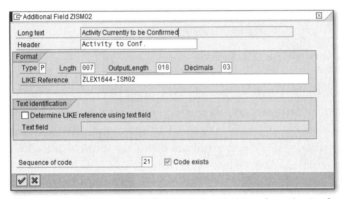

Figure 14.17 Additional Field for Displaying the Time from the Confirmation

Code for the
additional field

6. Confirm your data entry. Then position your cursor on the newly defined field, and choose 🔳 (CODE FOR EXTRA). You can now enter your own ABAP code for the purposes of data retrieval (see Figure 14.18).

7. The standard function module UNIT_CONVERSION_SIMPLE is available for the conversion of (time) units. You can use the ABAP command CALL FUNCTION to call the function module within the additional field. If you choose PATTERN, the SAP system can help you with the code. The system then displays the screen shown in Figure 14.19.

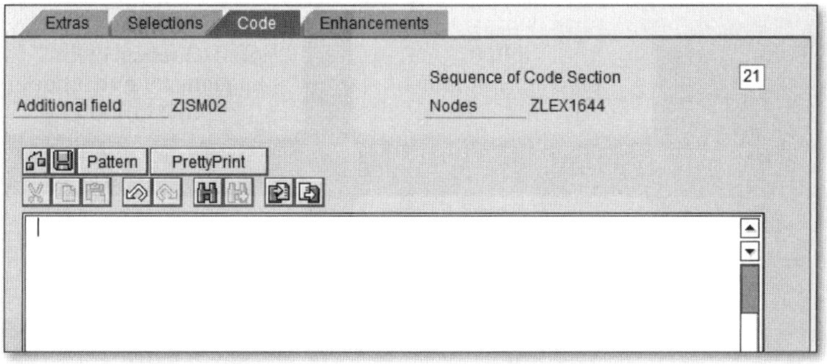

Figure 14.18 Code Screen for the Additional Field ZISM02

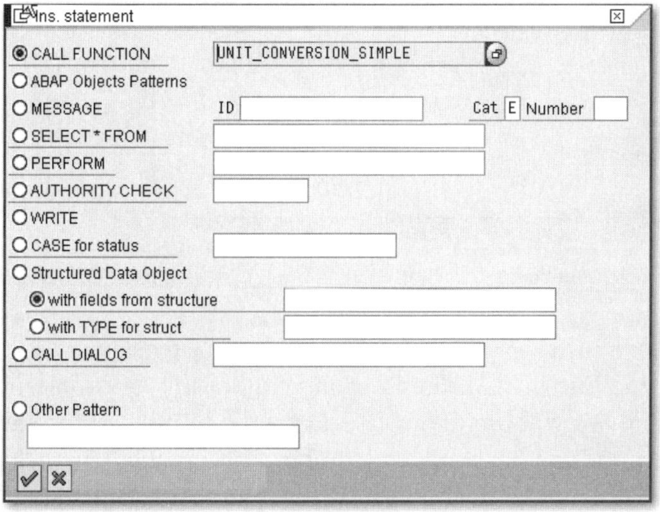

Figure 14.19 Inserting Sample Code for the Function Module UNIT_CONVERSION_ SIMPLE in an Additional Field

In real life, the main difficulty is finding the correct function module. After you have found the correct function module, the code is always consistent. You can use the CALL FUNCTION command to call the function module. The function module then contains the following three areas: EXPORTING, IMPORTING, and EXCEPTION. In the EXPORTING area, you specify the fields that you want to transfer from your InfoSet (ABAP program) to the function module. In the IMPORTING area, the result after processing the function module is transferred to your InfoSet (ABAP program). Finally, in the EXCEPTION area, the system lists the options available to you if the data access is unsuccessful (see Figure 14.20).

Structure of the function module

Figure 14.20 Sample Code for the Function Module UNIT_CONVERSION_SIMPLE

Export and import parameters of a function module

Most lines in the function module are preceded by an asterisk (*), which indicates that the line is marked as a comment, but the function will not be executed. We will use the table field ZLEX1644-ISM02 (Current Activity to Be Confirmed) to populate the function module. The field ZLEX1644-ISM02 contains the confirmed time from the table AFRU (Order Confirmations), while the field AFRU-ILE02 contains the time unit for the time entered. Enter the corresponding field ZLEX1644-ILE02 in the UNIT_IN column, and enter the issue unit in quotation marks in the UNIT_OUT field. You have now populated the function module with data content without any programming.

IMPORT parameter in the function module

In the IMPORTING area, the result after processing the function module is returned to the InfoSet. Therefore, enter the defined additional field ZISM02 in the OUTPUT line. It is important to remove the asterisk before the term IMPORTING so that the code is active. Furthermore, you must insert a period at the end of the line (Output = ZISM02.). The function module result is shown in Figure 14.21.

ZLex1644: Productivity Working area

ZLex1644: Productivity Working area

O...	S	Menge	Ziel	M...	StdVal	Activity to Conf.	Activity to Conf.	MAS %	P...	StdVal	Activity to Conf.	Activity to Conf.	PES %
1...	N	10	5	▢	86,200	45,217	40,983-	48-	▢	31,890	16,579	15,311-	48-
1...	N	33	28	▢	284,460	241,517	42,943-	15-	▢	105,237	88,556	16,681-	16-
1...	F	52	42	▢	448,240	363,800	84,440-	19-	▢	165,828	133,393	32,435-	20-
1...	F	95	0	▢	53,200		53,200-	100-	△	53,200	53,760	0,560	1
1...	F	70.127	70.127	▢	43.829,375	43.829,375			◉		8.035,385	8.035,385	100
1...	F	70.127-	70.127-	▢	43.829,375-	43.829,375-			▢		8.035,385-	8.035,385-	
1...	F	95	95	▢	59,375	59,375			◉		10,885	10,885	100
1...	F	70.127	70.127	▢	87.658,750	87.658,750			▢	7.304,896	4.382,938	2.921,958-	40-
1...	F	70.127-	70.127-	▢	87.658,750-	87.658,750-			▢	7.304,896-	4.382,938-	2.921,958	
1...	F	95	95	▢	118,750	118,750			▢	9,896	5,938	3,958-	40-
1...	N	95	116	◉	653,125	794,750	141,625	22	◉	32,656	39,738	7,082	22
1...	F	70.127	70.127	▢	43.829,375	43.829,375			◉	7.304,896	8.035,385	730,489	10
1...	F	70.127-	70.127-	▢	43.829,375-	43.829,375-			▢	7.304,896-	8.035,385-	730,489-	
1...	F	95	95	▢	59,375	59,375			◉	9,896	10,885	0,989	10

Figure 14.21 Productivity Report When Using the Function Module UNIT_CONVERSION_SIMPLE

In real life, the function module UNIT_CONVERSION_SIMPLE is used to display productivity in the production area. The report contains the following content in the relevant columns:

▶ Order: Order number.

▶ L: Indicator for the **L**ate shift (early shift and night shift).

▶ Quantity: Confirmation quantity.

▶ Target: Target quantity calculated on the basis of the confirmed time.

▶ MAS: Traffic light status for comparing the target time and actual time.

▶ MASS: Target time converted by the function module.

▶ MASI: Actual time converted by the function module

▶ MASA: Absolute variance between the target time and actual time.

▶ MAS %: Percentage variance between the target time and actual time.

When you use different time units and units of measure, you need to convert the data to display productivity. The data converted into a pre-assigned unit is stored in additional fields, thus making it possible to perform both a quantity and time comparison for each data record.

Using function modules is a simple way to populate your InfoSet with valuable information. In real-life situations, you may also want to display texts in your analysis.

14.3.2 Function Module for Displaying Texts

Displaying long texts in the Data Browser
In the SAP system, texts are stored in a special data type. Texts are stored in the tables STXH (STXD SAPscript Text File Header) and STXL (STXD SAPscript Text File Lines); in other words, the text is stored in both a header record and item record. You could now use a table join to display both tables directly. Instead, use Transaction SE16N to call the Data Browser, and enter the table "STXL".

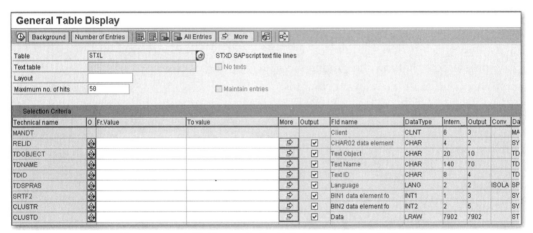

Figure 14.22 Initial Screen in the Data Browser for the Table STXL

Determining a text ID and text object
The texts are stored in a cluster field for the relevant data object. To display texts for the operations, enter "ROUTING" in the field TDOBJECT and "PLPO" in the field TEXT-ID. After you have called the data selection, the system displays the screen shown in Figure 14.23.

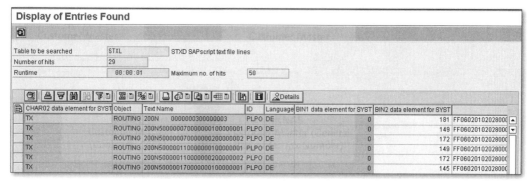

Figure 14.23 Displaying Texts from Operations

It will not help you to display texts (that contain more than one line). However, you can use a function module to display the texts in an analysis. Create an InfoSet with the tables CRHD (Work Center: Header) and PLPO (Routing: Operation). Let's assume that you want to analyze all operations for a work center. You can therefore use the work center ID (ARBID) to create a table link (see Figure 14.24) and then follow these steps:

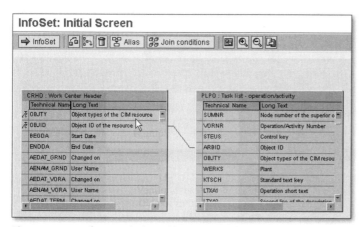

Figure 14.24 InfoSet with the Tables CRHD and PLPO

1. Switch from the FIELD GROUPS view to the EXTRAS view. On the EXTRAS tab, create an additional field for the routing texts (see Figure 14.25).

2. The additional field is used to save texts that contain more than one line. The field is of the type "character" and is defined with a length of

Sample code

500 characters. Confirm that you want to create your additional field, and then switch to the code view for the additional field.

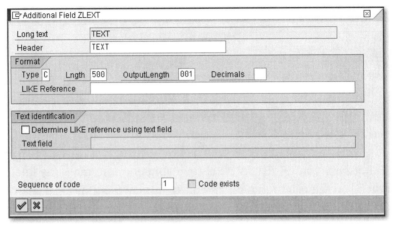

Figure 14.25 Additional Field Called "Text"

3. Choose the PATTERN button to enter the code for the function module.

4. Enter the "READ_TEXT" function module in the CALL FUNCTION field (see Figure 14.26).

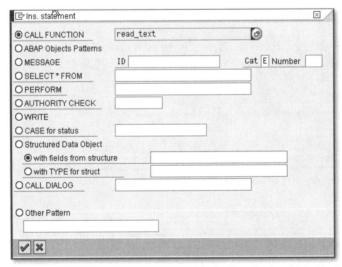

Figure 14.26 Inserting a Function Module for Text Retrieval into the Sample Code

The code for the READ_TEXT function module is now inserted into the additional field. The function module is also divided into the EXPORTING, IMPORTING, and EXCEPTION areas. In addition, the command SY-SUBRC is used to query whether the data access was successful, while the IF statement is used to determine if the data access was unsuccessful (SY-SUBRC <> 0) (see Figure 14.27).

Using the IF statement to query data access

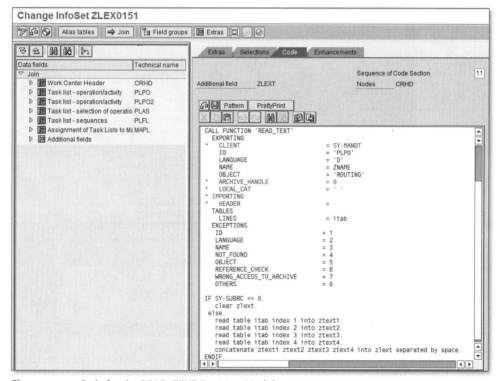

Figure 14.27 Code for the READ_TEXT Function Module

Let's take a closer look at the code for the EXPORTING and IMPORTING areas. You now need to populate the function module with content from the previous tables and then temporarily store the function module output. Your code could look like the code shown in Figure 14.28.

Exporting

```
CALL FUNCTION 'READ_TEXT'
   EXPORTING
*    CLIENT                      = SY-MANDT
     ID                          = 'PLPO'
     LANGUAGE                    = 'EN'
     NAME                        = 'ZNAME'
     OBJECT                      = 'Routing'
*    ARCHIVE_HANDLE              = 0
*    LOCAL_CAT                   = ' '
*  IMPORTING
*    HEADER                      =
   TABLES
     LINES                       = itab
```

Figure 14.28 Code for the READ_TEXT Function Module

You now need to specify the object for which you want to procure texts:

1. Use Transaction CA03 (Display Routing) to call a routing and then navigate to the order items.

2. Double-click the TEXT field to display explanatory text about the operation (see Figure 14.29).

Figure 14.29 Displaying Explanatory Text About the Operation

3. To display the internal text names, the text ID, and the text object, call the menu path GOTO • HEADER. The system then displays the screen shown in Figure 14.30.

Variable key   The text name, text ID, and text object are now displayed. The text name comprises the following information:

- ▶ MANDT (Client)
- ▶ PLTYP (Routing Type)
- ▶ PLNNR (Routing Number)

▸ PLNKN (Routing ID Number)

▸ ZAEHL (Routing Counter)

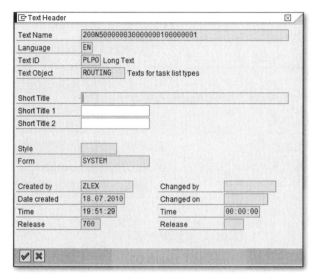

Figure 14.30 Displaying the Text Header for the Routing

4. Return to your InfoSet with this information. Then navigate to the code for your additional field. In the EXPORTING and IMPORTING areas, enter the values for the following parameters (see Figure 14.31):

▸ ID = 'PLPO'

▸ LANGUAGE = 'E'

▸ NAME = ZNAME

▸ OBJECT = 'ROUTING'

▸ LINES = ITAB

5. It is important to remove the asterisk in front of each entry so that the lines are no longer declared as comment lines. You previously used the menu path GOTO • HEADER to obtain the field values for ID and OBJECT from the application transaction. You permanently assigned an E for English to the LANGUAGE field. We will now consider the NAME and LINES objects in more detail.

Figure 14.31 Code in the Additional Field for Text Retrieval

The NAME export parameter represents a variable key whose structure differs according to the data selection. We have assigned the ZNAME variable to the NAME export parameter. We have also permanently assigned the itab entry to the LINES import parameter. Because the program does not yet know ZNAME and itab, a data declaration is still required. The type specified for the data is shown in Figure 14.32.

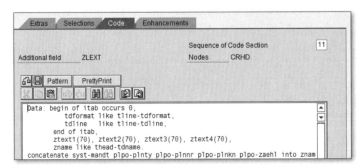

Figure 14.32 Data Declaration in the Additional Field

The ZNAME variable is declared directly in the additional field. For the declaration, we use the LIKE statement to refer to an existing field THEAD-TDNAME from the ABAP Dictionary. In the line CONCATENATE syst-mandt plpo-plnty plpo-plnnr plpo-plnkn plpo-zaehl INTO zname, we will populate the ZNAME field with data content. We will then use the fields as a basis for creating a flexible data selection. To ensure that we transfer the correct client to the ZNAME data field, we will refer to the field SYST-MANDT. The current client is always located in the field MANDT (Client) in the system toolbar. The CONCATENATE command is used to link individual table fields with each other.

CONCATENATE command

Because the operation texts in the routing contain more than one line, we require an output with multiple lines for the respective data object. We will therefore use an internal table to output the texts. The data statement and the BEGIN OF and END OF commands can be used to define the start and end of an internal table. When specifying the type for individual fields in the internal tables TDFORMAT and TDLINE, we also refer to existing fields in the ABAP Dictionary. The internal table is now defined, and the data can be transferred. To display the relevant lines in the internal tables, we defined four additional text fields called ztext1(70), ztext2(70), ztext3(70), and ztext4(70). All that remains is to transfer the content of the internal tables into the four defined text fields. Therefore, let's take a look at the code at the end of the additional field (see Figure 14.33).

The IF statement is now used to query whether the data access was successful. For example, there may not be any long text for the operation. In this case, the command CLEAR ztext. is used to clear our additional field. If the data access was successful, the first line in the internal table is now transferred to the data field ZTEXT1. Lines 2–4 in the internal table are then transferred to the data fields ZTEXT2, ZTEXT3, and ZTEXT4. Lastly, the contents of the four data fields ZTEXT1, ZTEXT2, ZTEXT3, and ZTESXT4 are transferred to our additional field ZLTEXT, separated by a blank character. In the InfoSet, the first four text lines in the long text for the routing are now available in this additional field, and the texts can now be read in the query. You can now output the text in a field. Alternatively, you can define several additional fields and output each text line in a separate additional field (see Figure 14.34).

Filling text fields

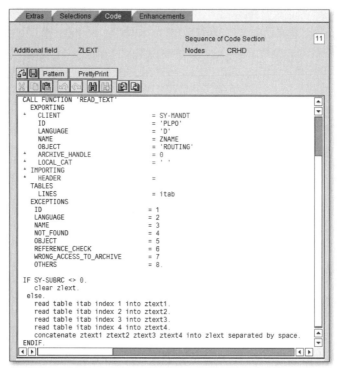

Figure 14.33 Code for Transferring the Content of an Internal Table to Additional Fields

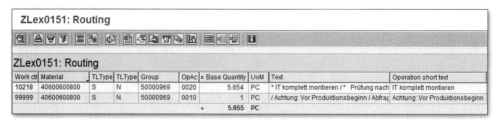

Figure 14.34 Displaying Routing Long Texts in the Query

Testing function modules

Function modules are extremely valuable in programming. Generally, the use of function modules makes it possible to retrieve data content without extensive programming. Frequently, the main difficulty with function modules is finding the correct function module. You can call Transaction SE37 (Use Function Modules) to search for function modules. Here, you can use the [F4] help to search for suitable function modules. You can also test the functions of a function module. Enter the function module "READ_TEXT" and choose ⊞ (TEST). The system then displays the following screen (see Figure 14.35).

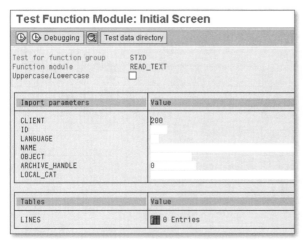

Figure 14.35 Test Option for Function Modules

You can enter import parameters here and test the effects of you entries. This test function enables you to ascertain the behavior of the function module. You can also easily identify the correct import parameters.

14.4 Summary

You can also use the extensive functions of the SAP system in query reporting. In particular, you can fine-tune your query reports in the area of data retrieval. If necessary, you can also use a secondary index to improve the performance of your selection.

Furthermore, for recurring table links, you can create predefined table links (database views) in the ABAP Dictionary. Database views can be used as a basis for your InfoSet. InfoSet maintenance is also easier because only the relevant table fields are available.

In an InfoSet, you can use function modules to implement complete SAP functions. For example, you can use a function module to convert units or to display long texts in your query analysis.

In this chapter, we will introduce you to the relevant transactions for query reporting and authorization objects. You will also learn how user groups affect authorization assignments. Finally, you will learn how to create your own transactions for calling query reports.

15   Authorizations and Transaction Creation

Advanced authorizations are required to use the extensive features in *query reporting*. If you want to use ABAP code to add additional fields to an InfoSet, you need developer authorizations and, if you want to create transactions, you need administrator authorizations. In this chapter, we list the relevant transactions for query reports. You can already restrict authorization assignment in query editing transactions. A separate transaction (SQ03) is available for managing user groups, or you can enter a separate authorization object in the InfoSet. The report call should be made as easy as possible for the user. Therefore, you can create a separate transaction for calling a query report.

15.1   Transactions in the Query Environment

When you edit queries, you use different functions because you are a report creator, developer, and/or Basis administrator, all at once. Table 15.1 lists the relevant transactions in the query environment.

Enterprise functions in query editing

Area	Transaction Code	Description
Report creator	SQ01	SAP Query: Maintain Queries
Report creator	SQVI	QuickViewer

Table 15.1 Transactions in Conjunction with Query Editing

Area	Transaction Code	Description
Report creator	SQ02	SAP Query: Maintain InfoSet
Administrator	SQ03	SAP Query: Maintain User Groups
Report creator	SQ07	SAP Query: Language Comparison
Administrator	SQ10	SAP Query: Role Administration
Developer	SE16N	General Table Display
Developer	SE11	ABAP Dictionary Maintenance
Developer	SE36	Logical Database Builder
Developer	SE85	ABAP/4 Dictionary Information System
Administrator	ST05	Performance Analysis
Administrator	PFCG	Role Maintenance
Developer	SD11	Data Modeler
Administrator	SARA	Archive Administration

Table 15.1 Transactions in Conjunction with Query Editing (Cont.)

Even without developer authorizations, you can create excellent analyses. However, your reports are only valuable when you add enterprise-specific information. You can create query reports for all application areas. Here, you can use individual ABAP code to format information from several user departments.

Flexible data access versus data sensitivity

Flexible data formatting is contrary to data sensitivity. With the relevant knowledge, you can easily export all table information from the system. If you know the correct tables, you can call data relating to the payment run, purchase prices, sales prices, and all master data, for example, in just a few minutes. It is therefore interesting to know how to restrict data access in the SAP system.

15.2 User Groups

User groups can be used to restrict authorizations. For query objects, for example, you can assign change only or display only authorizations to a user group (see Figure 15.1).

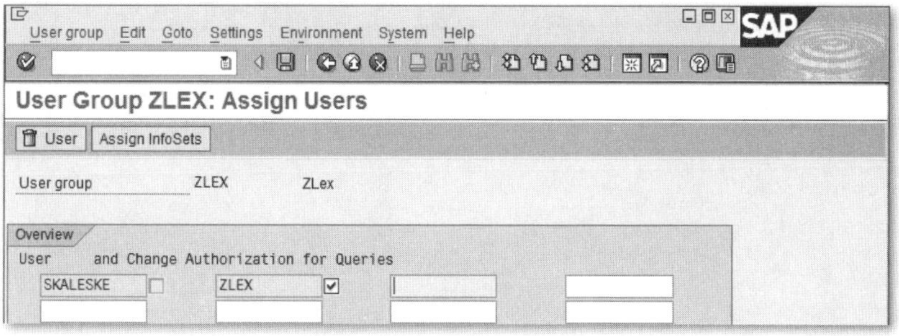

Figure 15.1 User Group with Change Authorization

The user group represents a grouping of users. The user grouping distinguishes between users with change authorization and users without change authorization. If you assign a user to a user group with change authorization, the user can execute and change all query objects. If you assign a user to a user group without change authorization, the user can only execute queries.

You can therefore use the user group to restrict access to data because data can only be accessed when an InfoSet is assigned to a user group. For each user group, you can only create queries for InfoSets that have a corresponding assignment to a user group. However, the use of a user group to assign authorizations is not yet flexible or restrictive enough. You can therefore use special authorization objects.

Assigning an InfoSet and query to a user group

15.3 Authorization Objects

During authorization assignment, user roles are assigned to users. A user role comprises all necessary transactions. Additional access restrictions for authorization objects are also defined there (see Figure 15.2).

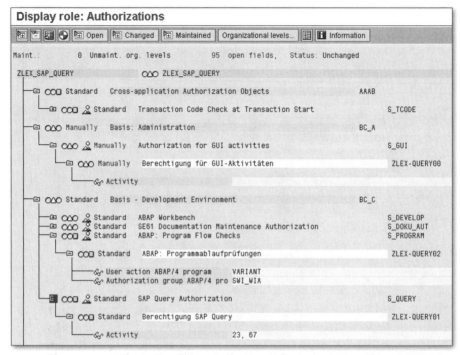

Figure 15.2 Authorization Objects in the User Role: Authorization Object S_TCODE

The authorization concept is a multilevel concept. In the first step, the authorization object S_TCODE is used to check the authorization for calling the transaction. If the authorization check is successful, the system checks access at the table and program level. When you call a program, the system checks, among other things, the authorization objects listed in Table 15.2.

Area	Object	Description
AAAB	S_TCODE	Transaction code
BC_A	S_GUI	GUI activities
BC_A	S_TABU_DIS	Table maintenance
BC_C	S_DEVELOP	ABAP Workbench
BC_C	S_PROGRAM	ABAP program flow checks
BC_C	S_QUERY	SAP Query authorization

Table 15.2 Authorization Objects and Descriptions

You can activate activities for individual authorization objects. The authorization object S_GUI refers to the SAP List Viewer display. You can activate four different activities for this authorization object:

Authorization object S_GUI

- ▶ 02 Change

- ▶ 04 Print, messages processed

- ▶ 60 Import

- ▶ 61 Export

To export the data from SAP List Viewer, you must activate activity 61 (Export) for the authorization object S_GUI. However, authorization assignment is not yet productive just by restricting the corresponding activity. For a particular user, you may want to permit a data export in some transactions and exclude it from others. Consequently, authorization groups are used to restrict data access further.

Data export

15.3.1 Authorization Groups

The SAP tables are assigned to approximately 550 different authorization groups. In Transaction SE54 (Generate Table Maintenance Dialog: Table/ View Initial Screen), you can display the tables assigned to the authorization groups. Consequently, you can use the authorization group and, in turn, the authorization object S_TABU_DIS within the authorization group to restrict access to the tables.

Authorization object S_TABU_DIS

The authorization groups are not always permanently preassigned in the SAP system. For example, you can assign any name to the authorization groups for the authorization objects S_DEVELOP and S_PROGRAM. Furthermore, you can assign a freely defined authorization group to an InfoSet when you create it. You can also enter the authorization group in the InfoSet retroactively. To do this, call Transaction SQ02 (Maintain InfoSet) in change mode. Then choose the menu path GOTO • GLOBAL PROPERTIES to access the screen shown in Figure 15.3.

Authorization objects S_ DEVELOP and S_PROGRAM

When executing an SAP query, the system checks, as part of its authorization check, whether the authorization group from the InfoSet is assigned to the user via the user roles for the authorization object S_PROGRAM, which is assigned to his user master. The authorization object S_DEVELOP controls whether additional ABAP code can be defined in an

Authorization check for authorization group

InfoSet. In the query environment, in particular, you can use the authorization object S_QUERY to further restrict data access.

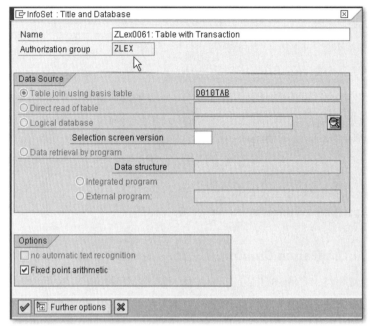

Figure 15.3 Assigning an Authorization Group Within an InfoSet

15.3.2 Authorization Object S_QUERY

You can maintain the following activities for the authorization object S_QUERY:

▶ 02 — Change

▶ 23 — Maintain

▶ 67 — Translate

You can use the activity for the authorization object S_QUERY and the user group from Transaction SQ03 to control query authorizations as shown in Table 15.3.

No.	S_QUERY Activity	User Group	Query Authorization
1	–	–	No authorizations in the query environment
2	–	×	User: Execute queries
3	02	×	Report creator: Change queries in a user group
4	23	–/×	Administrator: Create InfoSets and user groups, and perform a transport
5	02, 23	–/×	Super user: Complete query authorization
6	67	–/×	Translator: Perform a language comparison

Table 15.3 Authorizations for Authorization Object S_QUERY and User Group

In real-life situations, separate transactions are used to make created query reports available to users.

15.4 Integrating Query Transactions into a User Role

In the Customizing client, you can create transactions for your queries. The user can call his report by entering the relevant transaction in the command field or selecting it in the user menu. Transactions are created in user role maintenance. Call Transaction PFCG (Role Maintenance) (see Figure 15.4), and then follow these steps:

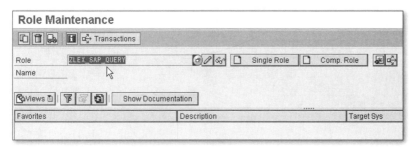

Figure 15.4 Creating User Roles for a Query Call

1. For your role, enter a name in the ROLE field, and choose the SINGLE ROLE button. The system now displays a CHANGE ROLES screen (see Figure 15.5).

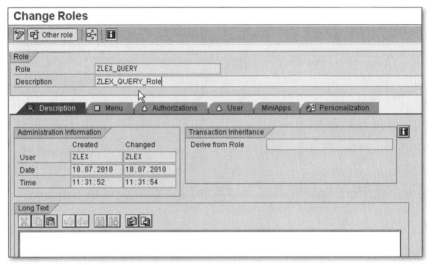

Figure 15.5 Describing a User Role

2. For your role, enter a description in the DESCRIPTION field. Then choose 🖫 to save your role.

3. Select the MENU tab to display the screen shown in Figure 15.6.

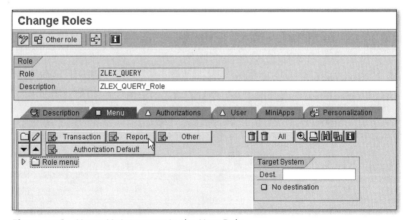

Figure 15.6 Menu Maintenance in the User Role

4. To insert a report, choose the REPORT button. The system now displays a window in which you can create the transaction code (see Figure 15.7).

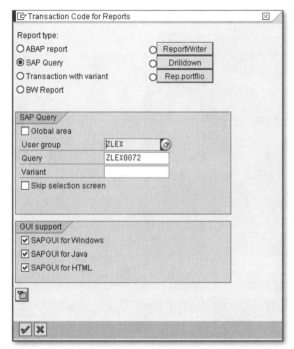

Figure 15.7 Creating a Transaction Code for a Report

5. Select SAP QUERY as the report type. Enter the USER GROUP and QUERY in the SAP QUERY screen area.

Assigning an individual transaction

6. To assign an individual transaction, choose ▣ (DISPLAY OTHER OPTIONS). Two additional input options are now displayed in the current window (see Figure 15.8).

7. Deselect the GENERATE AUTOMATICALLY option. You can now enter your transaction code in the TRANSACTION CODE field. Choose ☑ to confirm your entry. You will then be asked to enter a development package (see Figure 15.9).

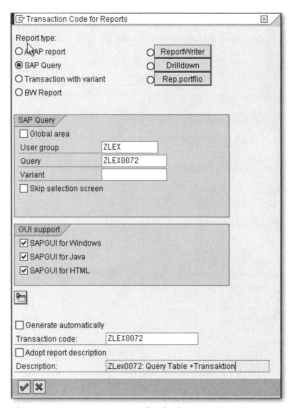

Figure 15.8 Assigning an Individual Transaction Name

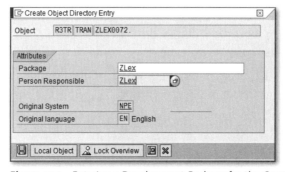

Figure 15.9 Entering a Development Package for the Creation of a Transaction Code

Development
package

Development packages are used to structure the developments performed in the system. The creation of a transaction not only represents a development, but it is also a cross-client setting. For the transport system, settings for the complete system are stored in Workbench requests (see Figure 15.10).

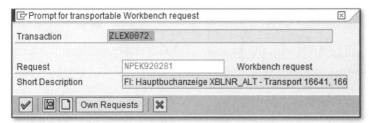

Figure 15.10 Creating a Workbench Request

8. Select an existing Workbench request, or choose ☐ (CREATE REQUEST) to create a new Workbench request. You will then return to the role maintenance overview (see Figure 15.11).

Workbench request

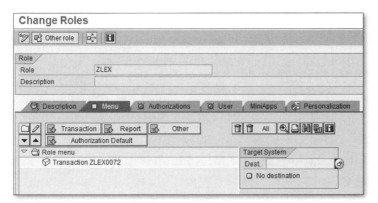

Figure 15.11 Role with a New Transaction

In this example, we created ZLEX0072 (Transactions with Tables), which you can now call directly with the transaction code.

15.5   Notes on Authorization Assignment

The SAP authorization concept offers you extensive options for restricting authorizations. You can restrict the most important authorization objects from administration and development, or you can set them to inactive. SAP is continually improving the authorization concept. This is reflected by the large number of SAP Notes that deal with the query authorizations topic.

15.5.1 SAP Notes

The following SAP Notes, in particular, contain additional explanations about authorizations in the query environment (see Table 15.4).

SAP Note	Description
24578	SAP Query: Authorizations
76545	ABAP/4 Query: Authorization for functional areas
89744	ABAP Query: Authorization for table accesses
173118	SAP Query: Authorization check at runtime
185286	SAP Query: Lock query download
324348	SAP Query: Special characters in names
339230	SAP Query: Message AQ 316 during construction

Table 15.4 SAP Notes for Assigning Authorizations in the Query Environment

SAP Note 24578 (SAP Query: Authorizations) describes the effects between the user group and the authorization object S_QUERY.

15.5.2 Authorization Objects for Administrators and Developers

Authorization objects from the administration area

In real-life situations, the following authorization objects from the administration area are set to inactive for query creators and developers:

▶ S_CTS_ADMI Administration functions in the Change & Transport System

▶ S_ASAPIA Implementation Assistant

▶ S_USER_AGR Authorization system: role check

▶ S_USER_AUT User master maintenance: authorizations

▶ S_USER_GRP User master maintenance: user groups

▶ S_USER_PRO User master maintenance: authorization profile

▶ S_USER_SAS User master maintenance: system-specific assignments

You can use the authorization objects S_TABU_DIS, S_PROGRAM and S_DEVELOP to restrict developer authorizations.

15.6   Summary

In real-life situations, query creators, developers, and Basis administrators interact well with each other. Frequently, reports are created by Controlling key users or another group of users who have extensive authorizations.

As a result of other SAP tasks, the authorization for query creators is already very extensive, irrespective of query reporting. In medium-sized enterprises, in particular, additional written agreements accommodate the issue of data sensitivity. The use of separate transactions for data queries is popular among users.

PART V
Real-Life Examples

In this chapter, you will learn which business processes and master data you can analyze. We will also explain which procedures are frequently applied in real life, which tables are queried, and which additional information is provided.

16   Real-Life Examples

You can use SAP Query to create analyses that are not available in the standard system. You can create reports without having extensive knowledge of ABAP. Furthermore, the analyses can cover all enterprise areas, and individual data records or summarized data are displayed in the form of statistics or ranked lists.

How do other enterprises create reports? Which tables or table relationships are queried repeatedly, and how is additional information added to the InfoSets? In this chapter, you will learn how enterprises create reports. We will provide three examples to show you which three query reports from the areas of Sales and Distribution (SD), Production Planning (PP), and Financial Accounting (FI) are frequently used.

16.1   Procedure When Creating Reports

There are various different procedures for report creation, depending on the situation. On one hand, for example, a particular group of users wants to analyze operational data. This involves analyses that will support daily tasks or will improve the quality of the master data. On the other hand, query analyses support the area of corporate management. Next, we will show you a typical procedure for report creation.

16.1.1   Brainstorming Workshop

Creation of a query report is not a technical process. Here, it is more about reconciling the reporting requirement with the user and agreeing

Specifying the reporting requirement

on the report content. A report is only fit for use when it is approved by the report recipient and the users who enter the data. For corporate management reports, it is especially important that management and the group of users responsible for the report content interact with each other.

Who is involved in defining a report?

To achieve a good level of reporting, you should involve three groups of users in your workshop:

▶ The *user department*, which is responsible for the data content and can use the data basis to improve processes

▶ *Management*, which holds discussions on the data content and, if necessary, makes decisions based on the reports

▶ An external *consultant* who assesses the reporting requirements, the technical feasibility, and, in particular, the requirements in terms of industry validity

The proposed reports are enriched with the input from the user department. Particular information can be entered in other data fields. Alternatively, it may be useful to pay particular attention to certain processes tailored to the enterprise.

Management is also central to successful reporting because management frequently brings numerous other approaches that will be evaluated further in shared dialogue. The goal should be for both management and the user department to use reporting. Therefore, it is very important to have a better understanding of the data basis and the origin of the data.

Using and adjusting industry templates

Enterprise-specific reporting is developed in most projects. The input of an external consultant is very valuable as a starting point for this type of reporting because many enterprises in the same industry often encounter similar issues. The feasibility of implementing the necessary reporting requirement can be assessed by an external consultant who, as a result of his experience, can bring a report template to the enterprise.

Documentation for the reporting requirement

Report names must be unique for all groups of users. A report overview that displays the results of the workshop should be created. A visual representation of the reports is particularly suitable here. For example, the results of a brainstorming workshop can be displayed graphically in a "report house" (see Figure 16.1).

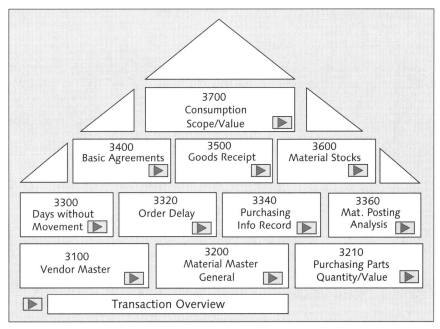

Figure 16.1 Report House for Materials Management

The report house serves several purposes. It is a clear representation of existing reports or reports to be implemented, and transactions can be assigned on the basis of the numbering used in the reports. You can also use the report house to display the status of the project. Various report boxes can be color-coded on the basis of their status. If this graphical display is created in PowerPoint, it is possible to interactively branch to a screenshot of the respective detailed report. Now we need to specify individual reports as described next.

16.1.2 Specifying Reports

In most projects, the speed at which reports are created is extremely important. Usually the enterprise wants to model its reports on reports

First-hand reports as a means to accelerating a project

by other customers in the industry. Consequently, the consultant introduces reports from past projects and actively incorporates these into the current project. A specific reporting requirement is then defined jointly in an enterprise-specific form (see Figure 16.2).

ZLex1800: Open Item Lists	
Reporting Requirement of User Department	
General Report Description	
Business Description	All open items of the customer (open item lists) are presented by various sales and distribution characteristics.
Background	Reducing the open item list directly impacts the company's success. You either require less credits or liquid funds are invested.
Standard Reports	FBL5N – Customers: Line Items
Explanation of which Functionality is Missing in the Standard Report	In the standard transaction, various sales analysis characteristics are not displayed. Additionally, the standard transaction doesn't provide the comprehensive functionality as the display of number of days in arrears.
Structure Selection	
Selection Variant	
Layout Variants	

Figure 16.2 Sample Extract of a Form Used to Define a Report

A concrete report definition simplifies report creation. It is important to strike a balance between adequate documentation and fast implementation of the reporting requirement.

Report output and processes are interdependent

Frequently, as a result of the required reporting information and the actual reporting specification, other issues arise in terms of the processes that are performed. Usually, the defined data is checked or an alternative scenario is considered for analysis. In the next section, we will take a detailed look at some real-life reports.

16.2 Sales Evaluation

Most customers want flexible sales evaluation. Here, the SAP Logistics Information System (LIS) or SAP NetWeaver BW are considered to be reporting tools. In real life, however, LIS frequently lacks transparency. It is therefore very difficult to achieve coordination among SD, FI, and CO user departments. Often, a certain amount of technical knowledge is required for report creation. Traffic light icons or a number of characteristics also limit the analysis options. Even though the SAP NetWeaver BW system is highly flexible, advanced knowledge of the system is required. Furthermore, the SAP NetWeaver BW system is often only updated at certain time intervals. SAP Query, on the other hand, makes it possible to query online data and drill down directly to the data record. In the case of operational sales evaluations, in particular, SAP Query is, for the reasons just outlined, the best solution for midsize enterprises.

In the next step, we will take a look at the table basis for our analysis. The following tables are the data basis for the sales evaluation:

Tables for sales evaluation

- ▶ VBRK — Billing Document: Header Data
- ▶ VBRP — Billing Document: Item Data
- ▶ VBPA — Sales Document: Partner
- ▶ KNA1 — General Data in Customer Master

We will assume that we are using SD tables for a sales evaluation. In real life, a sales evaluation is also performed in relation to values from FI or Profitability Analysis (CO-PA). We recommend an FI sales evaluation if sales are not generated by an SD billing document but directly by an FI document. If you want a sales volume analysis that considers differentiated margins, CO-PA can be a suitable data basis here. Figure 16.3 shows the relevant table fields for the sales evaluation.

The two tables VBRK (Billing Document: Header Data) and VBRP (Billing Document: Item Data) can be used as the basis for analyzing the most important characteristics. In real life, however, it is not so easy. The first issue arises when you consider the characteristic FKART (Billing Document Type), namely whether all billing document types are relevant for

Knowledge of table fields

analysis. You must answer this question in the context of the situation. All billing document types may be relevant for a process analysis.

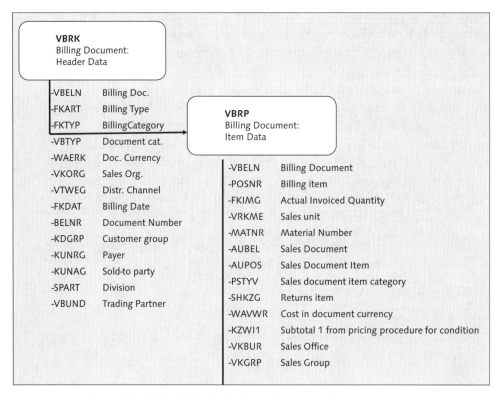

Figure 16.3 Table Fields for Creating a Sales Evaluation

The number of billing documents, for example, is frequently analyzed to consider the average value per billing document across a time axis. A decline in sales does not necessarily result in a lower volume in terms of sales order processing because the number of billing documents may remain unchanged when sales decline. This fact may point to risk concerns of the customer and can therefore be the necessary motivation for a bonus system when scale values are exceeded.

Let's take a look at a real-life analysis in relation to billing document types across a time axis (see Figure 16.4).

ZLex2301: sales of inventory

ZLex2301: sales of inventory

BillT	customer id	customer name	Σ	total amount	Curr.
F2	7003	Trust Ltd.	▪	740,90	EUR
F2	7003		▪ ▪	740,90	EUR
F2			▪ ▪ ▪	740,90	EUR
FAS	7100	NewActive GmbH	▪	21.239,60-	EUR
FAS	7100		▪ ▪	21.239,60-	EUR
FAS			▪ ▪ ▪	21.239,60-	EUR
FAZ	7100	NewActive GmbH	▪	21.239,60	EUR
FAZ	7100		▪ ▪	21.239,60	EUR
FAZ			▪ ▪ ▪	21.239,60	EUR
L2	7100	NewActive GmbH	▪	12.092,00	EUR
L2	7100		▪ ▪	12.092,00	EUR
L2			▪ ▪ ▪	12.092,00	EUR
S1	7003	Trust Ltd.	▪	219,40-	EUR
S1	7003		▪ ▪	219,40-	EUR
S1	7100	NewActive GmbH	▪	5.490,00-	EUR
S1	7100		▪ ▪	5.490,00-	EUR
S1			▪ ▪ ▪	5.709,40-	EUR
			▪ ▪ ▪ ▪	7.123,50	EUR

Figure 16.4 Number of Billing Documents Created According to Billing Document Type, Year, Customer, and Month

You can display your billing document types in Transaction VOFA (Billing Document Types) or in the table TVFK (Billing Document Types). Not all billing documents are relevant for the sales evaluation. It is therefore helpful to use another characteristic, namely the sales document category (VBTYP). The sales document category is used to classify billing document types. The sales document category groups billing document types as follows:

Billing document types

- ▶ M   Invoice
- ▶ N   Cancellations, debit memos
- ▶ O   Credit memos
- ▶ P   Debit memos
- ▶ S   Cancellations, credit memos
- ▶ U   Pro forma invoice

Pro forma invoice In real life, pro forma invoices are created for customs processing. In the standard system, these are the billing document types F5 (Pro Forma for Orders) and F8 (Pro Forma for Deliveries). The sales documents for these billing document types must be excluded from the sales evaluation. You can use the sales document category U, for example, to exclude pro forma invoices.

Display with the appropriate positive/ negative sign You may now be thinking that you can obtain the total sales simply by adding up all the billing document values. However, this is not the case because, in the SAP system, all key figures are saved with a positive sign irrespective of the actual business transaction. You would therefore also add cancellation billing documents and credit memo billing documents to the sales value. The respective billing document type or sales document category could be used to display the values with the appropriate positive/negative sign. However, this is not necessary because there is a much easier solution: The field VBRP-SHKZG (Returns Item) is provided. Depending on the characteristic SHKZG, the correct value can now be determined in an additional field (see Figure 16.5).

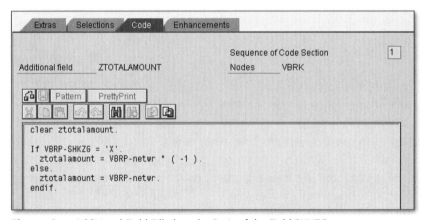

Figure 16.5 Additional Field Filled on the Basis of the Field SHKZG

Value credit memos and value debit memos The logic for the characteristic SHKZG also applies to other key figures. In an additional field, for example, the billing quantity must also be displayed with the appropriate positive/negative sign whereby the quantity display is somewhat more difficult to consider. In real life, there may be quantity credit memos and value credit memos. The evaluation should only take account of the quantity in a quantity credit memo. If you have a value credit memo or value debit memo, this document type does not affect the quantity. In the analysis, you must only adjust the revenue, not the values themselves. You should not adjust the costs either. SAP has provided a standard function in CO-PA for this purpose. If billing documents are displayed in CO-PA immediately (record type F), you can use Transaction KE4W (Reset Quantity and Value Fields) to fill the value fields on the basis of the billing document type.

In real life, it is common practice to read even more information from the customer master. In the case of a country analysis, the field COUNTRY1 (Country) from the table KNA1 (Customer: General Data), for example, is added to the analysis as an additional field. If the country analysis is based on partner roles that are not yet available in the analysis, these are first read into an additional field in the table VBPA. The ship-to party, for example, can be provided in an additional field via the code shown in Figure 16.6.

Additional fields from the customer master

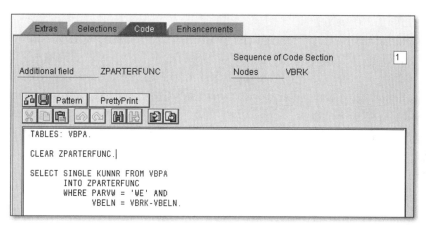

```
TABLES: VBPA.

CLEAR ZPARTERFUNC.|

SELECT SINGLE KUNNR FROM VBPA
       INTO ZPARTERFUNC
       WHERE PARVW = 'WE' AND
             VBELN = VBRK-VBELN.
```

Figure 16.6 Importing a Ship-To Party into an Additional Field

The SELECT SINGLE command is very useful for adding additional information from the customer master or material master to an analysis through the use of additional fields, or for adding data to sales documents. In real life, not only the country, for example, but also the industry is read from the customer master. The purchase order number, order reason,

SELECT SINGLE command

and product hierarchy, for example, are taken from the sales document and added to the analysis (see Figure 16.7).

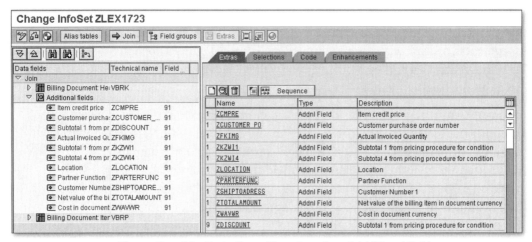

Figure 16.7 Sales Evaluation with an Overview of Additional Fields

Additional fields
with subfield
content

Both the IF statement and the SELECT SINGLE command can be used to add valuable information to the analysis. In some cases, however, it is especially helpful to make partial content from one particular field available in another field. For example, the month and year are taken from a date field and made available in other analysis fields. If, for example, the CO account assignment has a particular systematic approach, it makes sense to make the partial content of one field available in another additional field.

In the following example, an enterprise location is encoded in the third and fourth characters of a profit center. Furthermore, a two-character additional field called LOCATION has been defined. In the code for the additional field, the third and fourth characters in the PROFIT CENTER field in the billing document item are transferred to the additional field (see Figure 16.8).

Field assignment

The command VBRP-PRCTR+3(2) means that the field content as of the third character is transferred with 2 characters to the LOCATION field. In this view, the field is displayed with 8 characters, and the location is coded in the first 2 characters. The field is stored in the database with 10 characters, so that the field content as of the third character must actually be transferred to the additional field. Furthermore, the current arithmetic operations are executed in separate additional fields.

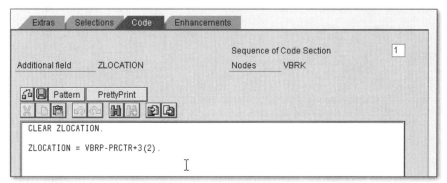

Figure 16.8 "Location" Additional Field Filled with Partial Content from the "Profit Center" Field

The contribution margin, for example, is determined in an additional field as follows:

Arithmetic operations in additional fields

```
Contribution margin = VBRP-NETWR—VBRP-WAVWR
```

The goods clearing value is subtracted from the net value for the billing document item. Value credit memos and value debit memos must be considered here. If there are different sales quantities, the price for 100 units is standardized in another additional field:

```
Price per 100 = VBRP-KZWI2 / VBRP-FKIMG
```

Subtotal 2 from pricing is divided by the invoiced quantity, while subtotals 1–6 from pricing are updated in separate fields (KZWI1–KZWI6) in the table VBRP (Billing Document Items). Subtotal 2 is frequently used because the net price (in other words, the gross price minus the discount) is saved here.

Subtotals

Depending on the contribution margin, a traffic light icon may also be inserted into the report. This traffic light icon can even be used as a query criterion (MARGIN: TRAFFIC LIGHT) on the selection screen (see Figure 16.9).

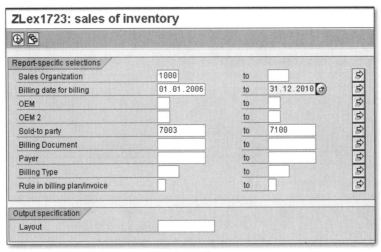

Figure 16.9 Selection Screen for Sales Evaluation

Selection variant in sales evaluation

The selection variant and its associated parameters are called via a transaction that was created for a report in the same way. Because the report is called ZLex1723, the transaction is also called ZLex1723. Certain fields are hidden in the selection variant (e.g., the selection of pro forma billing documents or statistical billing document items). The selection screen also enables you to make a selection using customer grouping characteristics. In this example, a two-level OEM hierarchy is used to group the customer masters. Preselections can be made in accordance with the OEM and/or OEM2 characteristics so that the list output can be structured in a specific way (see Figure 16.10).

Grouping in the list output

In the list output itself, you now have the flexibility to create any grouping. You can also filter according to specific characteristics. Furthermore, you can show or hide individual columns. If there is a large number of data records, you can format the data as statistics and ranked lists in addition to summarizing this data in SAP List Viewer. These functions are replicated in a similar form for other analyses.

ZLex1723: sales of inventory

ZLex1723: sales of inventory

BillT	custome...	customer name	invoice #		Σ	total amount	Curr.
F2	7003	Trust Ltd.	90000001			200,00	EUR
F2	7003	Trust Ltd.	90000003			182,00	EUR
F2	7003	Trust Ltd.	90000004			19,40	EUR
F2	7003	Trust Ltd.	90000005			9,70	EUR
F2	7003	Trust Ltd.	90000006			19,40	EUR
F2	7003	Trust Ltd.	90000008			24,25	EUR
F2	7003	Trust Ltd.	90000009			242,50	EUR
F2	7003	Trust Ltd.	90000010			43,65	EUR
F2	7003	Trust Ltd.				740,90	EUR
F2	7003					740,90	EUR
F2						740,90	EUR
FAS	7100	NewActive GmbH	90000046			21.239,60-	EUR
FAS	7100	NewActive GmbH				21.239,60-	EUR
FAS	7100					21.239,60-	EUR
FAS						21.239,60-	EUR
FAZ	7100	NewActive GmbH	90000000			21.239,60	EUR
FAZ	7100	NewActive GmbH				21.239,60	EUR
FAZ	7100					21.239,60	EUR
FAZ						21.239,60	EUR
L2	7100	NewActive GmbH	90000047			5.490,00	EUR
L2	7100	NewActive GmbH	90000048			5.490,00	EUR
L2	7100	NewActive GmbH	90000050			1.112,00	EUR
L2	7100	NewActive GmbH				12.092,00	EUR
L2	7100					12.092,00	EUR
L2						12.092,00	EUR

Figure 16.10 List Output for a Sales Evaluation Displayed with the Appropriate Positive/Negative Sign

16.3 Financial Accounting Analysis — Open Items

In real life, it is extremely useful to format open items (open item list) for SD. For this purpose, the standard system provides Transaction FBL5N (Customers: Line Items) in FI. Thanks to its many useful functions, FI employees tend to use Transaction FBL5N extensively (see Figure 16.11).

ZLex1820: Open Item											

ZLex1820: Open Item

Customer	Dun	Delay	Doc. Type	DocumentNo	Doc. Date	Periode	Year	Σ Net	Crcy	Amount in LC
1111555	0	1417	DR	18488008	01.08.2006	08	2006	0	CHF	2.320,00
1111555	0	1417	DR	18488009	01.08.2006	08	2006	0	CHF	4.500,00
1575757	1	1308	DR	18999998	18.11.2006	12	2006	30	EUR	100,00
1575757	0	1265	DR	18999999	31.12.2006	12	2006	0	EUR	100,00
7003	0	1388	RV	90000003	29.09.2006	09	2006	0	EUR	211,12
7003	0	1367	RV	90000009	20.10.2006	10	2006	0	EUR	281,30
7100	0	177	RV	90000050	23.03.2009	03	2009	60	EUR	1.289,92
1787878	0	1332	DZ	1400000000	24.11.2006	11	2006	0	EUR	72,16
1787878	0	1332	DZ	1400000001	24.11.2006	11	2006	0	EUR	100,00
1334455	0	1329	DZ	1400000010	27.11.2006	11	2006	0	EUR	300,00
1334455	0	1329	DZ	1400000011	27.11.2006	11	2006	0	EUR	300,00
1334455	0	1329	DZ	1400000012	27.11.2006	11	2006	0	EUR	350,00-
1334455	0	1329	DZ	1400000014	27.11.2006	11	2006	0	EUR	250,00-

Figure 16.11   Displaying Customer Line Items

Open item list with SD characteristics

The transaction has now been created for FI employees. However, this transaction contains a lot of information for employees from other user departments (SD), which may not be required or may demand some knowledge of accounting. You can therefore hide superfluous field content and save this view in a separate variant for your colleagues. However, additional information is frequently required. The customer name and other SD characteristics are displayed in the SAP list variant. Consequently, the selection screen differs greatly from the query in the FI open item list (see Figure 16.12).

Selection with SD characteristics

The sales employee can select SD data according to known criteria. For example, the employee can make a selection based on customers for whom he is entered as the employee responsible. Furthermore, a country-specific selection is possible or a selection based on customer records that have an order block. However, let's take another look at the data basis for our analysis (see Figure 16.13).

ZLex1820: Open Item List

Report-specific selections					
Company Code	ZLEX		to		⇨
Industry key			to		⇨
Industry Code 1			to		⇨
Debitor			to		⇨
Payment Block Key			to		⇨
Land			to		⇨
Open at key date			to		⇨

Output specification	
Layout	/ZLEX

Figure 16.12 Selection Screen for Querying the Open Item List

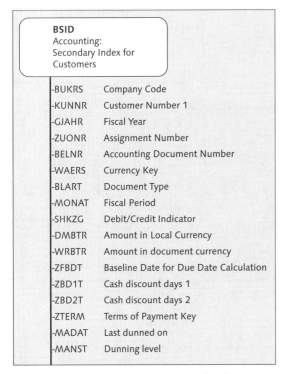

BSID
Accounting:
Secondary Index for
Customers

-BUKRS	Company Code
-KUNNR	Customer Number 1
-GJAHR	Fiscal Year
-ZUONR	Assignment Number
-BELNR	Accounting Document Number
-WAERS	Currency Key
-BLART	Document Type
-MONAT	Fiscal Period
-SHKZG	Debit/Credit Indicator
-DMBTR	Amount in Local Currency
-WRBTR	Amount in document currency
-ZFBDT	Baseline Date for Due Date Calculation
-ZBD1T	Cash discount days 1
-ZBD2T	Cash discount days 2
-ZTERM	Terms of Payment Key
-MADAT	Last dunned on
-MANST	Dunning level

Figure 16.13 Table BSID as a Data Basis for the Open Item List

Table basis for
open items

Once again, a crucial point in the analysis is the use of the correct table(s). FI contains the table BSEG (Document Segment: Accounting), which is a cluster table. This table could be used as a data basis by reading it directly in the InfoSet. For a data query, however, the database selects all document items. The table BSID, on the other hand, contains only current open items, which considerably improves performance. In contrast to the standard SAP transaction, you can use this table only to query the current status. This is usually sufficient in real life because the purpose of a query is to inform the user about current open item lists, not the entire history.

Displaying key
figures with
the appropriate
positive/
negative sign

When you evaluate open items, issues similar to those when you evaluate sales revenue arise. In other words, the amounts are not stored in the database with the appropriate positive/negative sign. Information regarding whether the amount is a debit or credit item and therefore a positive or negative amount is contained in the characteristic BSID-SHKZG (Debit/Credit Indicator). Consequently, the amount must be displayed in an additional field that is filled on the basis of the characteristic SHKZG (see Figure 16.14).

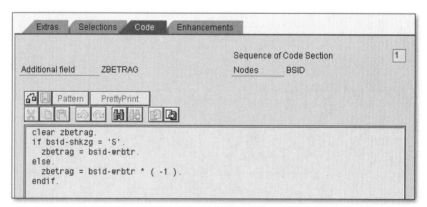

Figure 16.14 ZAMOUNT Additional Field Filled on the Basis of the Characteristic SHKZG

IF query for the
debit/credit
indicator

The IF statement is now used to query whether the content of the characteristic SHKZG is an S. In this case, the amount in the field BSID-WRBTR is transferred to the additional field ZAMOUNT. If the content of the characteristic SHKZG is not an S, but an H, the amount in the field ZAMOUNT is displayed with a negative sign. Field information from the customer master must now be provided in additional fields as additional information. For example, the SELECT SINGLE command is used to transfer the country of the customer to an additional field (see Figure 16.15).

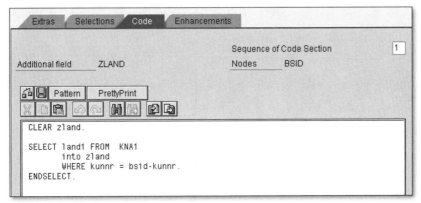

Figure 16.15 Selecting and Transferring the Country of the Customer to an Additional Field

The SELECT SINGLE command makes it relatively easy to read additional information from the table KNA1 (Customers: General Data). If you also want to display the name of the customer in the analysis, you must define another additional field and select and transfer the NAME1 field (instead of the LAND1 name) to the additional field. To select the dunning level, you must use the table KNB5 (Customer Master: Dunning Data). Until now, the selection was very easy because the company code is unique. Consequently, the company code in the table BSID always had a 1-to-1 relationship with the respective company code in the table KNA1, KNB1, or KNB5. If you select SD characteristics, there may be several sales areas for one company code. The sales area comprises the following organizational units: sales organization, distribution channel, and division. The sales data for the customer master is stored in the table KNVV (Customer Master: Sales Data).

Selecting other customer characteristics

There is now a "logic" among the sales organization, distribution channel, and division in the table KNVV and the company code in the table BSID. Mostly, there is a logical derivation between the sales organization and the company code. You must now consider which distribution channel and division you want to use for the data selection. If there is only one distribution channel and division, the code may correspond to the code shown in Figure 16.16.

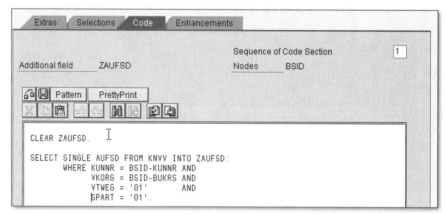

Figure 16.16 Transferring SD Characteristics to Additional Fields

Calculating the due date for net payment

The due date for an open item depends on the start of the payment period and the term of payment; in other words, the due date for net payment is not contained in the table BSID (Accounting: Secondary Index for Customers). The start of the payment period is based on the posting date, entry date, document date, or a manually entered date, while the term of payment can occur in three stages (e.g., 14 days 3%, 30 days 2%, and finally 60 days net). Alternatively, the term of payment can be just 14 days net. Consequently, the required information is stored in different fields because, depending on the term of payment, the first part only, the first and second part, or all three parts of the term of payment may be filled (see Figure 16.17).

Determining the days in arrears

For your evaluation, it is important (irrespective of the term of payment) to determine a specific date (e.g., the due date for net payment). To perform this query, you can use an IF command to compare date of required payment 3 (net period) with date of required payment 2. Date of required payment 2 is then compared with date of required payment 1. Because the payment days are entered in the fields "Date of required payment 1" (ZBD1T), "Date of required payment 2" (ZBD2T), and "Net period" (ZBD3T) in ascending order, this query is successful. To obtain the number of days in arrears, you must subtract the due date for net payment from the current date. When the program is running, the current date is available in the SY-DATE field. This gives rise to the program logic shown in Figure 16.18, which is used to determine the number of days in arrears.

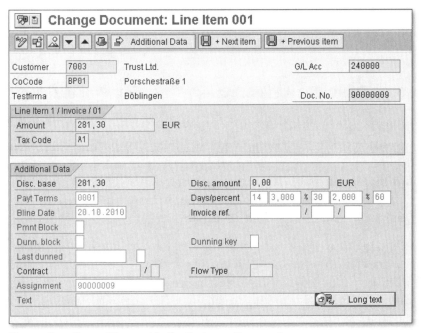

Figure 16.17 Term of Payment in the Customer Document

As a result of the days in arrears, you can now insert a traffic light status into the report, so that the critical open items can be identified immediately. You can also use statistics to create a receivables grid with individual criteria. It is therefore important to know the correct tables and processes so that you can create an excellent analysis in the standard system that corresponds to the needs of your enterprise.

Days in arrears as a basis for the traffic light status and receivables grid

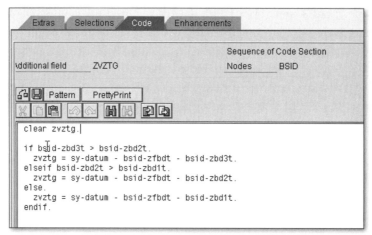

Figure 16.18 Determining the Number of Days in Arrears for an Open Item

16.4 Production Planning — Measuring Productivity

In Production Planning (PP), it is interesting to compare the standard times defined in the routing with the times that have actually been confirmed. The starting point for the analysis is table AFRU (Order Confirmations). The information stored in table AFVV (DB Structure of the Quantities/Dates/Values in the Operation) must also be queried. The resulting data basis is provided in Figure 16.19.

Table view as a basis for analyzing productivity

In the previous two examples in this chapter, the InfoSet was created using a table join (sales evaluation) and by reading an individual table (open items) directly. In this example, we will use a table view as the data basis. In the area of PP, you often need to query linked fields from the tables AFRU and AFVV. For this reason, a database view has already been created in the ABAP Dictionary.

The link between the two tables has been created using the fields AUFPL (Routing Number for Operations in Order) and APLZL (General Counter for the Order) (see Figure 16.20).

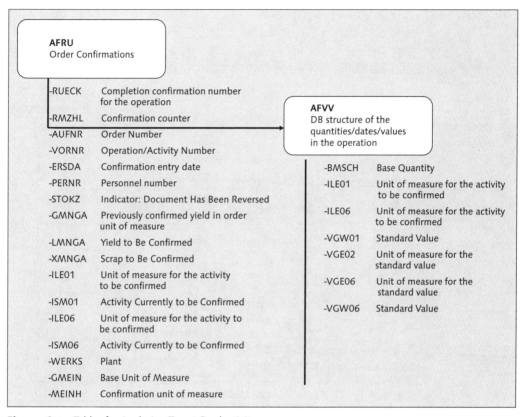

Figure 16.19 Tables for Analyzing Target Productivity

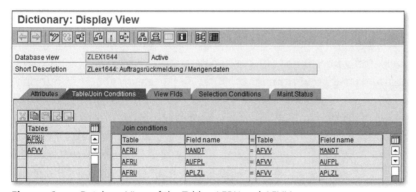

Figure 16.20 Database View of the Tables AFRU and AFVV

View fields After the tables have been linked with each other, the most important fields are inserted as view fields. Even though you can assign an individual name to the view field, we recommend that you use the original names in tables AFRU and AFVV (see Figure 16.21).

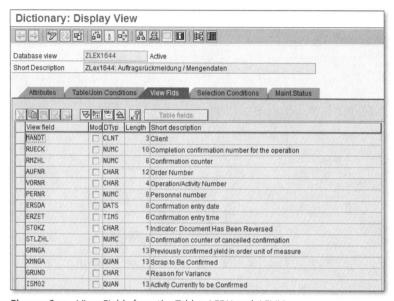

View field	Mod	DTyp	Length	Short description
MANDT	☐	CLNT	3	Client
RUECK	☐	NUMC	10	Completion confirmation number for the operation
RMZHL	☐	NUMC	8	Confirmation counter
AUFNR	☐	CHAR	12	Order Number
VORNR	☐	CHAR	4	Operation/Activity Number
PERNR	☐	NUMC	8	Personnel number
ERSDA	☐	DATS	8	Confirmation entry date
ERZET	☐	TIMS	6	Confirmation entry time
STOKZ	☐	CHAR	1	Indicator: Document Has Been Reversed
STLZHL	☐	NUMC	8	Confirmation counter of cancelled confirmation
GMNGA	☐	QUAN	13	Previously confirmed yield in order unit of measure
XMNGA	☐	QUAN	13	Scrap to Be Confirmed
GRUND	☐	CHAR	4	Reason for Variance
ISM02	☐	QUAN	13	Activity Currently to be Confirmed

Figure 16.21 View Fields from the Tables AFRU and AFVV

Table view in the InfoSet The InfoSet, as a data basis, is primarily based on the database view in the tables AFRU and AFVV. When you create an InfoSet, the database view is entered as a data source in the DIRECT READ OF TABLE area (see Figure 16.22).

Work center information In real life, you require not only the data in the tables AFRU and AFVV but also data content from other tables. In particular, you need information about the confirmation work center and the material number of the production order so that you can summarize the data. You can also use the work center to determine the cost center and its name as well as a cost center hierarchy for summarized analyses. The EXTRAS tab displayed in the InfoSet shows that the table that contains information about the work center (CRHD) has been added as an additional table. Many other additional fields have been added to the InfoSet (see Figure 16.23).

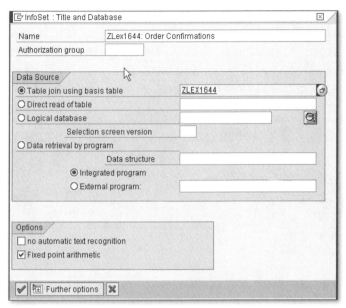

Figure 16.22 Data Basis for Productivity in Production

	Name	Type	Description	
1	CRHD	Additional tab.	Work Center Header	
12	ZGMNGA	Addnl Field	Gutmenge	
12	ZXMNGA	Addnl Field	Scrap to Be Confirmed	
21	ZISM02	Addnl Field	Activity Currently to be Confirmed	
21	ZISM03	Addnl Field	Activity Currently to be Confirmed	
21	ZISM05	Addnl Field	Activity Currently to be Confirmed	
21	ZISM06	Addnl Field	Activity Currently to be Confirmed	
22	ZVGW02	Addnl Field	Standard Value	
22	ZVGW03	Addnl Field	Standard Value	
22	ZVGW05	Addnl Field	Standard Value	
22	ZVGW06	Addnl Field	Standard Value	
23	ZFMASA	Addnl Field	Activity Currently to be Confirmed	
23	ZFPESA	Addnl Field	Activity Currently to be Confirmed	
23	ZMASA	Addnl Field	Activity Currently to be Confirmed	
23	ZPESA	Addnl Field	Activity Currently to be Confirmed	
24	ZFMASP	Addnl Field	FMAS %	
24	ZFPESP	Addnl Field	FPES %	
24	ZMASP	Addnl Field	MAS %	
24	ZPESP	Addnl Field	PES %	
25	ZKTEXT	Addnl Field	Short description	
25	ZMATNR	Addnl Field	Material Number for Order	
25	ZSCHICHT	Addnl Field	Schicht	
25	ZZIEL	Addnl Field	Ziel	

Figure 16.23 Extras for InfoSet from the PP Area

The material number for the order is stored in the table AFPO (Order Item). Because you need only one material number from the table AFPO, you do not have to include this table in the table join. Here, it is sufficient to use the SELECT SINGLE command to read the material number in an additional field (see Figure 16.24).

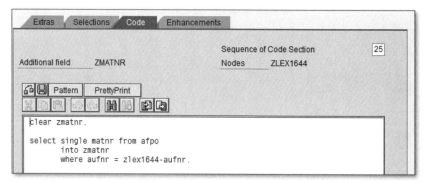

Figure 16.24 Transferring the Material Number from the Table AFPO to an Additional Field

Shift analysis The customer also wanted to provide other information in additional fields. In the TARGET field, a target quantity is determined on the basis of the confirmation time and standard value. The target quantity corresponds to the standard quantity, which corresponds to the confirmed time. The customer also wanted to summarize confirmations according to shifts. Consequently, the confirmation time is queried in a one-digit additional field, and, depending on the confirmation time, the confirmation is indicated as a confirmation from the early, late, or night shift. The relevant code is shown in the IF query in Figure 16.25.

Displaying the confirmation key figures with the appropriate positive/ negative sign As was the case with the two earlier analyses in this chapter, it is also necessary to display analyzed confirmations with the appropriate positive/negative sign. A canceled confirmation is also saved to the database with a positive value. Consequently, adding the confirmed quantities would produce a result that is too high. For confirmations, the quantities must be displayed with the appropriate positive/negative sign in conjunction with the field AFRU-STOKZ (Cancellation Indicator) (see Figure 16.26).

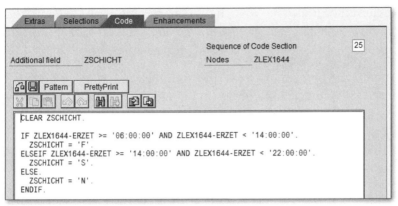

Figure 16.25 Additional Field for Displaying the Shift

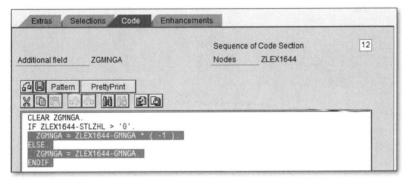

Figure 16.26 IF Query for a Confirmation Quantity Based on the Cancellation
Indicator

For quantities and times, it is necessary to consider dimensions. The
quantity, for example, can be confirmed in units, kilograms, or grams.
If you always use the unit of measure ST (Unit) for the confirmation,
this problem is solved for the confirmation quantity. However, the issue
of the unit of measurement arises for the (confirmed) time. In real life,
confirmations have different time units. Even in simple scenarios, confirmations with second, minute, and hour time units must be displayed
for a target/actual comparison with a time unit. This means that you
must convert the time unit of the confirmation. An IF statement can
also be used to convert the confirmation. If the time unit is seconds, the

Converting time
units and units
of measure

confirmed time is divided by 60; if the confirmation occurs in hours, the time must be multiplied by 60. This method makes it easy to convert time confirmations into a standardized display (minutes).

In real life, however, there are other time units, and, as a result, a function module must be used for a secure time conversion. The standard SAP system provides the function module UNIT_CONVERSION_SIMPLE for the conversion of time units. The function module must be filled with existing field information. It then displays the result in an additional field (see Figure 16.27).

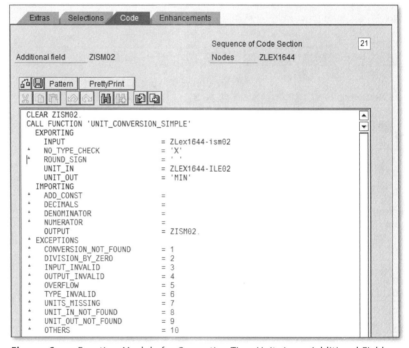

Figure 16.27 Function Module for Converting Time Units in an Additional Field

Function module for converting time units

In our example, both the confirmation time (Zlex1644-ISM02) and the confirmation unit of measure (ZLEX1644-ILE02) are transferred to the function module. The function module converts the time and transfers the result to the additional field ZISM02. Consequently, all confirmations are displayed in the report in minutes, irrespective of the time unit entered for each confirmation.

A simple arithmetic operation is used to display the variance between the target time and the actual time in another additional field:

Variance between the target/ actual time

```
zmasa = zism02 - zvgw02.
```

After the variance between the target time and the actual time has been determined as an absolute value, the percentage variance can be calculated in other additional fields. The percentage variance is used as a basis for the traffic light status. For this purpose, local fields are displayed in the query. If you want to use the percentage variance as a data basis for the traffic light status, you must assign a short name to the percentage variance (see Figure 16.28).

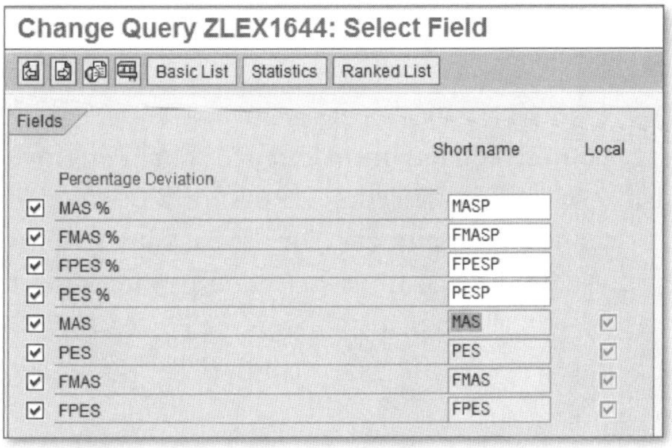

Figure 16.28 Local Fields in the Query

Additional local fields are created to display a colored traffic light icon. The local field must be selected and declared as an icon field. In the calculation formula, you can specify that a green traffic light will be displayed (ICON_LED_GREEN) when the percentage variance is less than or equal to 0% (MASP <= 0) (see Figure 16.29).

Traffic light icon in the query

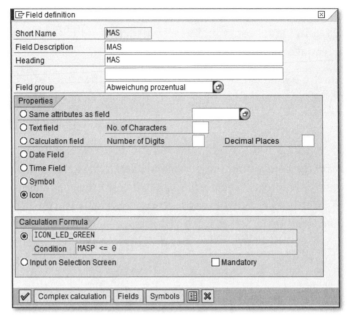

Figure 16.29 Defining a Traffic Light Icon in the Query

Selection screen for the productivity report

The way in which the selection screen has been designed should improve performance. In the background, the selection occurs for a predefined plant only, and only the confirmation numbers for the past few months are selected. You can fully hide the additional selection parameters, or you can choose 📖 (ALL SELECTIONS) to display them (see Figure 16.30).

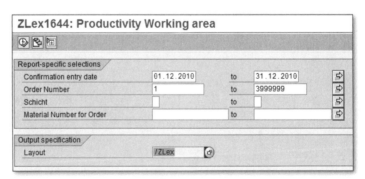

Figure 16.30 Selection Screen for the Productivity Report

Displaying data for the productivity report

You can display selected data in the already known SAP List Viewer. In real life, numerous statistics are defined and summarized for the following characteristics: material, order, work center, cost centers, cost center hierarchy, or plant. In SAP List Viewer, the traffic light status has already highlighted the critical data records (see Figure 16.31).

O...	S	Menge	Ziel	M...	StdVal	Activity to Conf.	Activity to Conf.	MAS %	P...	StdVal	Activity to Conf.	Activity to Conf.	PES %
1...	N	10	5	☐	86,200	45,217	40,983-	48-	☐	31,890	16,579	15,311-	48-
1...	N	33	28	☐	284,460	241,517	42,943-	15-	☐	105,237	88,556	16,681-	16-
1...	F	52	42	☐	448,240	363,800	84,440-	19-	☐	165,828	133,393	32,435-	20-
1...	F	95	0	☐	53,200		53,200-	100-	△	53,200	53,760	0,560	1
1...	F	70.127	70.127	☐	43.829,375	43.829,375			◎		8.035,385	8.035,385	100
1...	F	70.127-	70.127-	☐	43.829,375-	43.829,375-			☐		8.035,385-	8.035,385-	
1...	F	95	95	☐	59,375	59,375			◎		10,885	10,885	100
1...	F	70.127	70.127	☐	87.658,750	87.658,750			☐	7.304,896	4.382,938	2.921,958-	40-
1...	F	70.127-	70.127-	☐	87.658,750-	87.658,750-			☐	7.304,896-	4.382,938-	2.921,958	
1...	F	95	95	☐	118,750	118,750			☐	9,896	5,938	3,958-	40-
1...	N	95	116	◎	653,125	794,750	141,625	22	◎	32,656	39,738	7,082	22
1...	F	70.127	70.127	☐	43.829,375	43.829,375			◎	7.304,896	8.035,385	730,489	10
1...	F	70.127-	70.127-	☐	43.829,375-	43.829,375-			☐	7.304,896-	8.035,385-	730,489-	
1...	F	95	95	☐	59,375	59,375			◎	9,896	10,885	0,989	10

Figure 16.31 Displaying Data with a Traffic Light Status

In real life, different layout variants are created whereby the following data fields, in particular, are available:

▶ ORDER NUMBER

▶ MATERIAL NUMBER

▶ WORK CENTER

▶ COST CENTERS

▶ COST CENTER HIERARCHY

▶ PLANT

▶ SHIFT

▶ TARGET QUANTITY

▶ TRAFFIC LIGHT STATUS

▶ TARGET TIME

▶ ACTUAL TIME

▶ ABSOLUTE VARIANCE BETWEEN THE TARGET/ACTUAL TIME

▶ PERCENTAGE VARIANCE BETWEEN THE TARGET/ACTUAL TIME

For example, you can use the shift characteristic to display a summary of all confirmations for a particular time interval. The target quantity serves as a guide for the quantity to be confirmed in the standard time. The target time is the standard value (REFA time) multiplied by the confirmation quantity. For each customer, the target time, actual time, and the variance between both are displayed for the different activity types.

16.5 Summary

The three real-life examples listed in this chapter from the sales, open item list, and productivity areas demonstrate the highly flexible analysis options within SAP Query. Within a very short space of time, it is possible to create an analysis that satisfies the needs of a particular enterprise.

It is important to select the relevant tables and, in particular, to restrict the data selection. You do not have to include all relevant tables in the InfoSet. Instead, you must format additional information in additional fields. Data retrieval is generally achieved using the IF statement, the SELECT SINGLE command, simple field assignments, or a function module. If you drill down to individual data records and use (traffic light) icons, query reporting can offer you excellent online analysis possibilities.

A   Important SAP Tables

The following is an overview of the most important SAP tables for you. An enhanced table overview is available at *www.sap-press.com* or *www. zlex.de/query*.

A.1   General

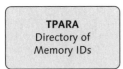

Figure A.1   General: Users

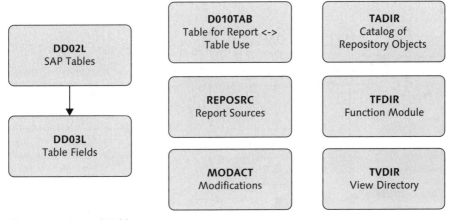

Figure A.2   General: Tables

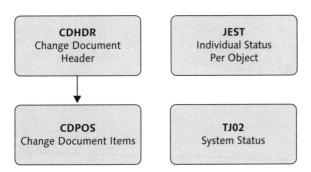

Figure A.3   General: Changes/Status

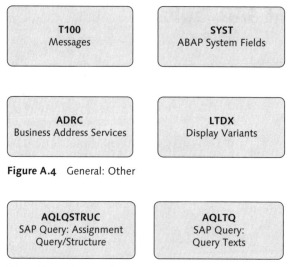

Figure A.4 General: Other

Figure A.5 General: Query

A.2 Sales and Distribution

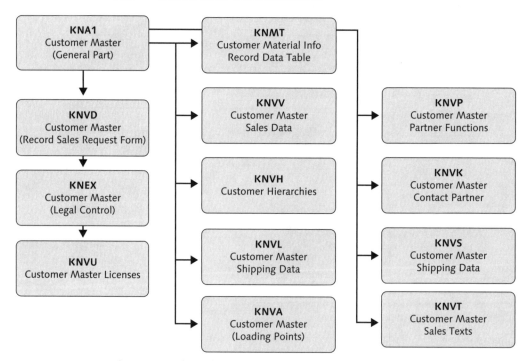

Figure A.6 Sales and Distribution: Customer

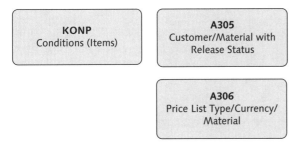

Figure A.7   Sales and Distribution: Conditions

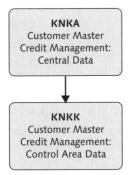

Figure A.8   Credit Limit

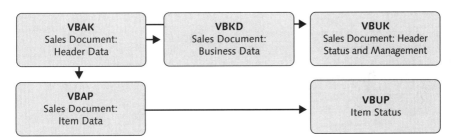

Figure A.9   Sales and Distribution: Sales Document

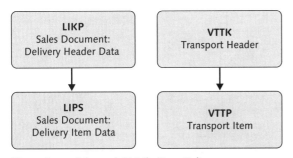

Figure A.10   Sales and Distribution: Delivery

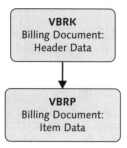

Figure A.11 Sales and Distribution: Billing Document

A.3 Production

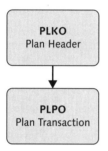

Figure A.12 Production: Routing

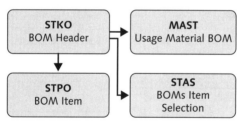

Figure A.13 Production: Bill of Material

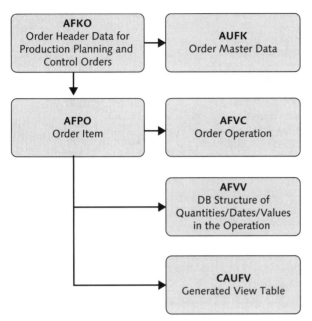

Figure A.14 Production: Order

A.4 Materials Management

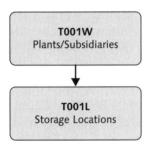

Figure A.15 Materials Management: Organizational Structure

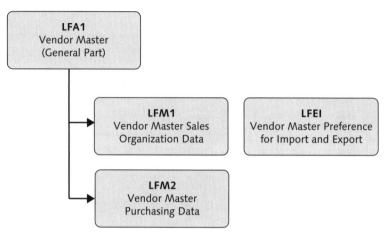

Figure A.16 Vendor Master

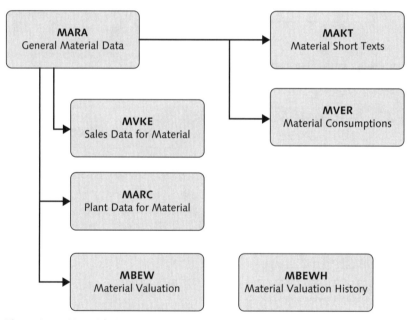

Figure A.17 Material Master

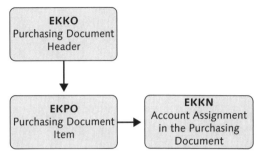

Figure A.18 Materials Management: Purchasing Documents

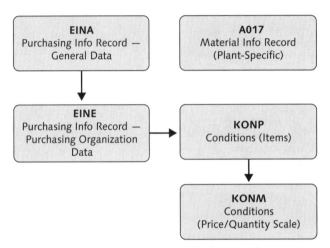

Figure A.19 Materials Management: Purchasing Info Records

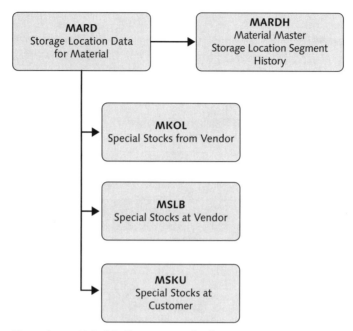

Figure A.20   Materials Management: Stock

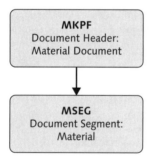

Figure A.21   Materials Management: Material Documents

A.5   Financial Accounting and Controlling

Figure A.22   Financial Accounting: Organizational Structure

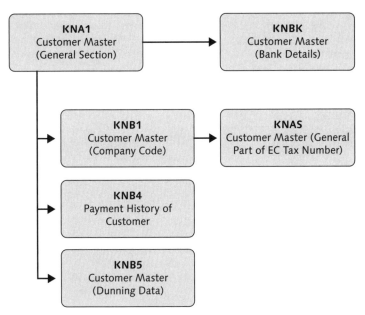

Figure A.23 Financial Accounting: Customer Master

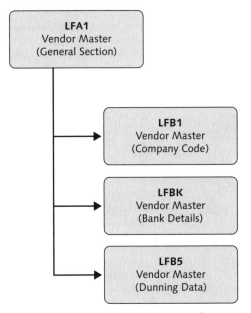

Figure A.24 Financial Accounting: Vendor Master

BNKA
Bank Master

Figure A.25 Financial Accounting: Bank Master

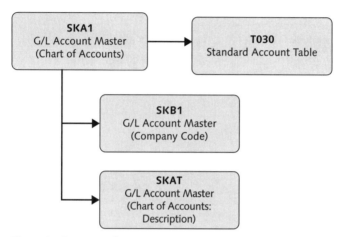

Figure A.26 Financial Accounting: G/L Account Master

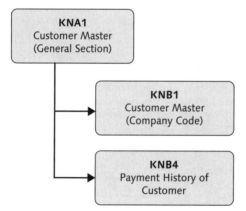

Figure A.27 Financial Accounting: Customer

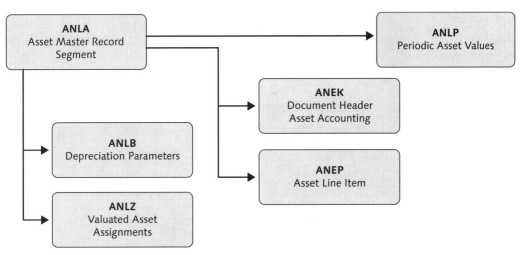

Figure A.28 Financial Accounting: Asset Master

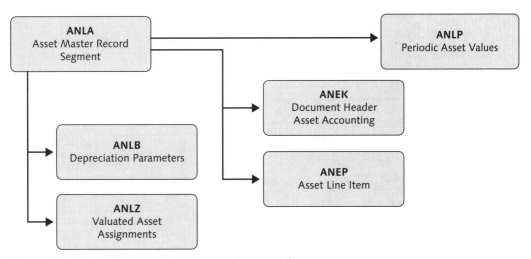

Figure A.29 Financial Accounting: Documents (Line Item I)

Figure A.30 Financial Accounting: Documents (Line Item II)

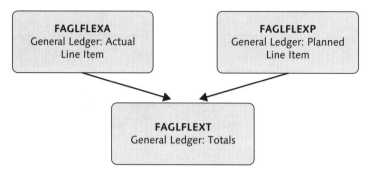

Figure A.31 Financial Accounting: Documents: New General Ledger (New G/L)

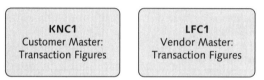

Figure A.32 Financial Accounting: Documents – Totals

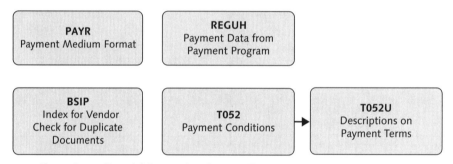

Figure A.33 Financial Accounting: Payment Transactions

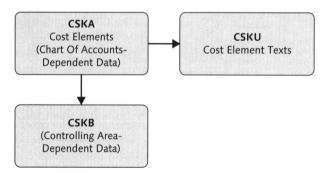

Figure A.34 Controlling: Cost Element Master

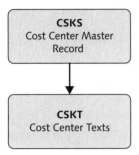

Figure A.35   Controlling: Cost Center Master

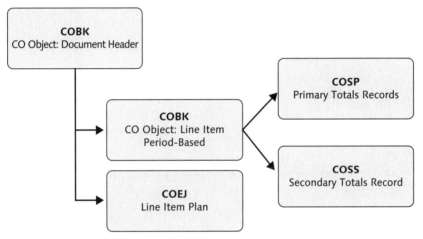

Figure A.36   Controlling: Cost Center Documents

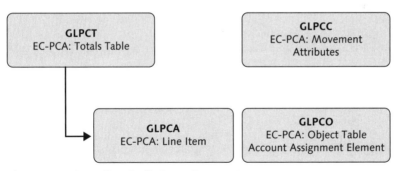

Figure A.37   Controlling: Profit Center Documents

B   The Author

 Since 1994, **Stephan Kaleske** has been working as a project manager and cross-module SAP expert for customers in the areas of mechanical engineering, plant engineering and construction, automotive, and services. He cites the modules FI, CO, IM, PS, TR, and FSCM as his particular areas of expertise. In challenging implementation projects, he not only performs actual analyses and drafts business blueprints (in particular, for the optimization and further development of business processes), but he also successfully implements SAP Customizing, performs integration tests, and holds training courses. Consequently, he not only understands how to map processes within an SAP system, but he can also present his ideas to all those involved in the project (key users, heads of departments, managing directors, and executive boards) and inform users about system operation. After completing his studies in business administration and working in the area of tax and external auditing for several years, Stephan Kaleske actively brought SAP premium customers to the fore through his enterprise consulting. To date, he has hosted more than 3,000 consulting and training days in the area of SAP ERP Financials. You can contact Stephan Kaleske at the following email address: *Info@ZLex.de*.

Index

T

U

V

W

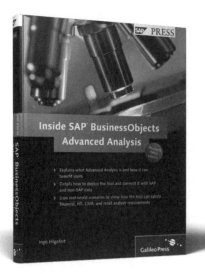

Explains what Advanced Analysis Office is and how it can benefit users

Details how to deploy the tool and connect it with SAP and non-SAP data

Uses real-world scenarios to show how the tool can work in financials,

HR, CRM, and retail

Ingo Hilgefort

Inside SAP BusinessObjects Advanced Analysis

Offers a comprehensive review of the product features/functionalities, as well as targeted guidance on installation, delployment, data connectivity, and usage scenarios. It also provides a side-by-side comparison of SAP Advanced Analysis Office with SAP BEx Analyzer, and a product road that outlines the main topics in the SAP BI roadmap for the Advanced Analysis Office version and the Web version as well touch on the migration topic.

343 pp., 2010, 69,95 Euro / US$ 69.95
ISBN 978-1-59229-371-1

>> www.sap-press.com

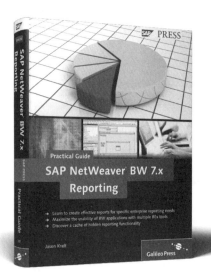

Learn how to create effective reports for specific enterprise reporting needs using NetWeaver BW 7

Build composite reports using multiple BEx tools with ease including report designer, Web analyzer, Excel analyzer, and Web application designer

Jason Kraft

SAP NetWeaver BW 7.x Reporting–Practical Guide

This book provides a detailed, how-to guide for anyone using NetWeaver BW and the BEx tools to generate reports. It will teach how to design effective, good looking reports that meet business objectives and provide an up-to-date resource covering the latest version of NetWeaver BW 7.0.

approx. 359 pp., 79,95 Euro / US$ 79.95
ISBN 978-1-59229-357-5, Nov 2010

>> www.sap-press.com

Discover how to develop and implement successful BW data models

Find complete explanations of key topics including: Architecture, Information Objects, Info Providers and SAP Business Content

Learn about Business Intelligence (BI) planning and related Business Object innovations

Frank K. Wolf, Stefan Yamada

Data Modeling in SAP NetWeaver BW

This book provides consultants, project/implementation teams and IT staffs with clear guidance on how to develop, implement, maintain, and upgrade SAP data models. The book starts by explaining the entire data modeling process, from the logical design of a model through enterprise requirements, technical framework, and implementation requirements. It then moves into a more in-depth review of the technical/component requirements and maps the technologies to the specific business requirements outlined in the first chapter. The next several chapters focus on the primary foundations of a data model (i.e. Info Ob-jects, Key Figures, Data Store Objects, etc.) and the principles of data modeling, including data architecture, data loading and transformation.

554 pp., 2010, 79,95 Euro / US$ 79.95
ISBN 978-1-59229-346-9

>> www.sap-press.com

 **PRESS**

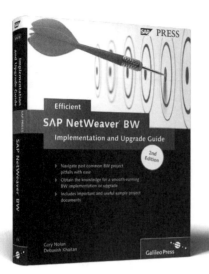

Explore the steps and components that ensure an efficient and smooth SAP BW implementation and upgrade

Learn about common practices and typical resource considerations for SAP BW projects

Leverage sample documents to help with your implementation/upgrade

Gary Nolan, Debasish Khaitan

Efficient SAP NetWeaver BW Implementation and Upgrade Guide

This book offers a clear and easy-to-follow path for efficient SAP BW implementations and upgrades. The book starts by defining a typical NetWeaver BW project lifecycle, followed by an examination of proper project management and upgrade strategies, including understanding common mistakes, resource requirements, and project planning and development. The topics are presented in a linear, intuitive, project-based scenario, to help you navigate easily through all stages of the project, including pre-project considerations, actual project guidance, as well as the Go-Live and Post-Live monitoring and maintenance considerations.

532 pp., 2. edition 2010, 79,95 Euro / US$ 79.95
ISBN 978-1-59229-336-0

>> www.sap-press.com

Explains how to use all of the features in Xcelsius

Teaches you how to build and customize interactive dashboards to effectively visualize your key business data

Provides guidance on using Xcelsius in an SAP environment

Ray Li, Evan Delodder

Creating Dashboards with Xcelsius–Practical Guide

Learn how to build your own Xcelsius dashboards, with this practical book. It explains how to use Xcelsius in an end-to-end, linear "common usage" manner, while highlighting typical scenarios where each feature can be used to solve business problems. It also gives you detailed, step-by-step guidance and best-practices for each feature, along with hands-on exercises that will help you begin creating dashboards and visualizations quickly. And if you're more advanced, you'll learn how to customize the Xcelsius components, themes, and data connections so you can use Xcelsius to the fullest extent.

587 pp., 2010, 49,95 Euro / US$ 49.95
ISBN 978-1-59229-335-3

>> www.sap-press.com

Interested in reading more?

Please visit our Web site for all
new book releases from SAP PRESS.

www.sap-press.com